LBJ

AN IRREVERENT CHRONICLE

LBJ

AN IRREVERENT CHRONICLE

BOOTH MOONEY

THOMAS Y. CROWELL COMPANY
ESTABLISHED 1834   NEW YORK

Designed by Abigail Moseley

Manufactured in the United States of America

Library of Congress Cataloging in Publication Data
Mooney, Booth, 1912-
    LBJ: an irreverent chronicle.

    1.   Johnson, Lyndon Baines, Pres. U.S., 1908-1973.
I.   Title.
E847.M58   973.923′092′4   [B]   75-33693
ISBN 0-690-01089-3

2   3   4   5   6   7   8   9   10

This book is
for
Betty, Ted, Joan

CONTENTS

Had I been present at the creation, I could have given some useful hints for the better ordering of the universe.

—Alfonso the Wise

($1221-1284$)

INTRODUCTION

The hill country of Texas, a far-reaching area west of Austin and south of old San Antonio, is a bleak, dusty region not friendly to living things. It is a land where all forms of life must, for survival, go armed against one another. Rattlesnakes slither over the usually parched earth, hard as biscuits baked over a cowboy's campfire. Saber-tusked *javelinas* snort their way through the useless mesquite brush and root around under stunted cedar and live oak trees. Horned toads, dragons in miniature, lie beady-eyed in the scorching rays of the sun, and terrapins bearing ancient armor on their backs plod tediously up the sloping sides of dry-bottomed arroyos. Buzzards circle in the fathomless sky, their lazy flight shifting abruptly to a steep downward plunge as sharp eyes spot below the carcass of a hapless animal that has not survived. Cactus plants thrust their vicious spikes outward to protect their purple juicy fruit. The soil fights a losing battle with sun and wind.

Hostile country.

A hard place to live.

I

A hard place for a man to make a living for his family during the first two or three decades of this century. No Texas oil wells here, no complacently thriving cities, no great cotton plantations. The ranches were small and most often profitless, the markets for cattle difficult to reach. The poor land did not encourage farming. Rainfall was meager. Such streams as existed dwindled away to hopeless trickles or faded altogether in the dry season, became sudden, short-lived torrents when thunderstorms struck the surrounding hills. Bumpy dirt roads connected the scattered houses with each other and with ugly ramshackle villages. Electric lights and gas stoves were for city folks. People in the hill country expected a hardscrabble existence and their expectation was generally realized.

In this barren land, near a straggling impoverished settlement called Johnson City in the valley of the Pedernales River, a son was born, August 27, 1908, to Sam Ealy Johnson, Jr., and Rebekah Baines Johnson. They named the firstborn of their year-old marriage Lyndon Baines.

Pictures sometimes tell long-lasting stories. A photograph of the new father shows a sharp-featured man with thin lips, strong outthrusting nose, and piercing eyes, a man whose volatile temper was reflected in the challenging gaze he directed toward the unnamed photographer. His wife, handsome enough in a stern-faced way, appeared every inch the elocution teacher and staunch Baptist she in fact was. Descendant of earlyday Texas statesmen, educators, and a gun-toting preacher, Rebekah Baines Johnson looked simultaneously ladylike and iron-willed. She was born and bred to be a doting, driving mother. Neither parent smiled for the photographer.

Nor was there a smile on the face of the son in a snapshot taken when he was four: a skinny boy with an absurdly large cowboy hat pulled down to touch his outsized ears as he sat on a drab front porch and stared squint-eyed into the camera, his lips parted slightly in a near-sneer. A rather grubby little boy who gave no impression of being childlike.

Sam Johnson, the father, was known to most of the 4,063 people who lived in the 719 square miles of the Texas hill country which comprised Blanco County. He was a schoolteacher, farmer-rancher on a small scale, businessman of sorts, state legislator. He fought all his life for financial security and several times momentarily attained it through real estate deals, but beginning with the farm depression of 1921, his fortunes slid steadily downhill. The lean times encompassed his first child's formative years.

Still, whether relatively well to do or living on the edge of poverty, the Johnsons were somebodies in Blanco County. The sizable frog in a tiny pond had a wife who gave no thought to resting in his shadow. Rebekah Baines Johnson was by no means content to be simply a housewife and mother of Lyndon and the four children who came afterward. At the time she may well have been the only female college graduate in the county, having determinedly worked her way through Baylor College, a Baptist institution, after her father suffered financial reverses. Now she variously taught her elocution classes, edited the little weekly newspaper in Johnson City, served on the town school board. She shared her husband's interest in political affairs, although not always his views of candidates and issues. Nor was she diffident about expressing her differences to him.

The union of these two was recognized by their Blanco County neighbors as a sound joining together of brains and guts. The Baineses, went the general opinion, were intelligent but unable to get things done. Some saw the Johnsons as unstable dirt farmers and half-assed politicians, but nobody questioned their ability to make things happen.

The family moved into Johnson City, established by and named for earlier Johnsons, and Lyndon grew up there rather than on the ranch. The town was not imposing. It consisted of the county courthouse, a few houses, several stores out of a Western movie set, a bank, a barber shop, a school building. Johnson City was an ingrown place where the inhabitants knew all about one another's personal problems. Neighbor tried to help neighbor when assistance was needed, but a prevailing spirit of pride and fierce independence led most families to stand stubbornly on their own feet. That spirit ran high in the Johnson family.

His mother pushed Lyndon. She taught him the alphabet from A-B-C blocks before he was two. When he was three he could recite from memory most of the Mother Goose rhymes and poems by Longfellow and Tennyson. At the age of four, when the snapshot was made, he was reading for himself. He started to school in Johnson City a year later.

He was no natural scholar. Learning was force-fed to him as much by his mother as by his teachers. Often she would not become aware that Lyndon was unprepared for a lesson until breakfast time on a school day. Then she would get the requisite textbook, place it on the table in front of her husband and devote the entire meal period to a discussion with him of what the boy should have learned the evening before.

Other less contrived conversation around the Johnson household also was educational. The talk often dealt with politics—a recurrent theme being what a poor chance the little fellow had to prevail against the big interests. A family heritage of populism had come down from the nineteenth century. Lyndon listened, his brown eyes thoughtful, to tales his father told about his fights for progressive measures in the Texas legislature. He often interrupted with questions, for he was not bashful.

Debate was one school subject in which Lyndon needed no urging to compete. The boy was a compulsive talker and had a tendency to turn a discussion on whatever subject into a contention. He would not give up the argument until his opponent conceded all points.

His interest in debate continued later when for a short period he became a schoolteacher. He coached a two-man team to victory in the debate competition in the county interscholastic league. The team advanced through the district contest to the state finals. And lost there. When the judges' decision was announced the young debate coach went to the men's room and vomited into

4

the toilet. A compelling will to win had become firmly set within Lyndon Johnson.

During his school years Lyndon engaged in the routine play and work of an active youth growing up in a backwater kind of place. He took pride in being the eldest of the family of five children and enjoyed helping his siblings through the vicissitudes of childhood—so long as they admitted they needed his help and deferred to him. They were good about doing that. His brother, four years younger, worshipped him. His sisters stood in awe of him. One of them later recalled that as a child Lyndon had always been "the bossy one" of the family.

After graduation from the tiny Johnson City high school and a fling at running away from home to California, Lyndon entered Southwest Texas State Teachers College at San Marcos in February 1927. In the unlikely setting of that bucolic educational institution, the young man's energy, his awakening ambition, his ego, and the Baines-Johnson genes coalesced to bring a sea change in his life.

He worked his way through college as janitor, door-to-door hosiery salesman, and, finally, secretary to the institution's president. He studied voraciously and his grades were outstanding. He became the college's star debater. He enjoyed his first success in the political arena, organizing students into a new faction to wrest control of campus politics from an entrenched group dominated by athletic jocks.

By the time he received a degree from the College in August 1930 at the age of twenty-three, he was on fire with a twofold purpose destined to last all his life: to obtain the financial security that had eluded his father and to become someone who amounted to something, the dream of his mother. The goals were not unique for a young man in the America of the 1930s. But the intensity with which Lyndon Johnson pursued them was, impelling him onward to become a superb professional in the field of politics.

He brought with him in his quest certain attributes not al-

5

ways associated with professional politicians. He had been shaped by an upbringing which gave him an awareness of the problems of others and a conviction that he should work to alleviate them. He believed in Horatio Alger, but he believed also in Thomas Jefferson and, for that matter, in James Stephen Hogg, the Texas antimonopoly governor who for a time had made a deep mark on the state's economic life. Lyndon Johnson understood what it meant to be poor and without much hope of ever being anything else. He had faith that man could better himself through his own efforts.

After a brief stint at teaching school, Johnson went to Washington, D.C., in 1932, as secretary to a newly elected Texas congressman. In that position he soaked up knowledge about government techniques and political personalities. He avidly cultivated politicians and men who worked for politicians, especially after this training ground for the political neophyte was enveloped in the stimulating atmosphere of Franklin D. Roosevelt's New Deal. He made friends in places as high as he could reach. His father's former colleague in the Texas legislature, Sam Rayburn, rising to power in the House of Representatives, took him under his wing.

Rayburn was instrumental in getting Johnson appointed Texas state director of the National Youth Administration in 1935. In Texas, this New Deal agency gave assistance to some thirty thousand young men and women. Among them were individuals who in the future would form a hard and active core of political support for Lyndon Johnson every time he ran for office.

The first time was in 1937. Johnson won a special election called to fill a congressional seat left vacant in Central Texas by the death of the incumbent. He was elected without opposition to a full term in the House of Representatives in 1938 and reelected in 1940, again without an opponent. After Texas senator Morris Sheppard died in the spring of 1941, the still youthful congressman became a candidate in another special election. This time, however, he lost, although by a narrow margin. He returned to his work in the House of Representatives.

6

When the United States went to war in December 1941, Johnson, a member of the Naval Reserve, asked to be called up immediately. He was on active duty, although not in combat, for seven months before Roosevelt ordered all members of Congress serving in the military forces back to their duties in Washington.

Roosevelt died, the war ended, and Johnson was again re-elected to the House in 1946. But he was becoming increasingly dissatisfied. In that year the Republicans gained control of both houses of Congress. Johnson decided he must go up in politics or he would go out. His goal was the United States Senate in the 1948 election.

Johnson was by nature single-minded, turning all his faculties to whatever situation lay immediately before him. He learned, and he needed the lesson, how to exercise self-discipline. He acquired shrewdness through observation, sometimes painful experience and determination not to make the same mistake twice.

These three qualities—single-mindedness, immense self-discipline, shrewdness that at times approached wisdom—constituted the base for his professionalism in politics. Successful political operations and power go hand in hand. The hill country of Texas, where life was a matter of root hog or die, left an indelible mark on Lyndon Johnson. He never outgrew it, nor wished to.

1

WHEN A BODY
MEETS A BODY

When meat rationing was still in effect after the war, one day Zephyr Wright, the Johnson cook, telephoned John Connally's wife (Connally was Representative Johnson's administrative assistant) to say her boss was unexpectedly bringing home six guests for dinner and there wasn't a meat stamp in the house. Mr. Johnson, she said, had told her to ask Mrs. Connally for some. Said Nelle Connally: "Zephyr, I don't have any and even if I did I wouldn't give them to him. He's got to learn he's just like everybody else."

Zephyr replied, after a thoughtful pause, "Miss Nellie, *you* know he's just like everybody else and *I* know he's just like everybody else. But I'm not going to be the one to tell him so."

Zephyr, a realistic and kindly human being, was rarely wrong in her estimates of people, but she made a mistake that time. Johnson was not like everybody else. Or anybody else.

I found that out for myself when I went to work for him at a time when his professionalism had been fully established.

9

It may be that I am the only one of the hundreds of persons who worked for Lyndon Johnson who was not afraid of him and was never directly on the receiving end of the sharp-tongued tirades with which he used to keep his employees on their toes.

My association with Johnson covered the last twenty years of his life. During six of those years I was a member of his Senate staff as sometime speechwriter, press liaison, political consultant, if the term isn't too grandiose, and general handyman. Since LBJ was not a man to turn loose of people easily, I continued to see him frequently while he was Vice-President and from time to time during his presidency and afterward. I knew both the public and the private Johnson and I can testify that they often contradicted each other.

At times, however, the two were completely merged. A spontaneous comment by him following a speech he made in Texas when he was a senator revealed clearly the two life qualities that most excited Johnson the politician and Johnson the man. His address was interrupted time and again by cheers, and as he finished the audience gave him a rousing ovation. Finally retreating backstage, his face glowing as his huge ears soaked up the still continuing applause, he chortled happily to an aide, "Oh, boy! Listen to that! It even beats screwing."

Nearly everybody agreed that Johnson was a hard man to work for and I suppose he was. I can only say that I did not find him so. This was due perhaps less to the mild, easygoing temperament I like to think I possess than to other factors.

For one thing, I was born and brought up under conditions not unlike his own in a rural backward Texas place where living was not easy. My formal education was not even as good as his. After finishing high school, I attended a junior college for just one year and then went to work on the local weekly newspaper. Other newspaper work followed, then magazine writing and editing, service in the Army Air Corps during the war, establishment of a public relations firm in Dallas, authorship of two or three books.

My background appealed to Johnson more than it did to me. In any case, there it was.

Also, as it happened, the circumstances under which I became a Johnson employee may have made life easier for me than others who worked for him. In the beginning at least, I enjoyed a "most favored nation" status.

The process began in 1948, which I did not know at the time. In that year Johnson was a candidate for the United States Senate. His strongest opponent was former governor Coke Stevenson, an old friend of mine. I was engaged by Stevenson to write speeches and handle his campaign publicity. I had never met Johnson and, so far as I knew, he was unaware of my existence.

That 1948 senatorial campaign was a hard-fought one in two Democratic primaries. Stevenson held an imposing lead in the first, but Johnson squeaked out a victory in the second. The final official count showed him winning by eighty-seven votes out of more than a million cast, earning for him a nickname, "Landslide Lyndon," which he purely detested. Anyway, he went to Washington after the formality of defeating a Republican in the general election, Stevenson retired to his ranch, and I returned to my public relations business in Dallas.

Later I learned that even during the heat of the campaign Johnson had made extensive inquiries about me. A friendly newspaper editor told me that LBJ had complained to him that his own staff was no good, the "Stevenson people" were outdoing him in publicity everywhere in Texas, Stevenson's speeches were better than his, somebody in the enemy camp was smart enough to pinpoint every stand he had taken during his eleven years in the House of Representatives on which he was vulnerable among Texas voters. My friend said Johnson gave me credit—or blame —for much of this situation and wished to hell he had heard about me before I went to work for his opponent.

I took this report with several grains of salt. I knew from listening to his radio speeches that Johnson was given to hyperbole. Besides, I was painfully conscious that he had won and we had lost. The bitterness of the Johnson-Stevenson campaign, intensified by the dubious outcome, was a long time fading from the minds of active participants.

Nevertheless, during the next three years, I became aware, somewhat incredulously at first, that I was being assiduously wooed by Johnson and his friends.

A cotton broker client of my firm, up to his ears in state politics, repeatedly told me that the senator thought highly of my ability. Walter Jenkins, Johnson's administrative assistant, came to Texas in 1951 to run for a congressional seat vacated by resignation, and I was hired to work in his campaign. He lost, but after he returned to his old job in Washington he kept in touch with me by letter and long distance telephone. He visited me in my office in Dallas one day to say that Johnson had instructed him to tell me he hoped I would come over to their side. In 1952, Johnson was responsible for my being called to Washington to participate in the effort of his friend and colleague, Senator Richard B. Russell of Georgia, to obtain the Democratic nomination for President. At that year's national convention in Chicago, Russell's support was confined with minor exceptions to the southern delegations and Adlai Stevenson was nominated. Later that year, Governor Allan Shivers led the Texas Democratic organization into the Eisenhower camp. I was closely allied with the formidable nd intensely human Sam Rayburn and, to some extent, with Johnson himself in the state campaign for the Democratic ticket. Adlai Stevenson lost Texas and the nation.

So I had on record four important losses involving Johnson in one way or another. One would think this would have been off-putting to a politician inordinately fond of success. But late in November 1952, after it had become apparent that Johnson was likely to be chosen as Senate Democratic floor leader in the 83rd Congress, Walter Jenkins telephoned to ask if I could go down to Austin, the state capital, to see his boss on a certain date.

Yes, I said.

It was a morning to remember. I met the senator at eight A.M. in an apartment he maintained in Austin. After coffee there we repaired to his office in the Federal Courthouse. He told his secretary he would see nobody and had telephone calls held up. For the next three and one-half hours he talked nearly nonstop. We left his office only once during the morning, to go to the men's room, and he continued to talk as we stood side by side attending to necessary functions.

The thrust of his nearly uninterrupted monologue was that the way he looked at it about half the voters of Texas were against him. He had to make a dent in that large body of citizens before 1954, when he would be up for reelection, and he knew I could help him do it. Coke Stevenson would never have run so well against him except for what I had done. He, Johnson, was not really the all-out-New-Deal-Harry-Truman-liberal that many Texans believed him to be. He wanted to—he must—project a more conservative image. If he was elected Democratic floor leader, he would have an opportunity to lead his colleagues in support of the Republican President when matters affecting the general welfare—and especially the welfare of Texas—were at stake. I would have a free hand to set my own course in his Washington office. He needed somebody to write his weekly report for Texas newspapers. He wanted to initiate a radio program from Washington. Nobody in his office knew how to compose friendly, down-to-earth letters in reply to communications from constituents. His relations with Texas newspaper correspondents in Washington were terrible and I was just the fellow to improve them.

On and on he went with a combination of thick flattery, urgent persuasion, appeals to my patriotism, and hints that many men who worked for him went on to high-paying jobs in private industry. I received a full dose of what later was to become famous as "the Johnson Treatment." It was heady, no doubt about that.

"Of course," he said when I, dazed and uncertain, was preparing to leave, "we may not get the floor leadership and if we don't I won't be able to expand my staff, so I'm not actually offering you a job. But," he added exuberantly, "it looks favorable and I sure want you to come up there with me and if you do you'll never regret it."

As I left he was snatching up the telephone and barking, "All right! Any calls I ought to take?"

Johnson may have thought he had made a sale, but he had not in fact nailed it down. I was in a state of vast indecision. After the early January caucus of Democratic senators unanimously elected Johnson floor leader, the job offer came through in solid form. I vacillated. To test the water, I sent Walter Jenkins a list of a dozen suggestions for activities that the senator's office might undertake in courting Texas votes. Back came a note from Jenkins saying, "The senator said to do everything on your list that we're not already doing," and adding, "He says the sooner you get up here the better for all of us." More flattery, of course.

Anyway, it worked, or something did. Things moved fast after Christmas. By early February 1953, the public relations firm of Mooney & Cullinan was out of business, my partner was on his way to a high-ranking job in the Eisenhower Administration, my wife and our fifteen-month-old son were ensconced in a rented house in Washington, and I was on the Senate payroll.

Johnson had assured me that I would never regret going to work for him. But for a couple of months or so I did regret it. Some radical readjustments were required in my thinking and my work habits.

I had never been employed in an organization where everybody was concerned solely with trying to advance the interests of a single individual. It was not, even then, a small organization. Johnson had some twenty-five men and women on his Senate staff and the staffs of the two committees he headed, the Armed Services Preparedness Investigating Subcommittee and the Senate Democratic Policy Committee. Employees of the committees had responsibilities to the whole Senate, to be sure, but there was never any question in their minds about their primary duty being to make Johnson look good.

That was my job too. I had known it would be, but I learned soon enough that the free hand Johnson had so straight-facedly promised me was a mirage. His personal direction of my work extended so far as instructing me how I should read Texas newspapers, of which several hundred came into the office every week.

"Get the heaviest-marking red pencil you can find," he ordered. "Leaf through the newspapers, don't waste a lot of time reading, just watch out for my name or any political story that we might be interested in. When you find something, draw a red circle around it and tear out the page and fold it so the story you've marked with your red pencil will be on top. Put everything on my desk by six o'clock every day."

I laughed as I told my friend Walter Jenkins about this detailed blueprint. "Hell," I said, "I've been reading newspapers to red-line stories all my adult life. Doesn't he think I know how to do it?"

Jenkins gave a restrained smile. "That's the way the senator is," he said.

So it was, and not only in connection with reading newspapers. I learned right away that he was a finest detail man.

One of my first assignments was to take over the composition of his weekly newsletter, a seven-hundred-word mélange of short takes about the senator's legislative activity, his political philosophy, and his contacts with any "important names" (especially President Eisenhower) that could be dragged in by whatever far-fetched means. The newsletter was mailed under the senator's frank to all Texas newspapers and radio stations and to thousands of Texans who had written him at one time or another to express approval of something Johnson had said or done.

15

The writing of this weekly report was easy. I spent ten minutes or so with the senator every Monday morning discussing subjects that might be included. Then I could turn out the newsletter in no more than a couple of hours. But this was only the beginning.

George Reedy, a United Press reporter who had been hired for Johnson's Preparedness Investigating Subcommittee in 1950, later being shifted over to the Senate Democratic Policy Committee, wrote the newsletter before I arrived in Washington. So I showed him my first effort. He said it looked fine to him.

"Will the senator want to see this before it goes to the mailing room?" I asked innocently.

Reedy actually turned pale. "My God, yes. Don't ever let anything go out until he's approved it."

I had been accustomed to tame clients who usually accepted speeches fifteen minutes before they were to be delivered and rarely changed so much as a word. Johnson was different, at least as far as the newsletter was concerned. He went over my reports with a heavy editorial pencil, usually marking them up to such an extent that the rewriting took more time than the original draft.

My pride of authorship underwent a severe bruising. But there were compensations. My office had been established in a large room on the second floor of the Senate Office Building. (There was only one then.) It was far removed from Johnson's tiny minority leader's office in the Capitol and was the length of the big SOB from his bustling senatorial office, so nobody bothered me much. The services of an excellent secretary were placed at my disposal. Johnson ordered the printing of a special letterhead with my name emblazoned on it as executive assistant, a title he created for me. This was not an effort to coddle my ego but was done, he explained, to make me sound important to Texans. The newsletter was mimeographed on this letterhead so that Texas editors, among whom I had a wide acquaintance, would see I was now working for Johnson.

The Texas Democratic primary of 1954 was eighteen months in the future, but the senator was already running for re-election as hard as he could every day. My job began to be fun, even though it was more demanding than anything I had ever undertaken before.

We started a radio program, taping a fifteen-minute talk by Johnson every week for broadcast over Texas stations. Interestingly, he hardly ever made any substantive changes in the scripts I prepared. He apparently regarded the spoken word as ephemeral in contrast to something appearing in print. At that time, anyway.

We tried an experimental television program. The screening in the congressional studio of the first film revealed Johnson as the only man I ever knew who could speak of himself in the first, second, and third persons in a single run-together sentence. He came out of the studio talking fast as he bent his tall form over me.

"We're going to have to do better than that. I'm not satisfied with the way it turned out. We slurred too many words, talked too fast, looked too damn serious, but I can't be one of those always-smiling fellows, you've got to get a lot more practice, that's easy to see, before you're ready to do a regular program."

He was still talking when we separated at the elevator.

Walter Jenkins and I lured a commentator for the National Broadcasting Company into coaching Johnson, but this effort came to little. The senator was too impatient to take kindly to instruction.

On a Sunday morning shortly after I had joined the staff, Johnson telephoned me at home and said he would like for us to have "a little visit." Although I grew up in Texas, I never became accustomed to the use of that phrase to mean a business conference, so confusion set in. I thought he was suggesting that I and perhaps my wife come over to his house—a social occasion. But no. He said he would come by in half an hour to pick me up and we'd go to the office for a while.

When his car drew up in front of the house and he tooted the horn, I went out to find the senator accompanied by Reedy

17

and Gerald Siegel, a young lawyer from Iowa and Yale Law School who was general counsel for the Senate Democratic Policy Committee. The senator was driving and talking, they were listening, and as I got in the car he interrupted himself only to explain, "We're discussing a speech we might make in the Senate." He rattled on all the way to Capitol Hill, a twenty-minute drive. We were joined in his office by Jenkins. Johnson continued to talk most of the time for the next three hours.

The speech he had thought of making in the Senate was forgotten. His restless mind turned to the political situation—*his* political situation—in Texas. He spoke, his eyes darkening behind thick-rimmed spectacles, a fierce frown appearing on his face, of people who would never forgive him for his support of Adlai Stevenson in 1952.

"Amon Carter's one of them," he said shrilly. "The Fort Worth *Star-Telegram* was always for me 'till last year. Strongest paper in the state and my best supporter. But when I was committed to Rayburn to introduce Adlai Stevenson when he appeared in Texas, Amon Carter called and asked me—no, he didn't; he *told* me—not to do it. I explained about my commitment and said I'd have to live up to it, and I did. Now Old Man Carter won't even accept my telephone calls. He even scratched me off his Christmas list."

He strode around the room, brooding over this rank injustice, and stopped in front of me.

"I'm gonna keep trying. Booth, first thing tomorrow morning I want you to write a letter to Amon Carter for my signature." A finger poked me in the chest. "Make it warm and friendly, but sad because of the difference that's come between us. Tell him I'm the same Lyndon Johnson I've always been. Tell him I'm working for Texas just the way he is and we can get a lot more done for the people—and for Fort Worth—if we work together. The way we used to do. Really pour it on, Booth, and let's see if we can get through that hard old head of his."

18

(I wrote the letter in line with the senator's instructions, but the obdurate publisher went to his death still hating Johnson. Later, however, after Carter's death, his daughter, Mrs. J. Lee Johnson III, was entertained frequently in the White House and both she and Amon Jr. were appointed to various commissions by President Johnson.)

The politician was in top form that Sunday. He hurled out orders to start immediately lining up a campaign manager in every Texas county that lacked one. Pep letters over his signature should go out to every manager every week. Ask for political intelligence from their areas. Tell them things to do. There had to be more press releases about what he was doing for Texas in the Senate. He wanted ideas. Everybody in the room should give him a short memo every day making some kind of constructive proposal.

"I'll do whatever you fellows tell me to do," he said with earnestness. "You're my brain trust. You're the ones who can get me reelected or let me be defeated. Gerry, don't think you're out of this just because you work for the Policy Committee. You've got to tell me what I can do in the leadership that'll help me in Texas. George, put a paragraph or two in every statement I make on the floor that Booth can turn into a release for the Texas papers. Gerry, get me up a list of all the proposals Eisenhower has sent up and tell me which ones we can praise for the benefit of all those folks at home who voted for him. All of you think every day about ways to win over as many as we can of that fifty percent of Texans who voted against me last time."

The senator stayed on his feet throughout the long harangue, striding back and forth, waving his arms, never still for a moment. Jenkins was seated at a desk frantically making shorthand notes. Siegel, Reedy, and I stood in a constantly moving semicircle, not saying much, but all of us trying to make what we did say sound intelligent and responsive. It was an entertaining scene.

"I want your wives to help too," Johnson cried. "Every one of them is bound to have good ideas about how to appeal to other women. Tell 'em I'm counting on them. Take them out to dinner, get them in a good mood, and pick their brains."

He paused to paw in a bottom drawer of his desk, drawing out several small packages.

"Give 'em some candy." He handed a package to each of us. "Tell 'em these are real Texas pralines and they're a present from Lyndon Johnson." For the first time that morning he smiled. "All women love to be given candy. Tell 'em it's from me for taking you away from home on Sunday."

I relayed this message to my wife after I reached home for a long delayed lunch. She was amused, although not excessively so, observing that she hoped I would not often have to go to the office on Sunday.

"I don't think so," I reassured her. "Walter told me this was unusual."

The pralines, she reported, were stale.

2

POSTGRADUATE COURSE
IN POLITICS

My political education, which I had considered rather thorough, was vastly extended during the next two years. The master politician under whom I served was engaged in two distinct campaigns in 1953 and 1954: to get reelected senator from Texas and to consolidate the Democratic forces in the United States Senate. Sometimes there were unavoidable conflicts between the two goals, but in the main the second was adroitly made to serve the first.

So far as Texas was concerned, Johnson gave high priority to overcoming or at least softening the petroleum industry's abhorrence of him. This opposition from the state's most powerful economic force dated back a long way. After all, he had been a Franklin Delano Roosevelt Democrat and the oil boys never cared for FDR after 1933. And at midpoint in World War II, Johnson had been one of only two Texas congressmen (the other was Wright Patman) to vote against a bill which had the effect of raising the ceiling price on oil.

"That vote hurt me politically more than any other I ever cast," Johnson told me. "The oil people have hated me since then. They were against me in 1948. You know that."

I did know it. H. L. Hunt, the eccentric multimillionaire independent oil producer from Dallas, had made what was in those days a substantial contribution to the Coke Stevenson campaign. Jack Frost, another independent, had sent me his personal check for $2,500 to be used for Stevenson. Charles E. Simons, executive vice-president of the Texas Mid-Continent Oil & Gas Association, had done all he could to try to defeat Johnson. The oil-rich moguls of Houston detested him.

Fortunately for the senator, the petroleum people needed him in 1953.

A Supreme Court decision had held that Texas lost local ownership of its offshore lands, thought to be rich in petroleum reserves, when it entered the Union. Two quitclaim bills passed by Congress were vetoed by President Truman. The tidelands issue overrode all others in the 1952 presidential campaign in Texas and was a leading reason for Eisenhower's victory there over Adlai Stevenson. Attorney General Price Daniel used the issue to gain the Senate seat being vacated by Tom Connally, who withdrew from the race after a group of former supporters told him pitilessly that he was through.

Daniel, in whose first campaign for attorney general in 1946 I had worked as publicity director, now was out in front in a new and determined effort to turn ownership of the Texas tidelands back to the state. A not-yet-dry-behind-the-ears member of the august Senate might be expected to run into considerable trouble in gaining approval of such a proposal. But Daniel had the Senate Democratic leader on his side. Not only on his side but constantly *at* his side, pouring out advice on strategy, telling how he personally would get this or that senator to vote with them, reminding Daniel that he should inform Texas oil men how much Johnson was doing to get the legislation through the Senate.

22

The quitclaim bill was duly passed and signed into law by President Eisenhower. In rejoicing Texas, there was credit enough for both senators.

"Those sons of bitches are going to have to come around to me, whether they like it or not," Johnson exulted.

Nor was he unwilling to go around to them. People in the oil business lived in perpetual fear that Congress would tamper with the precious depletion allowance, which was a significant factor in enabling them to hold down their tax bills. At Johnson's bidding, I wrote for him a series of brief statements, which he made in the Senate, extolling the merits of the depletion allowance. He liked them and even telephoned me one day from the Senate cloakroom to say several senators had told him he was giving the clearest exposition of the subject they ever heard. Naturally, Washington correspondents of Texas newspapers received advance copies of the statements.

Contrary to popular belief, however, Johnson was not one to roll over and do tricks at the command of the oil barons. I once heard him deliver a stern lecture to several of them in his office. He castigated them severely for their shortsightedness in automatically opposing every social welfare proposal advanced in Congress.

"You make it goddam hard for us to fight your battles up here," he said. "And it doesn't help any when stories come out in the papers about your private airplanes and your clubrooms with walls lined with the skins of unborn lambs and the fifty-grand parties you throw. You guys have about as much public relations sense as a tomcat on the prowl on Saturday night."

Some of his listeners snickered uncomfortably, but none undertook to answer his criticism.

Johnson was scornful, and not always secretly, of most oil men as dolts who had lucked into a great deal of money and believed that circumstance made them instant and unquestioned authorities on government, economics, social problems, and you

23

name it. I once saw him come into a room where several Texas oil producers were knocking back a few drinks as they bragged about big deals they had put over in the past.

"Give me a glass of scotch," LBJ demanded. "I want to get rich and smart in fifteen minutes like you guys."

The millionaires were not amused.

The alliance between Johnson and the petroleum industry was uneasy and marked by distrust on both sides, but it became a part of the Texas political scene. And at times brought the senator considerable opprobrium from liberals in the state, a sad bunch who had been knocked around so much by the ruling oligarchy that their heads sometimes seemed muddled. They never did understand Johnson even when, in the Senate and later in the presidency, he was getting legislation passed they liked but which had stymied their heroes.

Of course the campaigning was not confined to the petroleum industry. People there had money and money was necessary in politics, but votes were even more necessary. Johnson assiduously cultivated his constituency and I tried to help.

Four or five hundred letters a day—demanding, censorious, laudatory—poured into the office from Texas. All had to be answered, preferably within twenty-four hours. Most of those dealing with political issues or political prejudices were likely to come to my desk. Day after day I spent hours muttering into a dictaphone soothing, and sometimes responsive, replies to be signed by the senator—or to be signed for him by Jenkins or some other staff member who had become adept at forging the LBJ signature. This was not really what I had come to Washington to do. But Johnson liked the letters I composed and that was that.

Other members of the staff also wrote letters and Johnson often delivered lectures on the importance of making them warm, human, understanding. At one staff meeting, as he held forth on this subject, he suddenly ejaculated, "You can't write the kind of letters I'm talking about unless you've had hockey between your toes. Like Booth here."

After the meeting adjourned it was up to me, as a former farm boy, to explain to my more sophisticated associates that Johnson felt no one could empathize with common folk unless he had at times in his childhood walked barefoot through a barnyard and accumulated some amount of animal manure—hockey—on his feet. An enterprising, although ill-advised, staff member promptly announced formation of a secret society called the H.B.T.T. Club.

Not all letters to constituents had to be dictated individually. We used form letters whenever possible—to send birthday greetings, for example, or congratulations on a golden wedding anniversary. When a legislative issue drew a large amount of fan mail, for or against or both, we turned to the mechanical typewriters available to Senate staffs.

These machines were not the computerized marvels of today which can turn out "personal" letters at the rate of one every seven-tenths of a second. An operator had to type the name, address, and salutation, after which the machines would clatter away typing the body of the letter. One person could keep several machines going simultaneously.

One year, although I think this was somewhat later, Johnson conceived the insane project of sending a congratulatory letter to every high school graduate in Texas. Early in the year we instructed our country political managers to provide us with lists of seniors and eventually we had perhaps 50,000 names on hand. I composed five or six differently worded (warm) letters so that every recipient would not be getting exactly the same message, and they were prepared for the mechanical typewriters.

The senator sent word via Jenkins that all hands were to spend a couple of hours at least one evening a week manning the typewriters. They responded nobly if complainingly, not only secretaries but such incongruous figures as Bill Brammer, a brilliant future novelist (*The Gay Place,* which had a hero roughly modeled on LBJ), and Harry McPherson, a future counsel to the President of the United States. The basement room of the Senate

25

Office Building which housed the typewriters, thirty-five or so in number, became a hell of noise every evening and the Johnson staff a collective object of pity to other Senate employees.

One day Jenkins told me the senator had asked him if I was doing a stint. No, he truthfully replied. "Does he think he's too good to do that?" Johnson demanded incredulously. I suggested to Jenkins that he inform the senator I did think so. I doubt that my suggestion was followed, but in any case I heard no more about the matter.

On another occasion Johnson let me know directly that he was displeased. One day I wrote a statement for him to make in the Senate in support of a housing bill which, he pointed out, would prove beneficial to the large Mexican-American population in Texas. He spoke his piece, I delivered copies of the statement to news reporters, and it seemed to me a good job well done. But I was disillusioned the next morning when Johnson got me on the telephone as soon as he reached his office.

"Did you send my housing statement to the Spanish language papers?" he asked, as usual without preliminaries. "And to the officers of LULAC?" (That was the League of United Latin American Citizens, powerful in South Texas.)

I had not and said so, confessing, "I didn't think of that."

"Didn't think of it! Hell, do I have to think of everything?" His voice rose. "What's the use of working my guts out if we don't make use of what I say? If you can't do what you're supposed to do we'll have to find somebody who can."

"All right," I said, and we both hung up.

Much later that day I encountered Johnson and Daniel in the tunnel leading to the subway line that runs between the Senate Office Building and the Capitol. Johnson hailed me joyously.

"We just passed the tidelands bill," he exclaimed, "and that's the story for the front pages tomorrow." He put a hand on my shoulder. "Come on, Booth, walk over to the office with us."

As the three of us strode to the elevator he kept his hand on my arm, talking excitedly about being rid of this troublesome issue once and for all. I never knew whether he remembered our earlier telephone conversation, but I suspect he did. I already understood that LBJ was a man incapable of apologizing in so many words for anything.

Johnson was an expert needler. When he was in the mood he derived great satisfaction from taking light jabs at anyone within speaking distance— "joshing," in the idiom of the hill country. At a staff meeting one Saturday morning I became conscious that I had been selected as his target of opportunity. From time to time he interrupted serious discussions of political and legislative strategy to direct one-liners at me, his subject matter ranging from the color of my tie to the cigarette ashes I had allowed to dribble onto my lapel. I ignored his sallies. Finally he could no longer endure my lack of response.

"Goddammit, Booth," he exploded, "what's wrong with you? I've been trying all morning to make you mad and you don't even seem to know it."

Probably I should have been ashamed of myself for replying with calculated pomposity, "Why, Senator, what we're talking about is so important that my mind has been completely occupied."

He blinked twice behind his thick spectacles before returning, with a grimace of annoyance, to the business at hand.

At another staff meeting he lectured us rather sharply on our collective shortcomings, finally concluding, "Sometimes I think what I ought to do is get me a good smart Jewish boy as staff director and turn him loose to run things."

When the meeting was over I walked down the corridor with Gerry Siegel, one of the most competent and most unassuming men Johnson ever had working for him.

"You know," Gerry said, smiling, "I thought *I* was his good smart Jewish boy."

He was too, a fact of which Johnson was well aware most of the time.

An extracurricular activity I could not avoid came my way

when Johnson was elected president of the Texas State Society of Washington, D.C. This organization of approximately a thousand displaced persons from the Lone Star State—a great many of whom would vote in Texas by absentee ballot in 1954—had a secretary, but for the two years of LBJ's tenure as president I was in effect his administrative assistant for Society business.

It was at times a demanding assignment. We staged a number of affairs that could only be described as gala, beginning with a hugely attended brunch at the Mayflower Hotel honoring Texas-born Dwight D. Eisenhower and Mrs. Eisenhower. Other big-name honor guests included an old Houston friend of Johnson's, Oveta Culp Hobby, newly elevated to Cabinet status as Secretary of Health, Education, and Welfare, and Attorney General Herbert Brownell, who qualified because his wife was born in Texas. A summer barbecue out in the Virginia countryside drew a couple of thousand—men, women and children—who listened raptly to the western music of native Texan Gene Autry and his Cass County Kids. They also heard the Society president make a speech without any mention of politics, but reminding them that their organization was bigger and better and more active than ever under his leadership. There were coffee parties and dinners and receptions, all well covered by correspondents for Texas newspapers and also adequately recorded in Johnson's weekly newsletter.

With LBJ it was always politics all the way.

Meanwhile, that other campaign, the one starring him in the role of Senate Democratic leader, was being conducted with fervor and skill.

At the beginning of the first session of the 83rd Congress, the Senate was composed of forty-eight Republicans, one Independent (Wayne Morse of Oregon, who announced that he was abandoning the Republican party but would vote with the Republicans in organizing the Senate for the session), and forty-seven Democrats. This near-equality in numbers could not, however, be accepted at face value. The Senate Democrats were far from being a unified force as the session opened.

They were even divided in their opinions about their floor leader. True, the Democratic caucus officially gave him a unanimous vote, but it was not quite that overwhelming. Hubert Humphrey, the fire-eating liberal from Minnesota, had tried to line up votes among the liberals for the elderly James Murray of Montana, giving up only after Johnson had convinced him that the total vote for Murray would be humiliatingly low. But the holders of such votes as the Montana senator would have received remained darkly suspicious of their new leader.

Some of the Democratic senators were decidedly in a don't-care frame of mind. Kenneth Birkhead, assistant to Kentucky Senator Earle Clements, Johnson's whip, ran into aging Francis Green of Rhode Island one day shortly after the Senate reconvened and greeted him, "How're you feeling, Senator?"

"Just great," Green replied.

"That's wonderful," Birkhead said politely.

"Yes. No responsibility."

And with that, Birkhead reported, the senator strolled off down the hall.

Only a few senators would have expressed themselves so nonchalantly, and certainly Johnson was not one who felt any lack of responsibility. He was talking about "the politics of responsibility" from the day the session opened. He had not yet zeroed in on the word consensus, which later became so popular with him, but that was what he sought among Senate Democrats.

Mostly he got it. And in such a way as not to place himself in blatant, overt opposition to the Republican President who had won so handily in Texas the year before.

He soon had Senate watchers, and not long afterward the press, agape with wonder over how he did it. Birkhead, who had been observing the Senate for years, remembered an occasion early in the session when the Republicans planned to pass certain amendments to the Taft-Hartley Act.

"There had been agreement as to a time certain for voting," Birkhead recalled years later. "The time came, and Johnson had every one of the Democratic members sitting in their seats—an unheard of thing. Not just in the chamber, some of them back in the cloakroom, but every one of them sitting in their seats when the vote started. He had Paul Douglas and Harry Byrd sitting there waiting for the vote. I don't think anybody would have ever thought that you could get all those forty-seven guys together and get them there at the same time and have them taking a position in a sense opposed to the Taft-Hartley Act. He did, so help me," said Birkhead, still awed, "come up with every Democratic member sitting there waiting to vote."

Of course they were not always sitting there. One day Johnson called me urgently from the cloakroom for factual information about the Reciprocal Trade Agreements Act, which was up for extension, and said breathlessly into the phone, "Hurry up with it. I'm the only Democrat on the floor and they're letting me have it from all sides."

I hastened over to the Senate chamber, expecting to witness a hair-raising confrontation between the boss and a horde of harrying Republican senators. But I was disappointed. Johnson was indeed the sole Democrat to be seen, but there were only three Republicans in evidence and one of them was presiding over proceedings in the absence of Vice-President Nixon. Johnson, I concluded, was not without a flair for self-dramatization.

Yet he did bring Senate Democrats cohesively together during his two years as minority leader. The wiseacres who had predicted that he would be limited to administering a receivership in political bankruptcy were soon proved wrong. Somehow, he was able to convince his southern conservatives that liberal senators did not really come equipped with horns and a built-in gleam of wildness in their eyes. Somehow, he brought the liberals to understand that more of wisdom than they had thought could be found in some parts of the conservative philosophy.

Johnson himself, smiling his tight little smile, told me that Harry Flood Byrd, the prototype of the Virginia squirearchy, had grumbled to him, "Lyndon, I'll never understand how in the world you got me to liking Hubert Humphrey so much."

His methods were not all that mysterious. As political writers in Washington began to catch onto the fact that a new force was loose in the Senate, they developed a fondness for writing on the one hand about undocumented secret deals and on the other about the Democratic leader's penchant for the use of bullying tactics in dealing with other senators. There was an element of truth in both charges, but they did not contain the whole truth.

Nobody in the world was better than Johnson at man-to-man persuasion. He tugged senatorial lapels, just as the columnists said, and his big nose was often thrust alarmingly close to another's face. One day I saw him at the end of a Senate corridor talking to Senator John Pastore of Rhode Island and he was like a windmill in a gale. His long arms threshed the air, up and down and sideways. He bent from the waist as if picking up an unseen object from the floor with both hands. As I passed along I could not make out what he was saying, but I could see he was speaking without a pause, leaning over the much shorter Pastore and finally, yes, taking him by both lapels as he brought his face down to stare straight into his helpless listener's eyes.

Later that day I asked Johnson what he had been talking about so earnestly to Pastore.

"Oh, it wasn't much of anything," he said. "I was just convincing him of something he already believed."

The senator was indeed persuasive, to say the least, but the principal reason he prevailed so often was that when he talked to a man he almost invariably knew more about him than the man himself knew. Johnson understood, made sure he understood, that other man's strengths and his weaknesses, and he made effective use of the knowledge. He always had on his mental screen a chart showing the points of contact, the buttons that must be pushed to elicit the desired results.

The floor leadership was a high-risk proposition for him as

it affected his standing in Texas. More than once he reminded me that the two immediately preceding Democratic floor leaders, Ernest McFarland of Arizona and Scott Lucas of Illinois, had been defeated at the polls after holding the job. That could happen to him unless he was as wary as a barefoot man in rattlesnake country. His policy of "no opposition for the sake of opposition" to programs offered by the Eisenhower Administration no doubt was based on principle. It also had the advantage of being good politics.

Luckily for Johnson, many Republicans in Congress were unwilling or perhaps unable to give up their habit of automatically opposing almost any proposal coming from the Executive Branch. They had long since become accustomed to saying yes when the President said no and to saying no when the President said "please." They found it hard to change after a Republican moved into the White House.

This state of affairs enabled Johnson to stand with President Eisenhower on some important issues, and lead most of the Democrats with him, against a sizable and vociferous group of Republicans. He made sure that none of this escaped the attention of the folks back home, who certainly did "like Ike." In a typical radio broadcast, carried by many Texas stations, he gave praise to Eisenhower as "a good soldier" who was being protected by an unusual form of partisanship—a combination, said LBJ, "between the President, some elements of his own party, and the Democrats against large groups of Republicans who tried to sabotage his program up and down the line."

The senatorial campaign of 1954 was coming closer in Texas day by day.

In leading most of his Democrats to support the Administration on some highly visible legislative measures, Johnson simultaneously enhanced his stature among them. In the closing hours of the 1953 session, one senator after another stood up to praise his leadership. This was not unusual, for senators are inclined to

32

speak well of one another on such ceremonial occasions. Worthy of note, however, was the disparate nature of the men who rose to laud Johnson. Liberals, conservatives, men from north, south, east, and west—Russell of Georgia and Mike Mansfield of Montana, Lister Hill of Alabama and Green of Rhode Island, Albert Gore of Tennessee, Herbert Lehman of New York, a youthful John Fitzgerald Kennedy, Stuart Symington of Missouri—these and others stressed the spirit of harmony which had come to prevail among them, thanks to the leadership of the senator from Texas. Sitting in the gallery, I swelled with vicarious pride.

Still, on that day in early August, it looked as if half the big-name politicians in Texas were aching for a chance to run for the Senate against Johnson. None of them had forgotten that the federal judge who tried unsuccessfully to overturn his narrow 1958 victory had predicted from the bench that he would never be elected to a second term.

Nor had Johnson forgotten. Within a few hours after he listened to the plaudits of his fellow senators he was on an airplane headed for Texas. He had told me repeatedly he planned to run his campaign for 1954 a year early and that was what he did.

He staged a whirlwind tour of Texas during that fall, visiting every major city and many small towns. He made two or three speeches a day, attended barbecues, sat as honor guest at luncheon meetings, attended county fairs, rode horseback in parades, dedicated school buildings, appeared before school assemblies. It was just plain old county courthouse campaigning. His talks were labeled nonpolitical and, strictly speaking, they were; but Johnson did not neglect to tell about the product he was promoting. He informed me gleefully that he figured he had shaken a quarter of a million Texas hands before the end of the year.

LBJ on the campaign trail presented quite a spectacle. Reedy, a Chicago intellectual who had been one of radio's original "Quiz Kids" before he grew up and became a newspaperman, said he had never seen anything like it.

33

"He's a hero to the people in Texas," he reported to some of his co-workers on Capitol Hill. "We would hit some little town and the senator would be out on the street almost before the car stopped rolling. He'd start down the sidewalk, shaking hands, and pretty soon he would have a crowd following him—kids asking for his autograph, nice old ladies telling him what a fine young man he was, farmers grabbing him by the arm and saying they knew he'd look out for their interests."

Reedy also learned something about grassroots speechmaking techniques. Johnson insisted on having a different speech for each audience. Then he would usually get up in front of an audience and say, "Now this is a really fine speech. My staff worked on it all night and I'm quite proud of it. But here before homefolks I'm going to talk from my heart."

With that, Reedy said, "He'd throw the speech on the floor, then he'd give the speech that had been written for the previous occasion—whatever it was."

Corny? To be sure, but his audiences loved the homespun approach and him. By the time Johnson returned to Washington in January, many leading Texas newspapers were saying editorially that this great leader should be returned to the Senate for another term without opposition. He was given a nice boost with most Texas voters when Morse journeyed to the state to make a Roosevelt Day dinner speech and said: "Johnson has the most reactionary record in the Senate. Look at his voting record. If he should ever have a liberal idea, he would have a brain hemorrhage."

Johnson did have opposition at the polls in 1954, but it could be politely described as token in nature. Dudley Daugherty, a rich young Texas oil man with views that were far off to the right even for Texas, was a candidate for the Democratic nomination for United States senator. He had no knowledge of politics and no idea of how a campaign should be conducted. Johnson's brother found in the Washington files a letter from Daugherty in which the young man praised the senator's performance and said he deserved to be reelected without an opponent. We leaked the letter to the press all over Texas. Johnson made no campaign speeches and put out no campaign literature. But hardly a day passed without our being in touch with friends in Texas to suggest ways of continuing to wage the silent campaign.

"It was just knife, knife, knife all the time," Daugherty later complained.

Few Americans outside of government circles in Washington were paying much attention in 1954 to events taking place in far-off Indochina. In February, President Eisenhower ordered that two hundred and fifty Air Force technicians be sent there from United States bases in Japan. The move was part of a continuing effort to prevent the fall of French Indochina to Communist forces led by Ho Chi Minh. The United States had been financing the French army in the area since 1950 and sending over great numbers of warplanes, naval vessels and combat vehicles. But the Air Force technicians were the first American troops dispatched to Indochina.

The French fortress of Dienbienphu was under heavy attack and its fall seemed imminent. In March, the French chief of staff journeyed to Washington to warn that Indochina would be lost to the communists unless the United States intervened with armed forces.

Secretary of State John Foster Dulles, who favored intervention, met in secret on April 3 with a group of congressional leaders. He told them the President wanted Congress to pass a resolution permitting him to use air and sea power in Indochina.

Minority Leader Johnson and Senator Russell, ranking Democrat on the Armed Services Committee, were among those present. Both opposed intervention. They drew from Dulles an admission that he had not consulted other nations to see if they would join in standing against the Communist attacks. The Secre-

35

tary said he would find out and proceeded to talk with representatives of a number of potential allies. Their responses, in particular that of Great Britain, were negative.

With no allies and no congressional approval, the President refused to yield to pressure from Dulles and Admiral Arthur W. Radford, chairman of the Joint Chiefs of Staff, for intervention with air power. Dienbienphu fell. A conference of the world's big powers at Geneva brought a cease-fire agreement between France and the Communists and the "provisional" division of Vietnam into North and South.

The shooting stopped in Indochina on July 21. The first phase of the war was over. But the way had been paved for a second phase, far bloodier and infinitely more tragic not alone in casualties but in loss of United States prestige abroad and racking discord at home as well.

In the July primary Johnson easily won the Democratic nomination, then still equivalent in Texas to election. The vote in his favor was almost three to one.

The Senate was in session late that night. Staff members and a few friends held an election watch party in the minority leader's office in the Capitol. At midnight, although the outcome was clear, Johnson was still on the phone getting vote counts. Most of the visitors had left. House Majority Leader Sam Rayburn, who had become a great friend of mine after we worked together in Texas in the 1952 presidential campaign, said he was going home. He offered me a ride.

As we descended in the elevator from the second floor of the Capitol, the former and future Speaker grumbled, "That Lyndon! He knows he's got a runaway victory and he's still pestering somebody for precinct returns in a little box in the Panhandle."

It was true that as we left the office Johnson, sipping on a scotch highball, was bawling happily into the phone, "You say the vote there is fifty-seven to forty-three in my favor? That's great, really great! In 1948 I got only six votes in that box."

I also remembered 1948 and, as Sam Rayburn and I rode through the deserted streets of Washington, I thought with wonder of how much I had learned about practical politics since that year. Since coming to Washington, I also had learned something about Lyndon Johnson. Not enough, however, to cause me to feel I saw him plain or that I could make an accurate guess about what he would do under any given set of circumstances. There were still more questions than answers.

3

LET US NOW APPRAISE
FAMOUS MEN

Although Johnson loved the job of minority leader, he had little liking for the title. He instructed those of us who handled news releases and correspondence to refer to him as the Senate Democratic leader and that title was printed on his official letterhead.

After the congressional elections of 1954, the Senate would be composed of forty-eight Democrats and forty-seven Republicans—and Wayne Morse who, completing his phase-out from the GOP announced that he would join the Senate Democratic caucus in January. So Johnson would become majority leader. He could hardly wait.

To be precise, he did not wait. The Senate convened in a lame duck session shortly after the election to take care of a resolution censuring Joe McCarthy, the rambunctious Red hunter from Wisconsin. As soon as he returned to Washington, the majority-leader-to-be held a news conference to state that the Democrats would present their own program in the new Congress. He said he had stopped off in Bonham, Texas, on the way to

Washington to confer with Rayburn, who would again be Speaker of the House. They were in complete agreement, Johnson reported, on a detailed Democratic program covering foreign policy, defense, and domestic affairs.

"Out of deference to the President," he added rather grandly, "the program will not be presented until we have heard his State of the Union message."

LBJ was in top form. He exchanged wisecracks with old friends in the audience, observed sarcastically that the "cold war" between Congress and the Executive predicted by Eisenhower during the campaign would not take place, loudly hailed Senator Gore (whom he did not like) with jovial flattery as the Tennessean came in to stand at the back of the room.

The assembled news gatherers ate it up in spite of being so jammed together in Johnson's Capitol office that some had difficulty in getting enough elbow room to write their notes. Reedy had suggested that the press conference be held in the spacious Senate Caucus Room, an idea vetoed by the boss.

"There aren't enough reporters in the whole city to make a respectable showing there," he objected. "We want it to look like a real crowd on television."

It did and he was happy.

In the year that Johnson stepped up to the post of majority leader, the country was growing fast and the economy was booming. The population approached 164 million, up 2.8 million in a year. The stock market average reached an all-time high. Per capita income and individual spending were greater than ever before. Inflation had been halted, consumer prices having risen by less than one percent in the two years since Eisenhower became President. Johnson shrewdly judged that people generally were in no mood for bitter political warfare.

He also realized that Eisenhower's control of the government now extended only as far as the Democrats in Congress would permit. The center of effective power was no longer in the White

House but on Capitol Hill. Many Republicans, including Knowland, their floor leader in the Senate, were more fundamentally opposed to some presidential programs than were the Johnson-Rayburn axis and their followers.

The combination formed an ideal setup for the pragmatic Johnson. He took full advantage of the opportunity. Thousands of columns of newspaper and magazine space and numerous books have told the story of his first year as majority leader, so I shall not dwell here on his performance. It was, in a word, spectacular.

There he was, day after day, at the first little schoolboyish desk in the front row of the Democratic side of the Senate chamber, the prototype of a take-charge man, standing tall and confident, jangling coins or keys in his pocket as he talked. He was an arresting figure and not only because of his size. He had become a snappy dresser, given to the wearing of silk suits of bright and shining hues. I remember in particular an electric blue suit he favored, worn with a polka dot shirt and a bow tie cut from the same material.

Reporters began to write about his clothing as well as his legislative accomplishments. When the first stories appeared in print about his $200 suits, a considerable price in those days, he seemed more pleased than not. For only a short time, however. He soon began to complain that the reporters, not wishing to take the trouble to understand his miraculous way with legislation, preferred to deal in trivia.

One day I was in his office with Houston Harte, owner of several influential newspapers in Texas and a longtime LBJ supporter. He and Johnson were standing close together as they talked and Harte suddenly reached up to fondle the lapel of the senator's jacket.

"Lyndon, is that one of those $200 suits I've been reading about?" he inquired, smiling with friendly malice.

Johnson gave him a sharp look. "Yeah," he growled almost inaudibly.

The Harte hand came off the Johnson lapel in a hurry.

The Democrats held a margin of two votes in the Senate, counting Morse, but Johnson operated as if he had a tremendous majority and could count on it without fail. He was always a personal politician, not a book politician, and the quality served him well at this time. The majority leader of the Senate possesses little real authority in that capacity alone. The rules and traditions of the body give him only one advantage over any other senator on the floor, which is preference in obtaining recognition from the presiding officer. Otherwise, so far as the actual structure of the Senate is concerned, a majority leader has only the power that he can obtain and exert as an individual. It was in this respect that Johnson excelled.

He knew the territory and he knew the people who inhabited it. As majority leader, he operated on three distinct levels: at the front of the Senate chamber guiding procedures; with other senators individually, persuading, flattering, trading when necessary; in the privacy of his office, where he frequently gave brief and sometimes devastating appraisals of other senators and wickedly mocked their personal idiosyncrasies to appreciative members of his staff.

I picked up more knowledge about other senators by seeing them with Johnson or hearing him talk about them than I could ever have gained from watching them in action in committee rooms or on the floor of the Senate.

After LBJ became President and the Vietnam war was reducing his Administration to a shambles, he and Senator J. William Fulbright of Arkansas had no kind words for each other; but it was different in their Senate days. This was true even though Fulbright had not originally favored Johnson for floor leader, telling Justice Tom Clark that he was too young and had been in the Senate too short a time. Clark thought the fact that Johnson was a Texan also had something to do with Fulbright's attitude, but then Clark hailed from Texas and could have imagined this.

In any event, the two often worked together effectively in the Senate. It was interesting to see the graduate of Southwest Texas State Teachers College and the Rhodes scholar of Oxford University in collaboration on such mundane matters as a housing bill or something of the sort. Johnson was a man who, to the point of boredom, constantly exhorted people to "reason together." Fulbright was a man who appeared to harbor deep-seated doubts that such a thing was possible. He was articulately literate in a degree rare in the Senate, but he liked to go his own lonely way.

"He's so smart," Johnson said to Gerry Siegel after one conference with Fulbright. "If he wasn't the laziest son of a bitch in the world he could be President."

Perhaps Fulbright was indeed indolent by nature or he may at times have simply felt a sense of disengagement. Sitting in on a conversation between him and the majority leader in Johnson's office one day, I decided it must be the latter. Johnson was, as usual, passionately advocating a certain kind of action on a legislative measure in which both men were interested. Fulbright, gazing at him over the top of his glasses and speaking with calm logic, looked every inch a professor in some rather good small university. His sentences came out whole and Johnson listened. But on this occasion they reached no meeting of minds on strategy.

"He just doesn't seem interested in winning," Johnson said disgustedly after the senator from Arkansas had departed. "I don't get it. I disagreed with Harry Truman about a lot of things, but he sure as hell was right when he called Fulbright an overeducated S.O.B."

That was a sometime judgment. Johnson later developed a habit of telling senators who approached him on matters concerning foreign affairs, "See Bill Fulbright. He's my Secretary of State." He eventually persuaded the ninety-one-year-old Francis Green to step down as chairman of the Foreign Relations Committee so Fulbright could assume the post. The Arkansan served as chairman of the committee longer than any other man in the history of the Senate. In 1960, after Kennedy's election, Johnson urged that Fulbright be made Secretary of State in fact. The President-elect was agreeable until his brother Robert and others convinced him that the appointment would be unwise because of the southern senator's position on racial integration.

It was sad that these two men, who contributed so much to the nation when they worked together in the Senate, should have become irreconcilably alienated. But they did, and the alienation was deep and permanent.

Speaking before a large audience of Democrats in 1966, the President expressed pleasure at the presence of "so many of my very old friends" and then added unnecessarily, looking from the podium directly down at Fulbright, "as well as some members of the Foreign Relations Committee." On Fulbright's side, the bitterness lingered after his 1974 defeat by a constituency that had never really deserved him. In a newspaper interview in December of that year, he said Johnson's leadership of the Vietnam war was utterly misguided because of his lack of information. "The thing I resent more than anything about Lyndon Johnson wasn't his mistaken judgment," he went on to say. "It was his deception of me and the public on what his purposes were in '64. I don't see any excuse for deceiving other people with whom you are working."

Their friendship was one more casualty of the Vietnam war.

Paul Douglas of Illinois, a sober-sided economist, author and humanist, came to the Senate the same year as Johnson. LBJ had great respect for him and little rapport with him. He once expressed honest amazement to me that the older man—by some sixteen years—could have been so aggressive as a fighting Marine in World War II, but was unable to get things done in the Senate. He thought this inability resulted from Douglas' self-righteousness, which kept him from considering for a moment any compromise of what he believed in order to make a halfway step toward turning some of his beliefs into legislative reality. At the same time, as he told me, "I'm always glad when Douglas is on my side."

After Johnson became President they were closer than they

had been in the Senate. LBJ then pushed for the kind of civil rights legislation Douglas had always favored. Also, the senator from Illinois was a hard fighter in the Cold War against communism and supported the Administration on Vietnam. He became chairman of a national "Citizens Committee for Peace with Freedom in Vietnam," which was organized to support the war effort. Johnson appreciated that.

Morse was in some ways the most difficult senator for Johnson. The Oregonian possessed an ego to match LBJ's own and he was perpetually ready to speak his mind on any subject. Johnson paid court to him in many ways, mindful that Morse had provided the vote on Senate organization that made him majority leader. He even gave the Oregon senator the Foreign Relations Committee assignment he coveted, although Clinton Anderson of New Mexico, an old friend, also wanted the post. It was after this that Morse rose in the Senate to say (in marked contrast to his estimate of Johnson in his Texas speech the year before), "During the past year I have been the beneficiary of one kindness after another from Lyndon Johnson. I consider him not only a great statesman but a good man."

This sentiment did not endure for long. Morse was soon back at his old habit of rasping disagreement with the majority leader and, for that matter, with almost any majority. Reporters covering the Senate came to anticipate the flicker of annoyance that passed over Johnson's face when Morse—"the Five O'Clock Shadow," as he was dubbed in the press gallery—got up in the late afternoon to begin one of his long, drawn-out harangues.

Still, the two men were kinder to each other in private than they were in their public statements. This remained true even after Johnson became President and the senator was a leading critic of the Vietnam war. When Morse was in a tough fight for reelection in 1968 (which he lost), Johnson instructed about a controversial project proposed for Oregon, "Oh, let Wayne have it. Maybe it'll help him to get reelected." And in that same year Morse held my ear for ten minutes at a cocktail party to expound about the tragedy of events in Vietnam having obscured the great accomplishments of the Johnson Administration.

Gore was another Democratic senator with whom Johnson was frequently vexed. He thought Gore was too fond of hearing his own voice and often spoke in the Senate when he should have been listening. In the world of the Senate, which in a sense was the only real world to Johnson, the majority leader wooed the man from Tennessee and tried to keep him in line with his own objectives. He was sometimes successful, sometimes not.

During one of the failed attempts to bring Gore around, the Tennessee senator complained that a bill being pushed by the leadership smacked too much of partisan politics. The irritated Johnson promptly rushed the bill through the Senate. Back in his office later that day, he telephoned Arthur Krock of *The New York Times,* to whom he often talked in confidence, and gave him an off-the-record account of Gore's opposition to the legislation and his reason for it.

"Politics!" he exclaimed in high, good humor. "That little son of a bitch never had anything but political thoughts in his life. But we beat him! We beat him all right. I guess I showed him we're not about to take any chicken shit from Tennessee."

Johnson cared even less for Estes Kefauver, the other Tennessee senator. They had known each other in the House and both were elected to the Senate in 1948, but they were never bosom buddies. LBJ considered Kefauver a fake liberal, always willing to grandstand in the Senate for propositions that had no chance of enactment. "He's been running for President ever since he hit Washington," Johnson said. And he added, prophetically, "He's never going to make it." Kefauver had shaken the hands of so many prospective voters in presidential primaries that he always approached anybody, no matter who, with an outstretched hand, giving him the nickname among irreverent Senate pages of "the Hand."

Lehman, the liberal senator from New York, was often at odds with the majority leader. This was natural enough. Lehman liked to talk at length about doing good things as he conceived them. Johnson's forte was actually getting something done— something at least fairly good. They were often in conflict, and Johnson noted with asperity that on such occasions he was likely to get the worst of it in newspaper stories. He wanted Reedy to do something about that.

"Political columnists just liked to write about Lehman," Reedy told me in later years. "Not because he was effective, which he wasn't, or overly intelligent, which he wasn't, or a keen parliamentarian, which he wasn't. But they had to find something to praise. So they always called him sincere."

This was not the kind of label that would escape Johnson's attention. He informed Reedy, who dealt daily with the national press, that he himself would like to become known as "Mr. Sincerity" of the Senate. Reedy thought he was out of his mind and would have nothing to do with the project.

"But somewhere," said Reedy, "Johnson had heard or read about subliminal impressions, so when he was in the company of newspaper people he started saying things like 'I want to be *sincere* about this' and 'The *sincere* answer to that would be thus-and-so.'"

Needless to say, the strategy failed to work. Accused of many bad actions and rightly credited with many outstanding deeds of legislative derring do, LBJ was never charged in the press with overriding sincerity, one definition of which is freedom from simulation.

A senator Johnson never really understood was Leverett Saltonstall, the minority whip, a Massachusetts patrician who had made a career of politics. The two served on the Armed Services Committee from the time Johnson entered the Senate and rarely differed there. Saltonstall also was the ranking Republican member of Johnson's Preparedness Investigating Subcommittee, which never returned a minority report. They worked together amicably on nonpolitical matters, but the Bay Stater remained an enigma to the Texan.

"He's an able senator," Johnson mused to me, "a well-educated man, a fine gentleman of the old school. But he's so *unaware!*" he cried. "Why," he said, jabbing a finger into my chest, "you could be screwing every secretary in his office and he wouldn't have any idea that anything was going on."

Saltonstall and his very junior colleague, John F. Kennedy, came to the majority leader one day with an urgent request. They wanted the Senate to pass a resolution paying tribute to Arthur Fiedler, director of the famous Boston Pops, on the occasion of his twentieth anniversary with the orchestra.

"Who the hell is Fiedler?" Johnson demanded.

They explained, or Saltonstall did while Kennedy stood looking young and earnest.

"Goddammit!" Johnson exploded. "This is the United States Senate! Are we going to have to pass resolutions honoring every drum-and-fife man in the country?"

They stared at him speechlessly and started to turn away. Typically, Johnson relented.

"Oh, all right," he said. "Give me your resolution and we'll get it through."

At another time Saltonstall, who was a member of the Board of Regents of the Smithsonian Institution, suggested to Johnson that he approach the fabulously rich H. L. Hunt to see if that gentleman would be interested in giving money to build an air museum in Washington. Since Hunt was not known for philanthropic activity and since he and Johnson stood at opposite polls politically (except for the petroleum depletion allowance), the majority leader was not receptive to the idea.

"I didn't get very far with Johnson on that one," Saltonstall reported later. "I think he was being cautious."

On his side, Johnson thought Saltonstall was being more naive than necessary.

As for the other Massachusetts senator, Johnson looked on

47

Kennedy as a nice young fellow but lacking the prized get-up-and-go spirit. His principal complaint about John Kennedy was that he appeared to take little interest in the work of the Senate, which to LBJ was the cardinal sin. He said the young senator was never around when needed for a close vote and was harder to track down than anybody else in the Senate.

"He's just a playboy," the majority leader grumbled. "Always off with some girl."

As a matter of course, Johnson maintained his enduring ties with the southern dons of the Senate, the conservative men with seniority and power who regarded him with pride as their boy. He sought their counsel daily and flattered them shamelessly. At times I was a witness to their meetings and I never ceased to be impressed by the mutual understanding, making words almost unnecessary, with which they approached issues concerning the Senate. The southerners did not always agree with their leader, but they wanted him to do well and, when it was necessary, were usually willing to stretch their own convictions to support him.

One year some of the Senate Republicans were trying hard to make drastic cuts in Eisenhower's appropriations request for foreign aid. In the past, when such efforts were mounted, Johnson had been able to bring about restoration of most or all of the funds requested when the foreign aid bill came up for final passage. This time, he told Russell, who favored the proposed cuts, he was pretty well fed up.

"I'm thinking I might just sit back and let 'em go at it," he declared. "After all, he's their President and if they won't stay with him why should I stick my neck out?"

I was surprised to hear Russell reply thoughtfully in his deliberate southern voice, "No, Lyndon, you can't do that. You've made a record on foreign aid—I wish the record was different, but there it is—and you have to be consistent."

This may have been the advice Johnson hoped to get. Anyway, he followed it.

The silver-haired Walter George, also of Georgia, was another of Johnson's band of southerners, one who could be depended on to raise his magnificent voice in the Senate chamber at times when his support meant a great deal to the Democratic leader. John G. Stennis of Mississippi and Burnet R. Maybank of South Carolina were important members of the tried-and-true group of LBJ mentors. Johnson had great respect for Byrd of Virginia, who told him in 1960 that he had not voted for a Democratic candidate for President since 1936 and who opposed most Democratic programs. Although the apple-cheeked archconservative liked Johnson and was kind to the younger man in many ways, their relationship was always more personal than political.

Sam Ervin of North Carolina was one southern senator for whom Johnson had little regard, although he did not advertise his feeling. Ervin, who came to the Senate in mid-1954 to fill out an unexpired term vacated by the incumbent's death, was touted by the press as a great constitutional lawyer. He had a large fund of rural stories, neither as amusing nor as apropos as he evidently thought. Newspapers doted on publishing stories about how the simple country lawyer pose cloaked a deep knowledge of what the framers of the Constitution had in mind. Johnson doubted that this was true and if it was true thought it unimportant.

"Ervin's a lightweight, a windbag," he said flatly.

He held quite a different view of another southerner, James O. Eastland of Mississippi. He deplored Eastland's militant racism and laughed privately at his Internal Security Subcommittee's obsession with the subversive threat to America posed by international communism. But he admired the political astuteness of the man from Mississippi and knew he could depend on him for support of legislation designed to benefit the rural areas of the nation.

He sometimes entertained me and other staff members by telling us how he would expect Eastland to react to various situations. His Texas twang would disappear to be replaced by a heavy southern drawl.

49

"Jim Eastland could be standing right in the middle of the worst Mississippi flood ever known," he joked on one occasion, "and he'd say the niggers caused it, helped out some by the Communists—but, he'd say, we gotta have help from Washington."

Johnson paused, his half-smile appearing. "And I'd try to see that he got it."

Even such good and faithful friends as Clements, his second in command in the Senate, and Humphrey, who had been won over to become a pipeline between the liberals and the Establishment, could not wholly escape being subjected to more or less gentle ribbing from their leader.

Johnson and Clements, the quintessential Kentucky politician, enjoyed a complete mutual understanding. Both knew a great deal about politics and power, and each was fully convinced that there was no higher Heaven than the United States Senate. Clements was dog-loyal to the man and the leader. And he was enormously helpful to him because he had an inside track to both the national Democratic party and to organized labor that Johnson lacked at the time.

I know that Johnson truly loved Clements. Yet he could not resist, always in private, mocking the way the Kentuckian talked: "We've got the votes on this bill, Lyndon. I say, we've got the votes." And Clements did in fact frequently repeat a sentence, invariably prefacing the repetition with a resoundingly vacuous "I say."

Later, in 1956, when Clements was struggling to win reelection, Johnson sent me down to Kentucky to help however I could in publicity for the campaign. He telephoned me often from Texas that fall to get a firsthand report on how things were going, repeatedly emphasizing that for him, no less than Clements, this was the most important contest in the nation. He arranged, through me on a small scale and through Bobby Baker, secretary to the Democratic majority, on a much larger scale, for financial assistance to be pumped into Kentucky from other states. We did all we could, but Clements narrowly lost to Thruston Morton—probably because a vote he cast in the Senate, to accommodate Johnson, on a bill affecting the medical profession had infuriated the doctors in his home state and resulted in their organized opposition to his reelection.

After the election Johnson commended me for my work in Kentucky. I expressed appreciation, but pointed out that obviously I had fallen short of attaining the hoped-for goal.

"You shouldn't feel that way," he said. "Look at it this way. Your man ran way ahead of the national ticket in Kentucky. You did everything anybody could've done."

Sometimes Lyndon Johnson could be downright surprising.

LBJ's relationship with Humphrey was somewhat different. It was partly a matter of age. Clements was a dozen years older than Johnson, Humphrey three years younger. Whatever the reason, the majority leader worked with the Kentucky senator as an equal and with the Minnesota senator on another level.

Not that his attitude toward Humphrey was overtly condescending—he *needed* him. Besides, he felt a real affection for the man, wholeheartedly approved of his concern for the poor and disadvantaged, and admired with a tinge of skepticism Humphrey's ability to talk extemporaneously and at length on a subject picked at random. He also regarded Humphrey, rightly or wrongly, as a convert from impractical liberalism to his own pragmatism in legislative activity. He thought, as he said more than once, that they made a great team in the Senate of the 1950s.

One evening, staying later on the job than I usually did, I went by Johnson's office to find him and Humphrey and a pretty young secretary. The senators were discussing the next day's legislative agenda, but Humphrey was unable to refrain from spreading himself out to direct some of his remarks to the secretary and, occasionally, to me. The charm of his conversation was irresistible. His nimble mind darted here and there and his facile tongue uttered a thought as soon as it came to him. Johnson, who could be as silent as anybody when it suited him, listened with every appearance of interest, from time to time bringing Humphrey back to the subject. I was fascinated. The secretary was goggle-eyed.

When Humphrey finally departed with a cheery "Good night, see you tomorrow," Johnson got to his feet and looked down gravely at his two employees.

"That's one of the sharpest minds you'll ever be around," he said. "One of the best talkers too." He gazed sharply at the young woman. "And you," he added, his eyes glinting with mischief, "honey, if Booth and I hadn't been here ol' Hubert probably would've talked you right into bed."

At a different time, he remarked of Humphrey, "Hubert prepares for a major speech by taking a deep breath."

Another liberal, Richard Neuberger of Oregon, who became a senator the same month that Johnson assumed the majority leadership, was an intellectual journalist who wrote for periodicals as diverse as *American Magazine* and *New Republic*. Johnson campaigned for him in 1954 and they liked each other. The man of the land from the Texas hill country was particularly impressed by Neuberger's dedication to the cause of conservation.

Humphrey, Neuberger, Johnson were seen by some Senate observers as a strange and unlikely combination. All the same, when Americans for Democratic Action accused Johnson of going along with a Republican "assault on liberalism," Humphrey, a founder of the organization, spoke up in the Senate to defend the integrity of the Texan's own liberalism. And Neuberger said realistically, "I think Johnson is as liberal as he can be and still continue as the effective leader of the senators who sit on the Democratic side."

These two, Johnson thought, were the best choices to reply to the ADA attack. He made no statement in his own defense.

"Let the liberals talk to their own," he said. "No need to overdo it."

It was clear by now that Johnson, although he continued to depend heavily on the southerners, had become much more than a regional politician following his reelection in 1954. On some legislative issues he could put together nearly incredible coalitions consisting of the southerners, a far right Republican such as Nevada's George Malone, a liberal Republican such as Maine's Margaret Chase Smith, a maverick like Morse, and most of those Democrats who had viewed his selection as floor leader with undisguised dismay.

The western senators early adopted Johnson as one of their own—men like the venerable Carl Hayden of Arizona, both "Big Ed" Johnson and Eugene Milliken of Colorado, Clinton P. Anderson and Dennis Chavez of New Mexico, and the two Washington senators, Warren Magnuson and Henry "Scoop" Jackson. Some of them naturally had their own ambitions and all of them had their own ideas about legislative issues, but Johnson was uusually secure in the knowledge that they would be on his side when roll call votes came.

Another westerner, Mike Mansfield, a quiet and studious former professor of history at Montana State University, succeeded Clements as deputy majority leader. His style was in sharp contrast to Johnson's, but they worked well together. The professor never tried to second-guess the politician.

LBJ had a strong fellow-feeling for Robert S. Kerr, the Oklahoman who had come to the Senate at the same time as he. Their neighboring states were blessed, or cursed, with the same petroleum and agricultural interests. The two men, big and tough, were equally adept at looking out for themselves when the infighting became mean. Johnson considered Bob Kerr the most forceful debater in the Senate. He may have been, although it seemed to me that he most often made his points by bullying tactics that almost physically backed his opponents up against the wall. Johnson also admired his sense of humor, which was decidedly heavy-handed and consisted in the main of insulting his adversaries—as when, in a fiery speech, he called the rotund Homer Capehart of Indiana a "rancid tub of ignorance." But his mind undeniably was quick and incisive. He quickly became a power in the Senate, and after Johnson left to become Vice-President was generally regarded as the most powerful man in the body.

Tom Hennings, who served several terms in the House before his election as a senator from Missouri in 1950, presented a different picture. Kerr was a teetotaler, a table-thumping Baptist, a pragmatic businessman with a tinge of old-fashioned southwestern populism. Hennings was a liberal, a courteous intelligent man, and an alcoholic. He was popular in the Senate but not influential there, although he might have been except for his alcoholism. He often was absent from his official Senate duties for days at a time. This was a source of irritation to the majority leader, who nevertheless always treated the somewhat older man with the utmost consideration. Perhaps Johnson's attitude grew out of the fact that his own brother was overly fond of the bottle. Whatever the reason, it was a measure of his understanding of human qualities that he seemed equally at home with Tom Hennings and Bob Kerr.

It took more than his famed skill at twisting arms for Johnson to pull Congress out of the doldrums in which it had drifted for most of the time since Franklin D. Roosevelt's second term. He brought senators together not by seeking the lowest common denominator in legislation but by determining what was the utmost that he could get a majority to support. As Saltonstall pointed out, he dealt with different people in different ways.

"He knew how to go after a person, so to speak," Saltonstall remembered in an interview for the oral history collection of the Lyndon Baines Johnson Library in Austin. "He never put the whips on me, to use that expression, in any sense of the word. He would say, 'Help me.' "

The Massachusetts senator was not the only Republican to receive special attention from Johnson. When he became the minority floor leader, he went out of his way to establish a friendly relationship with Majority Leader Robert A. Taft. Their regard for each other, emerging slowly, had its genesis in the respect each felt for the other as a man. Neither entertained any doubts about the other's integrity. Both were men of their word. Both loved the Senate. Each valued a worthy opponent and neither had any use for the kind of aimless chitchat that Johnson jeered at as "just visiting" and Taft forthrightly scorned as nonsense.

Two or three weeks before the Republican senator's death in the summer of 1953, Johnson told me, "Taft is dying. Write me a short statement so I'll have it ready." When death came, Johnson stood up in the Senate and read from the sheet of paper he had been carrying around in his pocket, "No more honorable man has ever sat as a Senate leader for any party. I have lost one of the best friends I ever had." He choked over the words, tears in his eyes, and I could but marvel that the emotion was genuine.

He and William F. Knowland, the California senator who succeeded Taft as Republican leader, got along together well enough, but it was a different relationship. Johnson at bottom felt that his opposite number, decidedly a heavyweight in physique, was a lightweight in leadership. In his office he sometimes lumbered across the room in a slow, ponderous fashion, muttering inarticulately, to show how Knowland approached legislative questions. Sitting across the aisle in the chamber, he used to twit the Californian as a roll call vote neared on one bill or another, "Bill, you just don't have the votes." Knowing it was the truth, Knowland usually managed to summon up a weak grin by way of reply.

When Knowland left the Senate to run—unsuccessfully—for governor of California, he was succeeded in the Republican leadership by Everett Dirksen of Illinois. Johnson laughed at Dirksen's chameleonlike qualities, but made use of them when it suited his purpose. Dirksen was a ham actor of great ability and that also amused his Democratic counterpart.

Styles Bridges, senator from New Hampshire, was prominent in the top Republican leadership, and he and Johnson were an effective team in moving things along. They settled more than one issue in quiet conversation without riling up their partisans in the Senate. Both were splendid pros; they understood each other's motives and political necessities.

Nor did Johnson neglect other Republicans. He made a lifelong friend of Margaret Chase Smith, who was on the Armed Services Committee with him, by arranging for a special staff member of that panel to be named by her and to be responsible only to her. He had the greatest respect for both Vermont senators, George Aiken and Ralph Flanders. He was never able to devote much time to such Neanderthals as Burke Hickenlooper of Iowa, Herman Welker of Idaho and the two Indiana senators, Capehart and William Jenner. LBJ had to draw the line somewhere.

Between them, Johnson in the Senate and Rayburn in the House got Congress moving again and kept it moving through the years of the Eisenhower Administration. They propped up the President to a greater extent than most of their troops realized.

One of the most respected newspaper columnists in the country, an outspoken admirer of President Eisenhower, wrote: "I do not think it is any exaggeration to say that Mr. Eisenhower's success as President began when the Republicans lost control of Congress and the standing committees. In his first two years he had suffered an almost unbroken record of frustration and domination by the senior Republicans, and particularly the Republican committee chairmen in the Senate."

Thus spoke Walter Lippmann in the year 1955.

"We have to help him," Johnson said earnestly to me after one visit he and the Speaker made to the White House—in the cool of the evening, I should add, for conversation and a quiet drink with the President. "He's great at running for office, but he doesn't know beans about government. The Republicans will ruin him if he listens to them too much."

The senator gave a sudden short laugh.

"You know, when he talks about the way some of the Republicans fight against his proposals he wrinkles up his forehead so it looks like a washboard. He just can't understand them. It's sort of pitiful."

He shook his big head wonderingly, but his tone was not that of a man overcome by compassion. Johnson was a Democrat by birth and conviction. Eisenhower, to him, was a Republican only by happenstance. That made a great deal of difference to LBJ, who believed wholeheartedly that a man ought to know where he stood. Even if he did not feel a compulsion to say so at every opportunity and under all circumstances.

The Senate man and the Texas politician did not always add up to the same person. It occurred to me that Johnson often played the hypocrite in dealing with other senators—but then he was never hypocritical except on purpose, which rather removed the stigma. The keen delight he took in cajoling men to go in the direction he pointed them contrasted sharply with the unthinking abruptness with which he issued orders to persons he had no need to persuade. The earthy, frequently coarse, language of the Texas hill country that marked his private conversation was far removed from the smarmy piety of too many of his public addresses.

All these and other contradictions were essential parts of the whole man. They would become more evident, rather than less, as time moved him forward.

4

A HEART ATTACK, A BOOK

Lyndon Johnson's heart attack on July 2, 1955, as I told my wife when I heard about it, was the least surprising news imaginable. At least in hindsight. For six months Johnson had been going at breakneck speed. His usual day began at seven-thirty in the morning and lasted until eleven or eleven-thirty at night. He seemed always in motion. More than once I saw him literally run the few steps from a doorway in the Senate Office Building to his car waiting at the curb. Even when talking on the phone he was likely to stride back and forth beside his desk. For lunch he gobbled a hamburger, rarely sitting down while he ate it. Late at night when he finally went home after downing two or three stiff drinks of scotch, he devoured a large steak and immediately afterward fell into bed. He sucked in the smoke from sixty cigarettes a day.

At the office, he had grown increasingly snappish. His staff, always stepping lively, stepped livelier still in the hope of averting irritated outbursts from the boss. He even forgot at times to be kind to visiting constituents. One day a group of Texas "Minute

Women," an organization of the extreme right, called on Johnson to urge him to "help get the U.S. out of the U.N. and the U.N. out of the U.S." In about six minutes the little old ladies scurried from his room, followed by a tired enraged roar, "Just get the hell out of my office!" The day before the heart attack, a Saturday, a session in his office with half a dozen news reporters came to an abrupt and mutually acrimonious end after he flew into a tantrum when asked a perfectly legitimate question and unmercifully bawled out one of the least offensive of the reporters.

Still in control of the Senate, he no longer was fully in control of himself. He was riding for a physical fall and he fell.

The heart attack was medically described as "moderately severe." There was no possibility that he could resume his duties in the Senate for the remainder of the session. Clements took over for four listless and unproductive weeks until Congress adjourned.

The first time I visited Johnson in Bethesda Naval Hospital, about a week after an ambulance had brought him there, he appeared depressed and withdrawn. He gave me a weak "hello" and complained immediately with evident self-pity that Rayburn had not been out to see him.

"He told me your doctor said you shouldn't have outside visitors for two weeks," I explained. "He's waiting until then."

"Yeah," he grunted. "That's just like him. Well, tell him to come out when he feels like it."

He fell silent then, staring up at the ceiling as he lay on his back in the outsize hospital bed. An oxygen tent was visible in a corner of the room. The creases in Johnson's face had deepened since I last saw him. His eyes were sunken. He had no interest in talking. There was something especially pathetic about such a big man lying there like that. Prometheus bound. I felt far away and sorrowful and stayed only a few minutes.

Three or four days later he sent word that he wished to see me again. The second visit was remarkably different from the first. He was back in play. He had a project for me.

For months the press had been giving awed attention to Johnson's prowess in the Senate. The issue of *Newsweek* on the stands when he suffered the heart attack contained a laudatory story about the Senate record during his half-year as majority leader. On the day after he was stricken the Washington *Post* published a column composed earlier in the week by its chief political writer built around the idea that Johnson was "riding a presidential boom." On that same Sunday the Orlando, Florida, *Sentinel,* published by a former Texan and an old LBJ friend, carried a glowing front-page editorial endorsing him for President.

This calculated orchestration of publicity was thrown out of synchronization by the heart attack. But that hardly mattered, for now hundreds of newspaper stories and editorials about Johnson appeared in print. Without exception they gave high praise to his leadership in the Senate. Many pointed out that if he recovered he could well be a future candidate for the Democratic nomination for President. The stories dwelt on his personality as well as his legislative activities, reviewed his political career, and painted appealing word pictures of his wife and their two daughters.

All this publicity resulted in an avalanche of "get-well" letters, thousands of them from all over the country. It was the letters that occasioned the senator's summons to me.

"We're going to answer all of them," he informed me, his voice not as strong as it had been but decisive. "Every one has to have a personal reply."

Immediately aghast, I protested, "But all the newspaper people and everybody who reads the papers know you're not up to dictating letters. It would look fake."

"No, it won't," he denied. "Bird and I were talking about it last night and we've got everything figured out. She'll sign the letters—even write some of them, to really close friends, but we're asking you to handle most of them. You can do it better than anybody else. Make 'em short, just a few lines, but tender and grateful. You know how to do it and Bird and I are counting on you. Talk to her before you leave."

Those were my sailing orders for Project Impossible. For the next few weeks I kept three stenographers busy transcribing short notes to be signed by Lady Bird Johnson. Out at the hospital, where she had moved the night her husband entered it, she used the hours not spent with Johnson to read and sign these notes, often adding a handwritten postscript. Gracious and considerate lady that she was, and is, she told me several times that they were just right, expressing exactly what she thought and felt.

The letters to which we replied were amazing in their variety and content. They came not only from old friends and political supporters in Texas and from figures high in the government and business world but also from many other persons of whom Johnson had never heard. A letter from a group of Catholic sisters reported that he had been adopted as their personal senator. The president of Wiley College for blacks in Marshall, Texas, near the community where Lady Bird lived as a girl, wrote that the students were praying for Johnson's complete recovery. An elderly lady, an old-age pensioner who described herself as one who had been helped by Johnson's work in Congress, enclosed a dollar bill with her letter. She explained that she knew how much it could mean to receive money unexpectedly in the mail and thought perhaps he would wish to use the dollar to buy something to add a note of cheer to his hospital room. A German lawyer wrote—in German—that he had once suffered a heart attack, knew how to expedite recovery, and was willing to come to the United States at his own expense to pass on his knowledge "because of what you, as a leader in your country, have done for my country." An Indiana farmer and his wife sent a greeting card every day for three weeks, each bearing a different handwritten verse of encouraging Scripture.

Although I admired LBJ, I had never for a moment thought of the possibility that he might be a sort of loved-by-all figure. Now, reading all these letters and dictating replies to them, I wondered.

The letters were answered, all of them, just as Johnson had

said they must be. He told me, and I believed him, that the comforting messages sent to him contributed as much to his recovery as the efforts of his doctors.

Whatever the cause, his progress after the first two weeks was highly satisfactory. He organized his recovery like a political campaign, and as successfully. The doctors told him he should reduce his weight from 200 to 185 pounds; he announced his determination to take off fifteen pounds more. His daily intake of calories, they said, should be limited to 1,500; he asked Lady Bird to figure out a nutritive diet of no more than 1,200 calories a day. He gave up cigarettes, showing me with pride an opened pack which he kept on his bedside table as a way of testing his willpower. He even took a long nap every afternoon.

He was a changed man in other, less visible ways, he assured two or three favorite newspaper columnists who were allowed to visit him while he was still hospitalized. He evidently convinced them, for stories began to appear—which I scanned in utter disbelief—that he had resolved never to go back to his old driving ways. The Johnson who once had admitted or even boasted that he doubted if he had read as many as half a dozen books all the way through since leaving college was said now to be deep into Plato, not to mention innumerable volumes of American history. He had developed a new personal philosophy of life, he declared. "I've thrown away the whip," he said.

None of these heralded changes turned out to be of an enduring nature, although I think Johnson really believed in them at the time.

Five weeks after he entered the hospital he was permitted to go to his home in Northwest Washington. Soon he was asking Reedy and me to bring small groups of reporters out to the house so they could see for themselves—and write about—how well this changed man was progressing toward recovery.

One day I took several Washington correspondents for Texas newspapers to see him. Sporty in a tailored dressing gown worn over shirt and trousers, LBJ greeted each of them warmly from the big leather chair on which he half-reclined. It was the first time they had seen him since the heart attack and they were slow to ask questions, doubtful that he was in shape to deal with a full-dress press conference. No matter. He was ready to talk and he talked.

He started out in a philosophical vein, explaining thoughtfully to the friendly reporters that he had never realized how many good people there were in the world until he was laid low. The folks down in Johnson City always knew when you were sick, he said, and it looked to him as if the whole country was filled with people like them. He told of visits by President Eisenhower and Vice-President Nixon while he was in the hospital. He said he was going home to Texas as soon as the doctors would let him and take it easy on the banks of the Pedernales for the remainder of the year. As he talked, the adrenalin began to flow and his tone quickened until he was sounding like the LBJ of old. He got to his feet and started walking around the room, brushing aside the protests of a couple of reporters who expressed concern that he was overdoing. He displayed a copy of his latest cardiogram, explaining its intricacies in terms he had memorized from the medical report. He bragged about the weight he had lost.

"Look!" he exclaimed, opening the dressing gown and loosening his belt to show that his trousers were much too big around the waist. Then he dropped the trousers to mid-thigh, causing Sarah McClendon, one of the reporters, to give a delighted gasp. "Feel that stomach," he ordered the nearest reporter, grinning broadly as the man placed a hand on his flat front.

Before the meeting ended he presented each reporter with a transistor radio, then new on the market, each one accompanied by a humorous and personal note written by me and signed by him. Because all of them had been so good to him through the years, he explained.

When I left with the reporters Johnson was heading for the bedroom, saying heartily that it was time for his nap. "Thanks for coming!" he exclaimed over his shoulder.

Outside the house, Marshall McNeill, a Scripps-Howard

writer who had known Johnson for many years, looked at me with an unbelieving smile on his face. "That," he said, "was the damndest performance I ever saw."

The ensuing stories in Texas papers were tremendous.

Walter Jenkins telephoned me the next day to say I should come by his office and pick up my transistor radio. What radio? I asked. Walter said the senator had instructed him that morning to get a set for me. He quoted LBJ: "I looked around the room yesterday afternoon and suddenly it came to me that I was giving radios to all those people who don't really give a damn about me and I'd skipped Booth, who's been working his tail off. I felt like a dog."

He caused me to feel like one a few days before he departed for his Texas ranch early in September.

Jenkins had told me the senator was determined that I should be among the staff members accompanying him to Texas. His plan was for me to stay at the ranch, living and working there, until shortly before Christmas. This was not a prospect that appealed to me. Fortunately, I thought, I had the perfectly valid excuse of my wife's pregnancy for not leaving Washington. I informed Jenkins that it would be impossible for me to go and he should tell the senator so.

"He's not going to like that," Jenkins predicted glumly.

Nor did he. LBJ called me to his house the next day. He barely greeted me before launching into a flattering exposition of how important and necessary it was to him that I should be at his side during the fall months. He went on to say that the ranch was where the action would be. He expected such visitors as Adlai Stevenson, Speaker Rayburn, innumerable senators, and many other political personages. I would have a once-in-a-lifetime opportunity to get to know these high-up Democrats in informal surroundings. Besides, he added, there would be little real work for me to do. I would practically be on vacation all the time.

We were standing close together in his living room as we

talked, him looking down earnestly into my face. I was compellingly reminded of our first conversation nearly three years before. Here I was getting the Johnson Treatment all over again. But this time I put up resistance.

"I can't do it, Senator," I said. "My wife and I are expecting a baby in November and I feel my place is here."

He said I could return to Washington on a moment's notice. Certainly he would send me back well before the expected arrival of the baby.

"Something might go wrong," I continued to object, "and I'd never forgive myself if I weren't here."

This was true, but not all the truth. I doubted that my system could stand ten or twelve weeks of exposure, imprisoned on a secluded ranch twenty-four hours a day, to this geyser of impatient energy.

He may or may not have suspected I was being disingenuous. In either case, what he said was, "Bird has had miscarriages and I wasn't around."

Unable to think of any reply to that, I said nothing.

"You won't go then, is that it?"

"Senator, I can't," I said desperately.

"Usually if a man is working for another man he tries to do what his employer wants him to do."

The threat was unmistakable.

"I know that," I said, "and I won't complain about any decision you make."

For the first time he turned his gaze away from me and looked down at the floor. When he spoke again it was in a disjointed mumble to the effect that he had talked with his wife and she was grateful for the help I had given her with the letters while he was in the hospital and if I felt I shouldn't go to Texas she was on my side. But he sure as hell couldn't understand my attitude.

As I remained silent he suddenly brightened.

65

"I'll tell you what you can do," he said, his voice normal again.

A few months earlier I had suggested to Johnson that I would like to write a book about him, a short biography. Engrossed wholly in the work of the Senate at the time, his reaction had been decidedly negative. Now, he said, he had changed his mind. Since I was not going to Texas and there would not be much to do in the Washington office, I could spend the fall writing the book. He would help. All his scrapbooks would be available and I could consult files of the *Congressional Record* in the Senate Library and of course I should talk to people who had worked for him for years. Also, becoming steadily more enthusiastic, he said he and Walter would give me a list of old friends in Texas to whom I could write or telephone for further information.

"What you do," he concluded, in command again, "you study that little campaign biography you wrote about Coke Stevenson in 1948 and then you write a book like that about me. Except," he added quickly, "better and longer. You didn't have as good a subject in Coke."

More or less stunned, I went away. The next day I started getting together material for the book. I did not find it necessary to follow LBJ's unintentionally comic instruction for me to study the one I had written about Stevenson.

It was an agreeable assignment. I explored all the sources Johnson had suggested. And others, including a number of senators, newspaper people who covered Johnson, his brother Sam Houston, Bobby Baker, and Secretary of the Senate Felton Johnston. Also, I recalled stories about Johnson's boyhood told to me by his mother, Rebekah Baines Johnson. I had met this imposing lady for the first time that summer while she was in Washington during her son's convalescence. Then seventy-four years of age, she charmed reporters—and me—with her calm common sense and her tales of a younger LBJ.

The book admittedly was not as objective as it might have

66

been under other circumstances, although I tried hard to do a competent job. When Roger Straus of Farrar, Straus & Cudahy, as his publishing firm was then known, accepted the manuscript, he told my agent that I had written a "puff" book. I hoped it was not quite that, but Johnson unquestionably was portrayed in a light more favorable than not.

Not favorably enough, however, for Rebekah Baines Johnson.

LBJ asked me to send a copy of the manuscript to him in Texas, the Senate not being in session when I finished. Naturally, I did so. I have no solid evidence that he read it, but I do know he turned it over to his mother. And during the time that the original manuscript was in my agent's hands, she read the carbon copy and carefully noted her judgments in penciled statements in a stenographer's notebook which in due time she sent to me. (The notebook is now in the possession of the Lyndon Baines Johnson Library.) She definitely had some suggestions to offer about the book regarding her son.

The second sentence of the first chapter of my manuscript began, perhaps a trifle grandiosely, "The heart attack opened the way for the final stage of a metamorphosis that had transformed a brash young congressman from the brash state of Texas. . . ." Mrs. Johnson noted succinctly, "I question the use of the word brash." I wondered then, and wonder now, if any other person in the world would have raised the question.

I wrote: "Johnson's seizure . . . focused nationwide attention on him and the accomplishments of the Senate under his leadership." The mother said she preferred "attack" to "seizure" (no doubt because people were seized with fits in the hill country), but she was wholeheartedly in accord with the latter part of the sentence. "Excellent," she praised. "Well-expressed and epitomizing the feeling of the nation."

She was less taken with my statement that at the time of the heart attack Johnson's "full stature was not generally recognized."

"Think this statement is too strong," she observed, "as many have for a long time looked to him with confidence and hope for the betterment of the world."

In writing of Johnson's early career, I pointed out that when he was Texas administrator for the National Youth Administration in 1935–36, he received as a dividend for his outstanding work "a strong and lasting foundation of political strength." Mrs. Johnson took a dim view of the implications of this bald statement. "This *was* an asset," she conceded, "but Lyndon's work was not done with that in mind. He had a deep desire continuing from the beginning of his teaching to do something for the youth of Texas."

I came a real cropper when I set out to describe Johnson's first term in the House of Representatives. As a pet of FDR's, he was unusually successful for a freshman congressman in getting Federal projects such as dams and rural electrification projects for his district, which, I wrote, "was always first in his thoughts."

Rebekah Baines Johnson thought this was "very good" until she was brought up sharply by a sentence reading, "And, of course, as a matter of practical politics he knew the wisdom of doing everything for his district that he possibly could do." Such a thought never crossed his mind, in his mother's opinion. "He is first of all a servant of the people working for their interests," she penciled in her forceful script. "The ideas of political advancement for himself should not be played up or stressed. They are only incidental and advancement for himself is to be considered as further opportunity for service to the people and the nation. A statesman is selfless and devoted to the public good."

Again I ran into trouble when I gave some mention to a "well-publicized offer" by President Roosevelt to appoint Johnson to head the Rural Electrification Administration, which had been turned down. I had been told (by his brother), although I did not write, that the job offer was a presidential stratagem, discussed beforehand by Roosevelt and Johnson, to increase the prestige of

his favorite young Texas congressman, so I felt justified in imply-
ing that the ploy had been successful. But Mrs. Johnson asked
plaintively, "Couldn't this *well-publicized* be stated so the critical
eye looking for weak spots in Lyndon's character couldn't say that
he never lost an opportunity 'to blow his own horn'?"

Happily, my narrative about his campaign for the Senate in
1948 met with a more favorable reception. This was because I
quoted at some length from Johnson's statement on entering the
race. "The reasons for his decision stated in his own language
reveal his responsibility to the people and his self-abnegation," the
mother approved. "Here the advancement idea is played down as
it should be."

In fact, my manuscript uniformly received the mother's ap-
probation when I quoted from her son's speeches or from press
commendation of his work as majority leader. "Think this is an
excellent presentation of Lyndon's work, his goals, his strategy,
and his growth," she commented about one section. "These chap-
ters . . . relate graphically his development as a statesman and
record his achievement in his great field." Again: "Here the man
is most forcefully revealed in his own words on many great issues,
for 'as a man thinketh so is he.' "

At the end of her critique, after she had read the manuscript
in its entirety, she summed up her impressions:

"This book is smoothly written, excellent in continuity, accurate in statistical detail. It is a resume of what Lyndon has done,
but it lacks the color and drama and humor that his life has had in
great abundance. It is a story of superhuman energy, great abilities, administrative and legislative strength and unrelenting determination. . . . He has known many great personalities and
they have left a deep impress. The human touches would enliven
and greatly add to the charm of the recital of his story. All that
has been said of his great energy, his skill and ability is true, but
it is equally true that he is quite as great in human and endearing
qualities which are of interest to people."

Her conclusion about the book as a whole: "Factual but not fascinating."

She was probably right. The book sold only a few thousand copies, mostly to the senator's friends, his county campaign managers, employees, and lobbyists hoping to curry favor with the majority leader by presenting copies for him to inscribe. A revised and updated version did much better, because of its timing, when it was hastily issued by Farrar, Straus in January 1964. But, alas, Rebekah Baines Johnson, her son's best friend and my severest critic, was not alive to read the first biography of LBJ to reach print after he became the thirty-sixth President of the United States.

Johnson himself apparently liked the book well enough when it first came out in 1956. In the foreword signed by him—written, as I recall, by James E. Rowe, a Washington lawyer whose friendship with LBJ dated back to New Deal days—he said, "the author knows what he is writing about," and added, "I hope the reader will like this book. I have read it and I like it." After publication, his comments to friends as reported to me indicated that he was well pleased. The manager of his radio and television properties ordered a rather large number of copies, presumably with Johnson's approval. Many persons brought books to his office for him to autograph and he always did so willingly, usually inscribing a sentiment composed by me; we let the copies accumulate and did them half a dozen or so at a time. Sometimes at informal gatherings of friends, I was told, he would read aloud some portions of the book.

In view of all this, I was taken aback when, about a year after it was published, he suddenly broke off conversation on another subject to say, "That book of yours—I know you worked hard on it and the facts are right. But somehow, Booth, you just didn't catch my complete dedication to my job and all that."

His mother must have been talking to him.

Johnson never mentioned the book to me again. But he did show signs of restiveness when he learned that a new edition would come out a few weeks after his accession to the presidency. His unease was communicated to me by Jenkins, who said the President had expressed a wish that "Booth didn't have to do it." Having long since gone off the LBJ payroll, I felt free to say that I did have to because I had signed a contract. Also, I told Jenkins, I thought I knew what was bothering him and sent word not to worry. My idea, a correct one as I learned later, was that his concern grew out of some fairly uncomplimentary references in the original edition to various political groups on which he would now necessarily be depending for support. I removed them from the revised version.

It was wasted effort. Lawrence Stern, a sober writer for the Washington *Post,* looked up the original edition and carefully recorded in a column the changes I had made. He took special pleasure in noting that in the later edition I omitted the pejorative adjective "leftwing" in referring to Americans for Democratic Action. By this time I was working for the Hunt Oil Company, and Stern managed to link the President, Hunt and me together in a chain that, to him, rattled ominously. Oh, well.

No word ever came directly from the White House about the new edition of *The Lyndon Johnson Story.* There was, however, some minor indirect reaction. When John Barron wrote a special report for the Washington *Star* entitled "The Johnson Money," he quoted a paragraph from the book about LBJ's financial status in 1948. I wrote that he had contemplated getting out of politics altogether because he wished to spend more time with his family and "wanted to make money, which he knew he would never be able to do in politics." Barron's point was that he had made money anyway. He showed an unnamed presidential aide a draft of his story before it appeared in the *Star.* He could get no official comment. But Abe Fortas, Johnson's friend and personal legal adviser, was quoted, as a source "close to the White House." He insisted that the account of Johnson's thought of quitting politics was untrue.

All I can say in my defense is that I reported what Johnson

told me months before I wrote the book in 1955. And, although I was not really miffed by the public disclaimer, it tickled my authorial vanity that Barron added a parenthetical paragraph quoting Johnson's statement in the book's foreword that "I have read it and I like it."

5

WORKING ON
THE RAILROAD

The newsman to whom I had been introduced in the National Press Club by Walter Hornaday, head of the Washington Bureau of the Dallas *Morning News,* professed sympathy when Hornaday told him I worked for Johnson.

"It must be hell," he said, eyeing me curiously.

"Not that bad," I denied. "It's interesting."

"I'd starve before I'd work for him," my new acquaintance said heatedly. "He treats the people in his office like cattle. I know because I've talked to some of them. I hate the son of a bitch."

Hornaday, a crusty old fellow whose paper was usually at odds with Johnson, ventured a protest. "Lots of reporters feel that way," he said, "and God knows I've had my share of run-ins with him. But I will say he has the most loyal staff I've ever seen on the Hill. Some of them have been with him for years and they'll defend him against you or anybody else. I can't tell why it is—he overworks them and bawls them out if they make a mistake and sometimes when they don't—but they sure stick up for him."

73

When I gave an account of this conversation, or at least Hornaday's part of it, to Johnson, he typically slid away from the main topic to tell me that the *News* correspondent had reported several times how helpful I was to him and other reporters.

"Nobody who's ever worked for me has been able to become friendly with Hornaday," he said. "I don't know what you did to him, but if you can get along with that old bastard you can get along with anybody."

That was not the point I had intended to make, but I tried to accept the implied compliment, if it could be so labeled, without smirking.

What Hornaday said was true, even though Johnson drove his staff, from top to bottom, hard and unmercifully. He felt no hesitancy about calling on any employee to do the most menial chores. He went among his office workers to draft baby-sitters for the two Johnson daughters. He had been known to administer biting rebukes to Reedy in front of reporters and curt reprimands to Siegel in the presence of senators, the respective groups with which the two men worked every day. He sometimes reduced stenographers to tears by blowing up on detecting erasures in letters presented for his signature. Not a few offices around Washington harbored fugitives from his office, individuals who had come to stay with him briefly and to depart from him thankfully.

Yet there were employees who had been with him through many years. Walter Jenkins had never worked for anyone else. Mary Rather, his personal secretary in the Senate and later in the White House, entered his service when he was a member of the House of Representatives. So did Dorothy Nichols, who had known him during his brief career as a schoolteacher, although she was not his pupil. Willie Day Taylor had been a part of the LBJ menage for a long time before she became Reedy's assistant on the Democratic Policy Committee. Mildred and Glynn Stegall, a couple from West Texas, were faithful employees year after year. All of these assorted persons were accustomed to the ways of

74

their boss and seldom complained. They expected to feel the sharp edge of his tongue from time to time and rolled with the punches, knowing that smoother days would come.

Newer employees often did complain about hard work, long hours, lack of appreciation for their efforts, and the tension that enveloped them when the impatient Johnson felt that things were not going as well as they should—that is, perfectly. But these, like the older hands, were quick to defend him from outside criticism. They were proud to work for him, even vainglorious about the wound stripes they had earned in his service. One reason may have been that everybody in Washington knew who Lyndon Johnson was and some of the prominence rubbed off on his employees. Another was that he brought out the best in "his people," causing them generally to perform above their own previous estimates of their capabilities. The prevalent feeling among other Senate staffers was that if you worked for Johnson you had to be good. This made up in some degree for the humiliation of being treated at times like an errant and perhaps not very bright child.

His attitude toward members of his staff was one of extreme paternalism. His modest purpose was to govern their lives. Their personal appearance was a matter of genuine concern to him. He gave stern fashion advice to all female employees, once telling a young woman he was interviewing for a job, "You'd be a damned good-looking girl if you'd lose twenty pounds and get your hair cut." Neatness was a fetish with him. He would watch with growing irritation as the ash on my cigarette grew longer, chiding me when it fell on my jacket or to the floor, "Look what a mess you're making!" Naturally, he was a compulsive ashtray emptier. Sometimes he searched employees' desks when they were absent to see if they were hiding letters they should have answered. After all, they were *his* employees and he assumed that their desks were also his.

His paternalism worked in the opposite direction as well. When Rayburn, with the frankness of an old friend, said he heard everywhere that he treated his staff poorly, the senator was incredulous. Nobody, he protested, looked after his people better than he did. When a man who had been in his employ for years underwent an appendectomy, Johnson picked up the hospital bill. Jenkins bought a house in Northwest Washington and his boss handed him a check for a thousand dollars to apply to the down payment. He gave Reedy an automobile for a birthday present. Johnson could be a real Big Daddy when the mood struck him.

He liked to hire husband-and-wife teams when possible because if either was called on to work late, which happened frequently, the other would understand. "Keeps down friction at home," he told me. Perhaps, but it did not always keep down friction in the office. I overheard a husband snarling at his wife, "Goddammit, why didn't you say you had to go home and cook our dinner?" Without volition, I had come to be a kind of father confessor to some of the younger workers. I found myself listening to such grousings as that of the bride who said she certainly was fond of her husband but had never expected to be in his company, in the office and at home, for twenty-four hours every day.

Something LBJ heartily disliked was being pressured to put anybody or keep anybody on the payroll. This was strictly his own business and he did not welcome interference. After he was elected minority leader, a number of Democratic senators came to him to say he must, absolutely must, retain a young woman named Pauline Moore on the staff of the Policy Committee. She had been there from the time of Scott Lucas and, Johnson was assured, knew more about the details of every legislative measure than anybody else on Capitol Hill. These urgent recommendations actively prejudiced Johnson against Mrs. Moore and he planned to let her go. But he waited a while and was always glad he did. She stayed on the job, quietly and competently, through his tenure as Democratic leader and far beyond.

A spirit of competition among employees was openly encouraged. If Johnson told me to prepare a memorandum for him I could be fairly certain that he was asking someone else—not necessarily on the staff—to do one on the same subject. Everyone who dictated letters was supposed to originate at least five congratulatory notes to Texans every day—for birthdays, silver and golden wedding anniversaries, civic honors, 4-H Club awards, whatever—based on information in newspaper clippings I sent around. At staff meetings Johnson would single out for praise the person who had composed the largest number of such letters during the week. All stenographers were required to report to Jenkins at the end of each day the number of letters they had typed. This compulsory letter count was a sore point with them, especially so because the score card took no note of the varying length of letters. The girls were afraid to cheat, believing firmly that Jenkins was under orders to make occasional spot checks of their actual output.

Johnson wanted the people who worked for him to be one big happy family and thought they were. At least some of them shared this belief. Ashton Gonella, a pretty and gentle-souled young woman who was one of his secretaries in the Senate and went on to serve as Mrs. Johnson's personal secretary in the White House, wistfully recalled the days when she worked for the majority leader.

"One of the happiest things," she said, in recording her recollections for the oral history collection of the Johnson Library, "was that every Sunday a lot of the staff members would go out to the Johnson house and we'd sit and talk. They used to call it the 'Johnson togetherness' because we never seemed to have any outside friends. We just sort of stuck together. When I'd go to lunch I'd go with a staff member. We just seemed to be a little clan of our own."

It was a clan of which I never became a card-carrying member. My social life, such as I could find time for, and my work day were almost totally separated, although nobody was immune against receiving telephone calls from the boss at any hour of any

77

day or night. My self-imposed schedule was to work from nine
A.M. to six P.M., at which hour I almost invariably went home.
This did not please Johnson. He never told me so, but he mentioned the habit disparagingly to his friend and mine, Les Carpenter, who, with his wife Liz, ran a news bureau for a number of
Texas papers. Johnson did not approve of any of his top staff
people leaving the office before he left.

My conscience bothered me a little, but not painfully. His
choice, his driving necessity, was to put in work days of fourteen
hours or more. My choice was different. I realized that he worked
harder than I—or anybody else on the staff except Jenkins—but
then he had more at stake. Or so I reasoned. Once in a while LBJ
would say with a hint of reproach in his voice that he had tried to
call me at five minutes after six the day before only to learn that I
was already gone from the office. But it was another issue from
which we both shied away.

And I never, never joined in the happy Sunday times which
sweet Ashton Gonella remembered so nostalgically. Perhaps I
made a mistake. They were nice people and I liked them. Some
became my friends for life.

Johnson might dress down his employees in private and even
in public, but he was given to boasting to other senators about
their competence and reliability. He liked to draw comparisons
between his staff and Rayburn's, greatly to the disadvantage of the
latter. He grumbled that the Speaker ran his office "out of his hip
pocket" and received a minimum of assistance from the men and
women he had brought up from Bonham. The Rayburn people
simply were not workers, Johnson remarked with the scorn of a
workaholic for presumed idlers.

The differences between the majority leader's office and the
Speaker's could hardly have been more marked. Rayburn never
had a large staff, never felt the need for one. Neither the Speaker's
Room just off the House chamber nor his congressional office carried the air of purposeful urgency characteristic of Capitol Hill.

Rayburn would see anyone who was willing to wait until the previous visitor had gone and often answered his own telephone. He was apt to note his appointments on the back of an old envelope, which he then thrust into his pocket—indeed, his hip pocket. The reception room of his office was a leisurely place where visitors came and went, chatting among themselves or with the receptionist, placing telephone calls, reading newspapers, and altogether making themselves at home.

LBJ's outer office, needless to say and to coin a phrase, was a beehive of activity. Nobody lounged around out there. Visitors waiting to get in to see the senator talked in hushed uneasy tones. The receptionist answered an always buzzing telephone and typed letters in between calls. People dashed in and out waving papers desperately.

Having come to know the Speaker well, I thought he had exactly the kind of office staff he wanted and would have been decidedly uncomfortable with a bevy of eager beavers. Still, I could understand Johnson's feeling; he liked both action and the appearance of action. Rayburn, on his part, was convinced that his friend in the Senate "took things too hard" and he worried about him.

The Speaker was so fond of Johnson that he would go out of his way to avoid upsetting him. One day he telephoned me, as he did from time to time, and asked me to come over "for a visit." When I duly appeared in his office, he came at once to the point.

"You know I've never had a press man," he said, "but maybe I need one and I was thinking about you. Lyndon has a lot of other good men over there. How would you like to come to work for me?"

Flattered and thinking how much easier my life would be, I said I liked the idea.

"How much money would you have to get?" the Speaker asked with his usual directness.

I told him what I was being paid in Johnson's office and said

the same amount would be satisfactory. Rayburn professed ignorance as to whether the Speaker's office had a position open at that
salary. He called in John Holton, his administrative assistant for
many years, and asked him. Yes, Holton said, such a position was
available, had never in fact been filled.

"Well, that's all right then," the Speaker said, turning back
to me. "Now—have you got the nerve to break the news to
Lyndon?"

Knowing how Johnson hated to have anyone hired away
from him, I could only answer, "I'd rather not, to tell the truth."

Rayburn leaned back in his chair, turning down the corners
of his mouth and throwing up both hands in a gesture characteristic of him. "I can't do it either," he admitted. "Looks like we'll
have to forget the whole thing."

So I made my way ambivalently back to the Senate Office
Building.

When I told LBJ of this incident, some years later, he gave
me a sharp glance before grunting, "You wouldn't have liked it—
too slow."

Johnson himself showed no compunction about raiding
other employees. At a party in Walter Hornaday's home he offered
a job, which she accepted, to an employee of the Dallas *News*
bureau. On one occasion a successful candidate for a Senate seat
sent his future administrative assistant to Washington to get the
lay of the land in advance of his own arrival. Johnson took a
fancy to the AA-to-be and tried in vain to hire him for his own
staff. The young man was somewhat startled to learn this was the
way things worked in the gentlemen's club that the United States
Senate was supposed to be.

It was one of Johnson's few failures when he undertook personal recruitment. He usually got his man by one means or
another.

Charlie Boatner, a valued editorial employee of the Fort
Worth *Star-Telegram* whom LBJ had known for years, recalled

that in June 1961 he received a telephone call from the Vice-President. The conversation opened with Johnson asking Boatner whether he was ready to prove himself a man of his word.

The journalist professed bewilderment.

"Well," said Johnson, "in 1948 I asked you if there was any chance of your coming to Washington and working for me and you indicated that you wanted your boys to go to school and finish in Fort Worth."

Boatner agreed that he had no doubt said something of the sort.

Then Johnson said, "Your youngest son graduated from high school the night before last and I want to know whether you're going to be a man of your word."

Boatner went to work in the Vice-President's office a few weeks later.

The run-of-the-mill hiring was usually left to Jenkins. But not always. When his friend Max Brooks, an Austin architect, bragged to Johnson about his marvelous secretary, a young woman named Marie Wilson, the senator reached the instant conclusion that she was just what he needed as an addition to his Washington office. Brooks explained that Mrs. Wilson was married to a faculty member at the University of Texas and probably would not wish to leave Austin without her husband. Johnson solved that problem by offering jobs to both of them. The husband, Glen Wilson, who held master's and doctor's degrees in psychology, on his arrival in Washington was assigned the dreary task of helping to handle routine "case mail"—the communications every member of Congress receives from constituents needing assistance in wrestling with the Federal bureaucracy.

Mrs. Wilson turned out to be everything Brooks had said, but she was not altogether happy and made her escape after a couple of years to go to work in an oil company's Washington office. Johnson, in Texas when she quit, was furious. "If I'd been here," he told Jenkins furiously, "I would never have let her go."

81

A year or so later, after she had rejected repeated suggestions that she rejoin his staff, the senator resorted to blackmail. He sent word to her through his brother that unless she came back to work her husband would be fired. She returned.

One of LBJ's favorite recruiting tactics was to demand of a prospect he really wanted, "Don't you think it's time you did something for your country?" He had no trouble equating working for him with patriotic service and judged that hardly anyone would care to return a negative answer to his question.

It appeared to some observers that once Johnson had prevailed on someone to join up with him he was likely to lose interest in that person and too often failed to make full use of his talents. This happened sometimes, but not consistently or over the long haul. It was true that McPherson as a new employee had been sent into the dungeon to operate automatic typewriters; yet he stayed on to succeed Siegel as general counsel of the Senate Democratic Policy Committee and later to become a counselor to the President. Another young Texas lawyer, Lloyd Hand, who thought he had joined the senator's staff as a speechwriter, was assigned, like Glen Wilson, to the most uninspiring kind of work; but he was to be named President Johnson's Chief of Protocol. Wilson himself, the Ph.D., advanced to a high position with Johnson's Committee on Aeronautical and Space Sciences, remaining there after his onetime boss left the Senate. Warren Woodward, not much more than a boy when he went to work in the senator's office, graduated to the assistant managership of the LBJ radio and television properties in Austin and then to a vice-presidency of American Airlines when that company was headed by Johnson's old friend, C. R. Smith. There were others never forgotten by LBJ.

Possible future employment at Station KTBC was a carrot dangled from time to time before employees Johnson wished to keep around and who showed signs of becoming restive under the Washington grind. The carrot came within Gerry Siegel's reach after he announced his intention of resigning from his Senate job at the end of 1957. Mrs. Johnson, who was president of the broad-casting company, then talked with him about becoming general manager after a suitable training period.

Siegel and his charming wife, Helene, went down to Austin on an inspection tour. They were accorded a typically Johnsonian grand reception, introduced to the Jewish community of Austin, and made to feel in general that the good life awaited them. As they were driven by car around the pleasant city, LBJ enthusi-astically showed them the section where he knew they would want to live. He named clubs which they should join. He told them what kind of boat they would need for use on the several adjacent lakes.

Gerry Siegel, never one to be completely carried away, began to feel some qualms about his future life being so completely taken over. They could have been deepened, although he never said so to me, by an incident that happened as Johnson was pre-paring to take him and Helene on an automobile tour of the ranch after they had left Austin. LBJ was at the wheel of his white Lincoln Continental in front of the ranch house, Siegel in the car beside him. But Helene had disappeared inside. Johnson tooted the horn impatiently until Siegel said, "I think she's gone to the bathroom."

"Well, hell," said LBJ in great good humor, "if she's not ready we'll go without her," and they roared away.

Later, Siegel reported, his wife said laughingly, "If we do move down here I suppose we'll have to watch our bathroom habits."

He probably would have accepted the job, however, he told me, if Russia had not put Sputnik I into space while he and his wife were in Texas. When that happened he said to Johnson, who already was arranging for his committee investigation, that he would be willing to stay in Washington for another year. The senator said, "All right" and the matter was never mentioned again.

At the end of that additional year, Siegel did resign from the senator's staff to join the faculty of the Harvard Business School. At Johnson's urgent request, he took a leave of six months from that position in 1960 to work again in Washington. Later he became general counsel of the Washington *Post,* from which stronghold he was able to resist LBJ's persistent efforts to bring him into the White House.

Relations between Johnson and most members of his staff passed repeatedly through a wax-and-wane cycle. Nobody knew when or for what reason, none ever being mentioned, he might incur LBJ's temporary disfavor. When it came about, the unfortunate individual was apt to find his counsel unsought, his memos ignored. Then the tide would shift, probably quite rapidly, and the old favorite would become the new favorite, rarely knowing why.

After LBJ became Vice-President, I walked into his office one day to find that Juanita Roberts, a soft-spoken Texan, had been replaced at the front desk by a newer employee, Liz Carpenter (who after three months had succumbed to Johnson's importunities to come along and help him), also a Texan but not soft-spoken. When I went in to see the V.P., I mentioned the change, curious because Juanita had been with him for years.

"Yeah, I thought it was something I had to do," he said. "Juanita's so damned *nice.* She won't keep nagging at me to do the things I should do. I decided I needed somebody really mean like Liz who'll make me do 'em."

Walter Jenkins was the truly indispensable man on the staff. He was dedicated to Johnson's welfare above anything and everything else. Johnson knew this was true. He leaned heavily on Jenkins, who was more familiar with his personal, political, and business affairs than anyone else, possibly excluding Mrs. Johnson. He wanted Jenkins to be within easy reach at all times.

This invaluable aide's mother died soon after I went to Washington and he flew to Texas. The next morning when I saw the senator he growled that Walter was always gone when he needed him most.

"But, Senator," I remonstrated, shocked, "he's in Wichita Falls to attend his mother's funeral."

"I know, I know. And tomorrow it'll be his grandmother's funeral and the week after that it'll probably be his aunt's funeral."

This was a measure of how unreasonable this extraordinary man could be.

Paying a glowing tribute to Bobby Baker in a statement made at an affair in that young man's hometown, LBJ said, "He's my right hand man, the last man I see at night, the first man I see in the morning." In talking with me at another time, he remarked in passing about this same man, "Sometimes I think Bobby is just a cheap conversationalist."

And that is a measure of how inconsistent he could be.

He frightened a new girl on the staff into hysterical tears when, in response to his curt order near the end of a day to fix him a drink, by which he meant a scotch highball, she unbelievably poured sherry and water into a glass, added ice, and handed it to him. LBJ took a lusty swig, then flung the glass across the room, yelling, "You've poisoned me!"

That was how temperamental he could be.

One quiet afternoon, Johnson left the Senate chamber to go upstairs to his Capitol office, instructing a rather young McPherson, "Just be sure there aren't any roll call votes while I'm away from the floor." It seemed unlikely that there would be a demand for one. Only a few senators were present. After a time, McPherson decided it would be safe for him to go to the cloakroom to enjoy a cigarette. When he emerged he found to his consternation that a roll call vote was being ordered on an innocuous proposition—demanded by Senator Eugene McCarthy for the sole and rather petty reason of embarrassing Senator Margaret Chase Smith, who was given to boasting that she never missed a roll call vote. She was absent that afternoon, having been assured by the majority leader that there would be no such votes.

The horrified McPherson, when he saw what was going on,

85

rushed upstairs—to hell with the elevator—to break the news to Johnson. The senator listened, sitting back in his chair with his long legs spread apart and glaring piercingly at his young subordinate.

"Where were you?" he asked quietly.

By his own subsequent account, McPherson yammered a series of semicoherent phrases. Cloakroom, he said. Cigarette. Not a senator myself. Couldn't stop it. Humphrey, the assistant leader, didn't do anything.

"Do you turn your back," demanded Johnson in a hard tone, "when you see your little girl crawling toward an open fire in the fireplace?"

"Wha—?"

"You heard me. You wouldn't even look around if she kept getting closer and closer to the fire? That's what happened down there. I told you not to allow any roll call votes and now you've made me break my word to Maggie Smith."

McPherson was scared and thought that this time he would be fired out of hand. But he was not. He only had to endure LBJ's bad graces for a brief time.

So far as I was concerned, the ebb tide was decidedly in evidence immediately after I left Johnson's staff in the fall of 1958. I had given notice in June that I was resigning as of August 15, selecting that date because it was generally thought that by then Congress would have adjourned for the year. The senator quizzed me closely about the assignment I was to assume as Washington representative of the Hunt Oil Company. He asked detailed questions about the retainer I would get, whether I would have an adequate expense account, and what my duties would be. He advised me to get my agreement with H. L. Hunt in writing, because "that old man is tricky and you can't trust his word." I never doubted that his sharp questioning was motivated solely by genuine concern for my well-being. He accepted my resignation with every appearance of goodwill.

As it turned out, Congress was still in session on August 15 and evidently would be for several days longer. My wife and I had plane tickets to Bermuda and hotel reservations there for our first real vacation in several years, so we departed on the appointed date. On the advice of the senator's brother, Sam Houston, who served as a kind of buffer between the staff and the summit, I said no farewells but just got out of town.

When I returned to Washington soon after Labor Day, the congressional session was over. Johnson and a large part of the staff had gone to Texas. Sam Houston was still around, though, and I paid him a visit on Capitol Hill. He grinned amiably when I saw him.

"Let me tell you what Lyndon said when he found out you were gone. He said," and Sam Houston could give a perfect imitation of his brother talking, " 'I don't understand Booth. I don't see how he could do this to me. He's just like the bride who walks right up to the church steps and then refuses to go through with the ceremony.' "

This was palpable nonsense, for both LBJ and I knew that my presence was far from essential. Johnson simply disliked the thought of any staff member leaving Washington while he was still there. He went into a predictable sulk. Two or three months passed before he forgave me to the extent of asking me from time to time, via telephone messages from Jenkins, to do things for him.

On Bastille Day in 1961, I was taken to a hospital with a bleeding ulcer. It was serious, calling for a number of blood transfusions, but surgery finally was determined not to be necessary. I was still on a bed rest regimen when the telephone rang one day and a slightly awed voice from the switchboard informed me that the Vice-President was calling.

"Walter said you're in the hospital." As usual, no time wasted on a greeting. "What's wrong with you?"

I told him, adding lightly, "I know how you boast about not getting ulcers but giving them. But this is one you didn't give. It's been nearly three years since I stopped working for you. I got this ulcer on my own."

"No, you didn't. I caused that ulcer, Booth, sure as hell. It's just a delayed reaction. Do you need anything?"

"I don't think so, thanks, except maybe a cigarette."

"It's not a joking matter," he said sternly. "Are they taking good care of you out there?"

"Yes, everything's fine. I expect to go home in a few days."

"Come to see me when they turn you loose."

He hung up without saying good-bye. The flowers arrived that evening.

Soon after Johnson became President, stories began to seep out of the White House about his high-handed way with people working there. This development did not surprise me in the least. After the first shock of Kennedy's assassination had worn off, I remarked to my wife, "Johnson has always wanted to be in a position to tell everybody what to do and now he can tell them." As President, he was operating the way he had always done. But the circumstances had changed.

The close family atmosphere of his senatorship and even of the vice-presidency was gone. Now everything he did, every word spoken in public or overheard in private, was subjected to instant scrutiny by the press. He had many more people working for him than ever before. Some of them were bound to leak stories to friendly reporters if they were unhappy about working conditions in the White House. Moreover, as senator and Vice-President, Johnson was usually surrounded by persons whose personal loyalty to him had been tested and not found wanting. As President, he was faced with the situation that some of the holdovers from the Kennedy Administration he implored to stay with him still dreamed of a Camelot that never existed except in their imaginings. They were not kindly disposed toward this intruder.

What LBJ wanted in an employee was an unusually bright fellow who would work like a slave, had his own ideas, and was willing to be completely subservient, mentally and physically, to the boss. The self-contradictions in these standards inevitably led at times to conflict between employer and employee.

Even some of the old Johnson hands found the going rough in the different atmosphere of the White House. After Pierre Salinger, who had been Kennedy's press secretary, left to make an unsuccessful race for senator from California, Reedy was given the job—being summoned from a hospital bed, incidentally, to take over. It seemed a logical choice, but Johnson was not satisfied for long. Bill Moyers, who succeeded Reedy, had worked for LBJ off and on since the mid-fifties and was associated with the Peace Corps during the Kennedy Administration. He was a bright and shining star in the press secretaryship until Johnson became dourly convinced that he had become a spokesman for himself rather than the President. They parted by mutual consent. Finally, George Christian, a big unflappable Texan tough-minded enough to have handled press relations for Governor John Connally, was brought into the post. He proved to be exactly the kind of press secretary Johnson wanted. Christian told reporters what the President wished him to tell and nothing more.

"George knows he works for me, not for the press," Johnson said to me with great satisfaction.

He did not have such praise for most of his subordinates. Once he introduced Bob Hardesty and Will Sparks to an incoming staff member as "the best speechwriters any President ever had." Before they had time to preen themselves on the implied compliment to their writing abilities, he amplified the statement, "They're not temperamental, they don't miss deadlines, and they don't get drunk the night before a major speech."

He did not seem to be able, or perhaps he did not try, to keep from downgrading people who were giving all they had for him. One day, for no clear reason, he said offhandedly to a group of reporters that McGeorge Bundy was "a nice young man, and I mean young." This was at a time when the "nice young man" was putting in fourteen hours of dedicated work every day. Johnson even said toward the end of his Administration that McPherson and Joe Califano, two of his top-flight men, were "publicity seekers." Mrs. Katharine Graham, publisher of the Washington *Post*, recalled with distaste that the President "would bawl people out in front of other people and rake his staff over the coals." Mrs. Graham took note of Johnson's insistence that the press disliked him and the "Eastern Establishment" snubbed him because of his Texas accent. She did not agree. "I think it was his personality," she said.

Mrs. Graham's harsh judgment was oversimplified, for it begged the question of what lay behind the personality to which she objected. Johnson felt, truly and deeply felt, that he represented the real America, the vast grassroots America that lay out in the hinterlands beyond the Potomac and Hudson rivers. No matter the millions he had acquired, no matter the extravagant trappings of an imperial presidency, he was in his own eyes a man of the people, and when he went out over the country to yell out speeches and to "press the flesh" of as many individuals as could come close to him he was demonstrating his oneness with them. What he considered carping criticism of his provincialism annoyed but did not dismay him. Why should it? He knew he was right in a way that effete graduates of Ivy League colleges could never understand.

In the White House, LBJ continued to play his old game of getting people to come with him by promising them the world with a ring around it if they would only enter the service of their country—i.e., go to work in his Administration.

At a cocktail party I attended, John Connor, a successful business executive who had been persuaded to come down from New York to assume the Cabinet post of Secretary of Commerce, poured a familiar tale of woe into my ear. He had been assured, he said, that he would be expected to write his own ticket in working out ways to strengthen ties between the Administration and the business community. But now he was hardly ever given the opportunity to present his views personally to the President. He said that at Cabinet meetings he was treated like an office boy and so was everybody else except Rusk and McNamara, the State and Defense secretaries. Connor wondered if I, as someone who had known the President for a long time, could explain the situation to him.

There was no comfort I could offer. Connor soon returned to the world of business.

Douglass Cater, a brilliant magazine writer who had joined the White House staff at Johnson's insistence, was another who received more promise than fulfillment as a member of the White House staff. I encountered Cater on a morning plane to New York early in the Johnson Administration. He was carrying a briefcase and wearing a harried expression. I asked him what he was up to.

"I'm supposed to be a special assistant to the President," he replied, "but what I'm really doing is act as a messenger boy. We're trying to get together a book of the President's speeches and of course he's not satisfied with the typeface the publisher is using and he's not pleased with the page margins and he keeps turning down jacket designs. Along with all that, he's pushing all the time to get the book out in a hurry. He doesn't know the first thing about the publishing business."

I undertook to make soothing sounds, saying I knew how it was but nobody was going to change Johnson.

"He's a tough man to work for," Cater said with an air of desperation.

But he stayed on to the end.

So did Peter Benchley, although without trauma. Benchley, who a few years afterward wrote a best-selling novel about a great white man-eating shark, was a member of the White House speechwriting team in 1967-68. According to Harry Middleton, also a presidential speechwriter during that time (later to become the director of the LBJ Library), Benchley was unique among

White House staffers in that he put in a strict nine-to-five day, with time out one day a week to take guitar lessons. One evening Califano tracked him down by telephone and ordered him back to the White House to help work on a project that must be completed by the next morning.

"I can't do that," said Benchley. "I'm at a party."

He stayed at the party and the next day Califano furiously told the President what had happened. "Well, fire him," LBJ instructed.

Califano, who had a reputation as the White House hatchet man, went to Benchley with a soft approach. He said, "You've been doing some fine work for Betty Furness on consumer affairs. The President thinks it would be a good idea for you to move over to her shop."

"Why, no, I don't want to work for Betty Furness," Benchley objected.

"But this is the President's suggestion."

"Why would he go through you?" Benchley inquired mildly. "I don't work for you, I work for the President. If he wants me to move somewhere else, he'll tell me."

Califano reported back to LBJ, who then told McPherson, head of the speechwriting team, "Joe can't seem to fire this Benchley fellow. You do it."

But McPherson also found Benchley immovable. The young writer remained in the White House until the day of Nixon's inauguration.

There is a postscript to the story. Shortly before Johnson was to go out of office, he gave a dinner party for selected members of the staff. Benchley was not on the original invitation list, but Liz Carpenter, who thought him amusing, added his name. So, Middleton reported, there at the party, to the intense irritation of Califano and McPherson, was Peter Benchley.

There is also a PPS. When Liz Carpenter's book on the Johnson presidency, *Ruffles and Flourishes,* came out, it was

Benchley who reviewed it in less than favorable terms for *Life* magazine.

So far as I know, Johnson never personally fired anybody. He had other ways of accomplishing his ends, as McPherson and others knew. When McPherson went to the White House early in 1965, he was kept on his former payroll as an assistant Secretary of State. He understood the procedure, realizing that this meant if things did not work out in his new position he could be sent back to State without fanfare or publicity.

He was accordingly appalled when a physical examination revealed the need for a hernia operation—and immediately, declared his doctor, who added that it would be three weeks before McPherson could go back to work. The young man, all too familiar with Johnson's impatience, saw the chance of the White House post he badly wanted flitting away. He glumly went to his office and typed for the President a four-line note of explanation.

His brief memo came back at once from the Oval Office, with a long handwritten note from Johnson at the bottom of the page. LBJ said arrangements were being made to transfer McPherson to the White House payroll before the operation. This, he explained, would make it possible for the patient to enter Bethesda Naval Hospital, where the cost would be appreciably less than in a private hospital. And the President went on to offer further suggestions for meeting problems that McPherson said, in telling me of the incident, he thought "would have occurred only to a staff man with a not too munificent salary."

This was a side of Johnson not known to such persons as the reporter with whom Hornaday and I had a drink that day in the National Press Club. There was no point in asking which was the real LBJ. Both were. The anomaly was a fit subject for the Sunday newspaper supplement psychoanalysts.

6

PLAYING FOLLOW
THE LEADER—MOSTLY

One of the reporters who went down to interview Johnson while he was officially recuperating from his heart attack on his ranch in the fall of 1955 was Douglass Cater, who wrote from Washington for *Reporter* magazine. Cater came to the Capitol to talk with me before departing for Texas, and he was troubled. He said he had read a story in *The New York Times* by William S. White to the effect that Johnson was using his time during the congressional recess to build a centrist coalition with which he hoped to set the government's course in the following year. Cater thought the story implied that the coalition would be less centrist than one dominated by southern conservatives. This disturbed him, especially since White was reputed to have an inside track to Johnson's thinking.

I urged Cater not to approach the senator with any preconceived idea of what he was up to, citing my own experience with him as evidence that he was by no means a southern demagogue. Cater, who hailed from Alabama, said he had been dismayed in

the past to see promising men from the South come to Washington
with the best of intentions only to be sucked into going along with
the Dixie congressional Establishment. I assured him this would
not happen to Johnson. Cater obviously wished to believe what I
said but was not sure he could. I talked freely, knowing that this
conscientious man was not only a perceptive observer of the political scene but also was completely trustworthy. He would find
out for himself, I promised him, that Johnson was not a sectional
politician and cared deeply about the United States and the welfare of the whole people.

After Cater left the office I telephoned the senator and re-
counted our conversation. He was noncommittal, but said he
would tell Reedy, who was commuting between Austin and the
ranch to bring the writer out when he showed up. I was a bit disappointed by his reaction, or lack of it, for I thought I had set the
stage for at least a minor coup in a respected national magazine.
But I need not have worried about whether LBJ would rise to the
occasion.

Cater later reported of his visit: "I asked Johnson about the
story and spent the whole day with him and came away much impressed with the man, impressed that he was not by any means
going to follow the traditional route of the southern senator but
really did have a national vision." His article in *Reporter* glow-
ingly reflected that impression.

Johnson did indeed return to Washington with a proposed
program of national legislation, which, I regret to say, he insisted
on calling "a program with a heart." It was carefully planned. His
program was set forth in detail in a speech he made in the small
Texas town of Whitney one day in December. He and Reedy, with
help from others, worked on this speech for weeks at the ranch.
When the final version was ready it was dictated to one of the girls
in the Washington office and Johnson instructed me to hand-
deliver it to a number of leading columnists and political writers
in the Capital. He also told me to inform them that they would

not be left out on a limb if they speculated that the LBJ program was a clear indication that the Democratic majority in Congress was preparing to take over the leadership of the government from the Executive Department.

"The Republicans are busting a gut to get Ike to run again in spite of his heart attack," he told me on the phone. "If he does run he'll win. But if he bows out we've got to be ready."

He did not explain whether the "we" was an editorial reference to himself or a political reference to the Democratic party.

The speech had something for everybody. Johnson said his Democratic majority would push for an expanded social security system, tax revision to benefit low income groups, aid to medical research and grants for hospital construction, the building of more highways, extension of farm subsidies, an expanded housing program, water resources development, aid for depressed areas, liberalization of immigration and naturalization laws, a constitutional amendment to eliminate the poll tax as a voting qualification requirement, and natural disaster insurance.

The program with a heart made a single bow, although a deep one, to Johnson's Texas constituency as such. It included a proposal to abolish Federal control of natural gas prices at the wellhead.

This was the stickler so far as the eastern press and senators from the East and North were concerned. They foresaw that removal of Federal price control would result in higher rates for consumers in their states. Support came from representatives of the gas-producing southwestern and western states.

The oil and gas lobby was out in full force. The bill was being overlobbied, Johnson warned John Connally, his one-time administrative assistant who was now associated with an independent petroleum producer in Texas. He also urged Connally to register as a lobbyist inasmuch as he was highly visible around Capitol Hill every day touting the merits of the decontrol bill. But Connally blithely responded that he was only trying to do good for his own industry and therefore was not required by law to register. Nevertheless, he checked out of his Mayflower Hotel suite and left town immediately after Senator Francis Curtis, South Dakota, rose in the Senate chamber to charge that an oil company lobbyist had attempted to bribe him. Not that Connally was implicated in the charge—but he had been seen almost daily in the company of an industry representative who had hired the man fingered by the senator.

Despite considerable uproar, the bill passed, only to be vetoed by President Eisenhower on moral grounds. Johnson fumed and swore over the veto, although he found grim humor in the fact that the nullification came from a President who had been supported by the petroleum industry with might and money.

As to the bribery charge, Johnson and Knowland agreed on the appointment of four senators of unquestioned probity as a special investigating committee. I attended all the committee hearings on Johnson's orders and gave him a detailed report at the end of each day's session. He was worried, more deeply than I had ever seen him, that his name or John Connally's would come up in the course of the investigation. But that did not happen and the majority leader was free to move on with other elements of his legislative program.

Which he did, as records for the sessions of Congress up through 1960 will show in case anyone wishes to examine them.

During these years Johnson nailed down his position as the most effective floor leader the Senate had ever known. He was the King and he gloried in his reign and all its perquisites—the chauffeured limousine, the haste with which elevator operators conveyed him upward or downward in the Capitol and the Senate Office Building (and if the haste was not sufficient the operators heard about it), the awe with which junior senators approached him, the way he could speed up proceedings by twirling his finger. It was all rather inspiriting for a boy-grown-into-man from the Texas hill country.

These were trappings of his office and he obviously enjoyed them. Yet he remained a man with deadly serious purposes, not all of them connected with his own ambitions. Harry Truman once said, "Washington is a very easy place for you to forget where you came from and why you got there in the first place." Johnson never forgot.

He surprised many people, including me, by the insistence with which he sought passage of the Civil Rights Act of 1957. Looking back, I realize I should not really have wondered at this. I was taken in by the circumstance that on the subject of civil rights he sometimes talked like a racist. When he campaigned for the Senate in 1948, he attacked Truman's civil rights program as "an effort to set up a police state in the guise of liberty." He specifically expressed opposition to an antilynching bill—"because the Federal Government has no more business enacting a law against one kind of murder than another"—and to the Fair Employment Practices Commission—"because if a man can tell you whom to hire, he can tell you whom you cannot employ." As floor leader, he successfully led resistance to any significant change in the Senate rules to make it difficult or impossible for southern senators to filibuster civil rights bills to death.

Also, I remembered suggesting in vain that he issue a statement on the Supreme Court decision of May 17, 1954, holding that racial segregation in public schools violated the Constitution. He was in Texas at the time and I wrote a brief suggested statement and telephoned it to him. It was innocuous enough, simply pointing out that the Court's decision was final and all good Americans should obey the law of the land.

There was a short silence at the other end of the line after I finished reading. Then Johnson said, his voice going high as it often did when he was troubled, "I don't see why I have to say anything." Nor did he, to my disappointment.

I felt better when he refused to add his signature to a "Southern Manifesto" deploring the decision. It was signed by all senators from the states of the old Confederacy except him. His cover story for Texas and the South was that as Senate leader of all Democrats he should not openly take a stand on so divisive an issue.

He was not talking that way in private conversation during the spring and summer of 1957. His efforts were directed at modifying civil rights legislation submitted to Congress by President Eisenhower so that its defeat would not be a do-or-die proposition with the southerners and it would still be acceptable to the other side. Aided by Siegel and Reedy, he went tirelessly from faction to faction conveying messages to each about what the other would accept, however reluctantly. This back-and-forth continued for weeks without the majority leader making any public statement about civil rights legislation. Although there was much speculation in the press about what he would do, he resolutely kept his own counsel.

One day after the bill had finally been brought before the Senate for action, I was walking down the hall with Senator Russell and asked him what he thought the outcome would be.

"It's in the hands of the Senate, Booth," he said with a sobriety unusual even for him.

There may have been an implied rebuke for my temerity in his tone, but there was resignation as well and I knew that LBJ had arrived at a winning compromise. I said as much when I reported Russell's brief sentence to him.

"Yes, I know," he said gravely. "It's all worked out on both sides." He suddenly smiled. "Why, I wouldn't have let it come up if we didn't have the votes."

Of course.

After a prolonged filibuster, giving the southern senators an opportunity to make a record for their constituents, Congress went ahead to enact the first civil rights legislation to be approved since Reconstruction.

I was assigned the task of replying to the subsequent letters from indignant Texans, who variously charged Johnson with being a turncoat, a traitor to the southern cause, a tool of the NAACP. Actually there were not as many of these vitriolic communications as we had expected. The senator's sense of timing again had served him well.

Allan Shivers, the Texas governor who on occasion was a bitter antagonist, once noted that people all over the United States were constantly asking him if Johnson was what is unflatteringly known in political circles as a wind rider. No, said Shivers: "He can smell the wind changing and he changes before the wind does."

That, it seemed to me, was the essence of political leadership—the ability to run ahead of the winds of change.

Johnson displayed that gift dramatically when he grabbed the reins of the nation's space race after Russia launched Sputnik I into infinity in the fall of 1957.

He was shocked by the lack of shock shown by the Eisenhower Administration. The President himself told reporters that the Russian satellite "does not raise my apprehensions, not one iota." Sherman Adams, his chief of staff ("coldest human being I ever met," Johnson once told me), loyally said the Administration was not intent "on attaining a high score in any inter-space baseball game." Charles Wilson, the former head of General Motors who was on the verge of retirement as Secretary of Defense, downplayed the Russian accomplishment as "a nice technical trick." Clarence Randall, a former steel company executive serving as White House adviser for foreign economic policy, dismissed the satellite as "a silly bauble." But many an American shivered at the thought of Communist missiles carrying nuclear warheads hurtling down from space onto the North American continent.

Johnson saw the situation as one involving the national defense and moved promptly to take charge. Russell and Styles Bridges, respectively chairman and ranking Republican of the Armed Services Committee, agreed to his eager proposal that the

Preparedness Investigating Subcommittee should conduct an investigation of what the United States was doing—and not doing—about space. Johnson had not paid a great deal of attention to his subcommittee since becoming majority leader, but it was a ready-made vehicle for this purpose.

With the country excited and fearful about the Russians' success, an intense spotlight was focused on the subcommittee's probe. It went on for two months. Reporters and television camera crews daily crowded around the committee room where the investigating senators heard testimony from eminent scientists and high-ranking military officers that the United States was far behind in the effort to conquer space. Johnson ordered FBI investigations of several members of his staff so they would receive clearance to look at material classified top secret. Later I learned with amusement that the investigation of me reached back as far as the small Texas town where I had spent the first twenty years of my life.

The senator enlisted an old friend, New York lawyer Edwin Wiesl, to serve as special counsel to the subcommittee during the investigation. Wiesl brought along as his assistant a young lawyer from his firm named Cyrus Vance, who later would become President Johnson's undersecretary of defense and international troubleshooter. Arthur Godfrey, who lived in nearby Virginia, hung around a lot for no known reason except that he was an airplane buff and regarded the space bit as a logical extension of his hobby.

It was all most exciting, and naturally LBJ was on the front pages and on the television screen every day. The final outcome included creation of a special Senate committee on space, later made the permanent Committee on Aeronautical and Space Sciences with Johnson as chairman, and passage of the Space Act of 1958 establishing the National Aeronautics and Space Administration.

Johnson had a great love for unanimous committee reports. Every report issued by his Preparedness Investigating Subcommittee in the past had been formally approved by all members and the report on the space investigation was no exception. To accomplish this took some maneuvering, however, for Senator Symington wished the report to be more critical of the Eisenhower Administration than Johnson thought wise or necessary.

"He wants to get politics into it," the consummate politician snorted with righteous indignation.

He delighted in telling how he outwitted the Missouri senator. First he got the draft report approved by Bridges ("I read it to him over the telephone one morning while he was still in the bathtub," LBJ reported gleefully), then by every other committee member, before approaching Symington, who held to his argument for adding the stinging comments he had espoused earlier. All right, said Johnson, he had the privilege of filing a minority report if he wished and if he felt it should be a political document. But he would find himself the odd man out in a seven-to-one division of the subcommittee. Wouldn't it be better, he asked, to sign the report along with the other senators? And after that, of course, he could always have his say on the floor of the Senate.

Symington, thus backed into a corner, reluctantly gave in. The upshot, however, was that he and Johnson were less friendly afterward than they had been in the past.

The senator was as fond of lists of legislation passed under his leadership as he was of unanimous committee reports. Near the end of one congressional session he instructed Reedy, a man of many talents, to prepare a summary of the ten most important legislative measures passed that year. The assignment presented no difficulty, but then the majority leader decided it would be better if twenty-five bills were listed for distribution to the press when Congress adjourned. Reedy produced it. The boss, his appetite growing, upped the ante to fifty bills—and finally to a round hundred. Reedy searched around desperately and eventually came up with ninety-nine.

Not enough, said LBJ. He must have one more. How about that bill providing for Federal inspection of poultry products?

"Senator, I know these reporters," Reedy protested, pain in his voice. "They'll start horsing around with the list and finally they'll write that you had to dig so deep you ended up with a chicken bill. And even that won't be as bad as the jokes they'll make among themselves."

His protest was in vain. LBJ had his list of one hundred progressive, constructive, reasonable legislative measures enacted during that session.

During all the time of his leadership, some of the legislation boasted about by Johnson and he personally were viewed dimly by a handful of Senate Democrats and party functionaries. They continued to complain about too much compromise, too much cooperation with the Eisenhower Administration. Some of them even blamed the majority leader for Adlai Stevenson's second defeat, worse than the first, in his 1956 campaign for the presidency. Herbert Lehman, who retired from the Senate that year, spoke for them when he said the 1956 election was lost before the campaign began, because "the Democrats in Congress failed to make the issues during the eighteen months we were in control." The statement ignored the indisputable fact that Stevenson was a remarkably inept candidate in 1956 while Eisenhower was more popular than ever. Joseph Rauh, national chairman of Americans for Democratic Action, offered the remarkable observation that under Johnson's leadership "the congressional Democrats have become practically indistinguishable from the party they allegedly oppose."

Paul Butler, an abrasive and rather vainglorious Indiana politician who occupied the post of Democratic National Chairman, regularly attacked the way Johnson ran the Senate and Rayburn the House. Butler even created a Democratic Advisory Council, composed of Democratic politicians in and out of Congress, to take over leadership in formulating programs for presentation to Congress as the official voice of the party. Johnson and Rayburn refused to accept proffered membership on the body. They considered it redundant.

The aggressive Indianian was always spoiling for a fight, although he appeared at times not to know what about or in which party. One time, after trying in vain to smooth over an intramural conflict among California Democrats, he came out with this astounding statement: "The most significant aspect of the whole business is, I believe, that virtually all of the issues have deep roots, and are all the more consequential for that reason." To Johnson and Rayburn many of his other comments and suggestions were no less meaningless.

Although he gave little public attention to criticism of his strategy and tactics, LBJ never welcomed it and he especially resented the charge that he was rendering poor service to the party. After a time I noted with amusement that his automatic reaction whenever I mentioned Butler's name was to respond, "That puddinhead son of a bitch!" I laughed about this to Rayburn, who said with a grimace on his rubbery old face that Lyndon was right about that but the best way was to ignore Butler.

Not many Senate Democrats joined in badgering their leader or gave any indication that they felt the same way as the dissidents. A few did. William Proxmire, elected in Wisconsin as a successor to Joe McCarthy, was one.

Proxmire's attitude represented an interesting turnaround. When he first came to the Senate after winning a special election in August 1957, he received such attention from Johnson as was rarely lavished on a freshman senator. The majority leader made a flattering speech of welcome, saw that Proxmire was assigned to three standing committees, and had him included in a group of senators making a junket to West Germany only a few weeks after the Wisconsin man had taken his oath of office. Warren Duffy, who for years had covered the Senate for the United Press, told Reedy, "I can't believe it. I've never seen any new member of the Senate get so many goodies."

Proxmire's initial reaction was to follow LBJ around like a puppy dog. He loved to tell how he had called Johnson the day he was elected, Johnson's birthday, to say, "I'm the best birthday present you ever got." His praise for the majority leader, expressed in page after page of the *Congressional Record,* was so fulsome as to cause some of the more sensitive members of Johnson's staff to feel embarrassed.

The honeymoon between the two was of brief duration. Proxmire prided himself on being a maverick, a man of independent spirit, and before long he joined Paul Butler in attacking control of Congress by Johnson and Rayburn. "When you get these two men together," he said in one Senate speech, "with the power of making committee assignments, you see the obsequious, bowing, scraping senators and congressmen around them." The cause of that outburst was the majority leader's refusal to assign him to the Finance Committee. Proxmire also stridently criticized what he called Johnson's high-handedness in setting Democratic policy. The young man from Wisconsin, publicity conscious to the nth degree, enjoyed the newspaper headlines that had him leading a revolt against the majority leader. And he reported with manifest self-approval that his attack on Johnson drew more citizen mail than anything he had ever done.

Fifteen years later, in a radio interview, Proxmire showed that he had forgotten nothing of his early days in the Senate. He said great pressure had been put on him as a new senator "to be pretty much self-effacing and anonymous," adding unsurprisingly, "That just never appealed to me." He recalled Johnson "trying to change my view, saying you've got to be careful about being in the minority, that the constituents are going to feel you're ineffective and it's going to hurt you." Johnson was wrong, Proxmire declared, "because when you vote alone, you stand out." The flamboyant senator from Wisconsin never got over his craving to stand out.

I noted with interest that LBJ, while deeply resenting criticism from Proxmire, let similar statements from Morse roll off his back. These two, regardless of their many differences, were old

Senate hands together. They had been through too much to get really angry with each other. After yelling back and forth on the floor, they could be found a few minutes later in the cloakroom talking in barnyard terms, to the accompaniment of raucous har-hars, about the lusty breeding performances of the bulls in their respective cattle herds. Morse once made an hour-long speech vitriolically attacking Johnson's practice of passing legislation by getting a certain time set for the vote. Bobby Baker, who nearly always reflected Johnson's viewpoint, lightly discounted the significance of the speech. "It's easy to understand," he explained to Harry McPherson. "Senator Morse has a speaking engagement back in Oregon that would have paid him a big fat honorarium and he's going to miss his engagement because he'll have to stay here to vote."

Baker also advised Johnson not to be upset when Senator Joe Clark of Pennsylvania made a fiery attack on the majority leader for his cooperation with the Eisenhower Administration. LBJ listened to the speech without saying anything in rebuttal, but he told Baker it made him mad.

"Joe Clark's never going to like you, Mr. Leader," said Baker, who had attained a position almost equivalent to a senator's except for votes and committee assignments. "You ought to tell him you've learned there's no way you two can work together and then tell him to go straight to hell and never talk to you again!"

According to Baker, Johnson simply shook his head and said nothing. But a few minutes later the secretary to the Senate majority saw the two senators exchange a few brief remarks which he could not hear. Later, Baker reported, Johnson called him over to his desk and said, "All right, you smart bastard, I told Joe Clark to go to hell and he says he won't go. So what do I do now?"

When he told me of this incident, Baker laughingly admitted that for once he was speechless.

Clark wrote Johnson a letter demanding that "liberals" be

given more voice in making policy. LBJ might have accepted the letter calmly, but he was enraged when its contents were leaked to the press and put forward as another sign of the mythical revolt against his leadership. Another senator, Michigan's Pat Mc-Namara, in the process of making a completely undistinguished record in the Senate, came up with a charge that Johnson was blocking attempts to broaden unemployment compensation. Other scattered shots came from here and there. The majority leader was accused on the one hand of one-man rule and on the other of failing to use his position to wage all-out war against Administration policies.

Although stung by what he regarded as unfair representations of his methods and motives, Johnson suffered in silence for some while. Then one day, sore and fed up, he got to his feet in the Senate to protest a new attack from Proxmire. "This one-man rule is a myth," he said sharply. "It does not take much courage, I may say, to make the leadership a punching bag." When matters in the Senate were not to the Wisconsin senator's liking, "He puts the blame on the leadership."

Proxmire, no doubt seeing more headlines in the offing, jumped up to say, "I challenge senators to tell me what our policy is on the budget, what our policy is on taxation, or what our policy is on almost any issue."

LBJ continued to scoff at his critics, asking with heavy irony, "Do they expect a fairy godfather or a wet nurse to get a majority to deliver into their hands?"

Proxmire finally took his seat. The best living example of a Senate leader's problems, snapped the exasperated Johnson, "has just sat down."

The leader's problems now also included the junior senator from Texas. Price Daniel resigned from the Senate in January 1957, having been elected governor. A special election in April gave his seat to Yarborough, the man Daniel had beaten for governor and decidedly no friend of Johnson. Yarborough was the darling of the segment of the Democratic party that in Texas was called liberal. A Yarborough Democrat was almost automatically an anti-Johnson Democrat.

"He's not on my side," LBJ said glumly of the new senator. "He'll undercut me every time he gets a chance."

Trying to stave off that possibility, he gave a welcoming reception for Yarborough in the historic old Supreme Court chamber in the Capitol. He delivered an effusive speech before an audience of other Democratic senators and the Texas delegation in the House, speaking highly of "Ralph" and even more highly of the United States Senate. Yarborough was red-faced and sweaty as he listened, a fixed smile on his face. It seemed to me he felt far from comfortable in the presence of so many members of the Establishment he had made a career of denouncing.

Johnson's effort proved largely futile. The two senators maintained a surface amity and cooperated on matters affecting their state, but Johnson's pipeline soon brought him word that Yarborough was consorting with the enemy, an offense not taken lightly by LBJ.

The leader's control of the Senate was never seriously threatened, but control was harder after the Democrats' stunning victories in the 1958 congressional elections gave them a majority of nearly two to one in both houses. The voter turnout for the Democrats was helped along by an economic recession early in the year, with unemployment figures reaching their highest point since 1941. Farmers were restless over the policies of Secretary of Agriculture Ezra Taft Benson. One of the recurrent crises in the Middle East caused the President to send United States troops into Lebanon. The President's chief of staff, Sherman Adams, generally regarded in Washington as an unassailable symbol of integrity in government, was accused of accepting favors from a New England industrialist in return for intervening with Federal agencies on his behalf. Adams maintained that he had done nothing wrong and the President believed him. But he eventually resigned, mainly because of the uproar from Republicans who thought their candidacies were being hurt by his continued presence in the White House.

Whatever the cause, Democratic candidates for Congress won so widely that Rayburn predicted the hefty majority would be hard to handle. Johnson found this was true in the Senate at times, but it was not until the beginning of the presidential election year of 1960 that an open effort at rebellion came to the surface.

The January caucus of Senate Democrats was not in the pattern that had been accepted since Johnson assumed the leadership. The usual procedure was for him to make his own State of the Union speech to the applause of the senators. This time Douglas, Proxmire, Clark, and McNamara jointly offered a resolution deploring the LBJ custom of calling a perfunctory caucus once each year. They demanded regular and frequent party caucuses so all senators could have a hand in making policy instead of everything being left to the LBJ-controlled Steering Committee.

The majority leader, forewarned that the resolution would be offered, reacted quickly and calmly. Of course, he said, speaking with unwonted softness, the senators could have as many caucuses as they wanted. He added, however, that in his experience the main effect of such meetings was to give rise to party disputes. But he said he would call conferences when asked to do so and the resolution was withdrawn.

No more Senate Democratic caucuses were held during the session.

Although his detractors continued to snipe at him for not fighting the Republicans hard enough, he was in fact more occupied with making a record for the Democratic party than Butler and others realized or cared to admit. He was as desirous of getting the moon and sixpence as they were. But, unlike his critics, he would gladly accept only the moon if that was what he could get and he would settle for sixpence in preference to nothing. He had no thought of building a record, either for himself or the party, based on defeat. He saw no value in advancing and raising a big fuss over proposals that could not possibly win congressional approval.

"Sure, I'd rather win big," he said one day when I, visiting his office from my downtown headquarters, brought up Butler's most recent attack on his leadership. "But I'd rather win part of what we want than lose all the time. What legislation did Paul Butler ever get through Congress?" he demanded rhetorically.

None of this is to say that LBJ was above using his position in the Senate to gain political advantage for the Democratic party. He was a partisan in domestic affairs and never pretended to be anything else.

In 1959, when the country again was experiencing an economic recession, the AFL-CIO sponsored an unemployment rally in Washington. Johnson was the only congressional leader to appear. He made an impassioned speech to the approximately seven thousand delegates, announcing a plan for a legislative-executive commission on unemployment. They whooped and cheered when he told them he was returning to the Senate chamber to introduce on that very day a bill establishing the commission. It would be instructed to hold hearings on the jobless situation around the country and report back to Congress within ninety days.

I happened to be in Johnson's office when he came back from the meeting. He was accompanied by Andrew Biemiller, lobbyist for the labor organization, who nodded in approval as the senator told him, winking at him and me, "We'll just introduce this resolution and send it down to the White House and let him veto it, which he will, and then we'll see."

It was all politics—Democratic politics. Johnson did introduce the resolution and within forty-eight hours it sailed through the Senate on a voice vote. In the end, however, organized labor took a second look and decided an employment commission was not such a good idea after all, for it could give the Administration an excuse not to take any immediate action to combat unemployment. On Rayburn's recommendation, the resolution was allowed to die in the House without so much as committee consideration. But the Senate Democratic leader had made a point for his critics to mull over.

Eisenhower vetoed many measures passed by the Democratic majority, usually with the help of a few Republicans, and for the most part the vetoes stuck. But late one day in the summer of 1960, his veto of a bill raising the pay of postal workers was overridden due to Johnson's strenuous efforts and effective lobbying by William C. Doherty, president of the National Association of Letter Carriers.

LBJ and Doherty, old buddies for many years, retired to the majority leader's office and began to celebrate their hard-won victory with a few drinks. Word came that several hundred letter carriers in uniform, who had been sitting in the Senate gallery throughout the tense day, were gathered in the auditorium of the association's headquarters building and lusted for a chance to see and applaud their senatorial hero.

The two responded to the call. Still exchanging effusive congratulations, they rode in the leader's limousine down Capitol Hill to their destination. According to Gerald Cullinan, executive assistant to Doherty, by the time they walked into the midst of the cheering postmen, LBJ was clinging rather desperately to the head letter carrier's arm. At last, after getting his eyes into focus, he delivered the shortest and by all odds the most inaccurate speech he ever made.

"My friends," he bawled, "all I can say is—in the words of a great *American:* 'We came; we saw; we conquered.' G'night all."

And out of the building he and Bill Doherty sashayed, to the accompaniment of loud huzzahs from the mailmen.

It was not always so much fun. Some of the reporters who covered the Senate grew bored with writing about Johnson as a legislative miracle man and became more interested in discovering and depicting feet of clay. What they had regarded in the past as political acumen they now portrayed as unprincipled wheeling and dealing. A few columnists who formerly praised his self-confidence now deplored his arrogance. Some writers found pleasure in giving satiric descriptions of the greatly enlarged and splendidly furnished quarters he had commandeered in the Capitol from the Senate District of Columbia Committee. His new office was decorated in green and gold. One of LBJ's secretaries told me, giggling happily, that he even sent the Capitol custodian on a search for matching green toilet paper for the bathroom.

My own impression was that his new surroundings could comfortably have accommodated an Oriental house of ill fame. I did not tell him so the first time I visited him there, contenting myself with saying jokingly that I would rejoin his staff if he would give me such a place to work. He managed a small grin, but I could see he was not amused.

Sometimes he raged in private about his critics, but outwardly he remained unmoved, with rare exceptions, and went about his business of running the Senate. Still, he was despondent at times. He told me, and no doubt others, that he might not stand for another term and even if he did, might refuse the leadership another year. I never took such talk seriously, for I had long since learned that he had steep ups and downs and I knew he would feel different on another day. The bumpy road along which he led others was one he himself traveled, never pausing to consider that he could if he would make the way smoother for all. The man from the hill country knew in the marrow of his bones that good things never come easily.

7

SOME CONVENTIONS

Attending a political convention with or for Johnson was a traumatic and exhausting experience. It entailed days of operating under constant pressure, a minimum of sleep, food snatched at odd hours, and drinks, if any, gulped down in one's hotel room. My first such go for Johnson was a state Democratic convention in Texas in the spring of 1956. It toughened me up for the national conventions at which I would subsequently find myself.

The state convention was preceded by a no-holds-barred fight between the Johnson-Rayburn axis and the conservative forces of Allan Shivers, in his last term as governor. At stake was control of the Texas delegation to the coming national Democratic convention. So far as the Speaker was concerned, the war with Shivers had been going on since 1952. In that year, he thought he had a pledge from the governor that he would support the Democratic nominee for President, whoever he was. On the basis of this belief, Rayburn had seen to it that the Shivers delegation rather than a contesting liberal group was seated at the Chicago convention. He regarded the governor's subsequent support of Eisenhower as a personal betrayal, which he never forgot nor forgave.

"That piss ant's not going to get a chance to lead a walkout this time," the Speaker told me one evening in his office. "We've got to beat him."

His solution was to put Johnson forward not only as chairman of the state delegation to the 1956 national convention but also as Texas' favorite-son candidate for President. This twin bill, if it could be presented successfully, would bring about the selection of a loyalist delegation by appealing to state pride in offering a real live candidate for the presidential nomination.

Shivers was willing for Johnson to go to the convention as the state's favorite son, but he wanted the delegation chairmanship for himself. In that position he could expect to be able to keep the Texans from voting for Adlai Stevenson, who obviously was the front runner for the nomination.

LBJ at first did not think highly of Rayburn's plan for him. He knew it would mean a bruising scrap with Shivers in the precinct conventions, which would choose delegates to the county conventions, which in turn would elect delegates to the state convention. From their ranks would be chosen the Texas representatives at the national gathering of Democrats. Johnson saw that a confrontation with Shivers in a statewide campaign to carry the vitally important precinct meetings might well alienate the conservative support he had so painstakingly cultivated in Texas.

"And I just might lose," he said gloomily. "Then what?"

He agonized for weeks about whether to step off the brink. Finally, Rayburn pushed him. While on a visit to Bonham, the Speaker gave a statement to his hometown newspaper that he and other loyal Democrats were going to run Johnson for both favorite son and delegation chairman. The wire services leaped on the statement and reporters in Washington besieged the senator. He fended off their questions for a time, still hesitant to take the ir-

114

revocable step. At last, muttering in an aside, "Well, sometimes a man has to be a damn fool," he read a prepared assent to the double candidacy.

John Connally took time off from his job with the oil producer to put his organizational genius to work in the precincts. He was able to draw away some of Shivers' conservative support. Brass collar Democrats and liberals—although these liked LBJ no better than before—followed Rayburn's lead. Organized labor threw its full strength into the campaign, less for Johnson than against Shivers.

The Shivercrats, as they were scornfully dubbed by the loyalists, had dominated state politics for half a dozen years through ready access to the moneybags and by following policies designed to appeal to Texas' plentiful supply of rockribbed standpatters. In this bitter campaign they tossed charges around with reckless abandon. Americans for Democratic Action! Labor's Political Action Committee! The CIO! The National Association for the Advancement of Colored People! These dread organizations, Texans were shrilly assured, held their senior senator captive.

The campaign, lasting about four weeks, engendered intensive personal antagonism between the leading figures. It was, as Johnson said later, "a campaign of hatred and prejudice." A mutual friend of his and Shivers, who at times in the past had been LBJ's political ally, suggested that when the contest was over the two men would shake hands and make up.

"No, we won't," Johnson denied. "Allan hates me now. He really does. There's nothing in the world he'd like better than to cut off my balls and throw 'em on the table and say, 'Look, Lady Bird, there they are.' "

This metaphorical event did not occur. The Johnson side swept the precinct and then the county conventions by overwhelming margins. The state convention, a one-day affair to be held in Dallas two weeks later, remained to make the victory official.

I had stayed in Washington during the campaign, but along with several other Johnson staffers I flew to Dallas a couple of days before the convention. We learned immediately that trouble was threatened. I was told about it at a conference with Johnson, Rayburn, and Connally.

They assigned me to write a speech for the senator to deliver at a Democratic rally the night before the convention. Johnson said the speech must be a plea for party unity. He proposed to make peace with those who had opposed him. Many delegates had their minds set on undertaking a drastic overhaul of the Texas party structure, beginning with the ousting of the Shivers-controlled Democratic executive committee. Johnson maintained that such an action would divide the party worse than ever and probably would end in an embarrassing fight in the courts.

I went back to my room and my portable typewriter and composed a speech beginning, "We should not come here in bitterness and anger." Johnson liked that and approved the entire speech.

Unfortunately, when he uttered the opening words in an appropriately reasoning tone at the rally in the ballroom of the Adolphus Hotel, some wretch in the gallery immediately bawled, "We do, though!"

This set off a chorus of boos and jeering laughter that could not be drowned out by the determined applause of Johnson friends. LBJ's face reddened with anger and he started shouting out the sentences counseling moderation and togetherness. Nobody went away from that Democratic rally in a happy frame of mind.

Johnson's concern showed plainly at a meeting he held later that night with his floor managers for the convention. More than a hundred men and a few women jammed into his hotel suite to receive his last-minute instructions. He addressed them in a voice gone hoarse, dispensing with oratorical flourishes to tell them in a direct fashion that he had done all he could and victory or defeat was now up to them.

"Don't leave the convention hall until it's all over," he pleaded. "Don't even leave the floor except to go to the bathroom —and don't go there very often."

He had further orders. Don't stay up late and get drunk. Don't stay up at all; go to bed as soon as you leave here. Don't sleep late tomorrow. Get out to the convention hall early.

"Just remember," he concluded solemnly, "they'll screw us nine ways from Sunday if they see an opening."

The next day LBJ's cohorts prevailed in fighting down the effort to throw out the executive committee. But in spite of all his floor managers could do, many of his dependable delegates drifted away from the convention hall before the long day, extending into the night, came to an end. Not enough of them stayed around to prevent the defeat of Johnson's choice for national committee-woman. One of his most outspoken enemies among the self-styled liberals, a talkative Houston woman named Mrs. Frankie Randolph, got the post. The senator said angrily he had been double-crossed.

In any event, we returned to Washington without the whole loaf but with more than half of it. LBJ would go to the national convention in Chicago as chairman of his state delegation and as Texas' favorite son candidate.

Some of his Senate colleagues, mostly southerners, took the line that he was a full-fledged candidate and issued formal endorsements. There was speculation in the press about the seriousness of his candidacy, although he assured reporters he would make no effort to get the support of delegates from other states. He told Jenkins, Reedy, and me the same, declaring that he would never become a sectional candidate as Russell had done with such negligible results in 1952.

I believed him and yet I could not keep from feeling at times that he thought pensively of what might be. He gave eager attention to every press mention of his candidacy. He had Reedy and Jim Rowe, now temporarily attached to the Democratic Policy Committee staff, keeping him closely advised about all the preconvention activities of the openly announced candidates. And he did not endorse Stevenson, clearly in the lead, or anyone else.

He even asked some of us on the staff to think up campaign slogans for political buttons to be passed out before and during the convention. The slogan he liked best, "Love That Lyndon," was contributed by me. I volunteer this information with extreme modesty inasmuch as Rowland Evans and Robert Novak, in their excellent book on Johnson,* characterized it as "ludicrous."

No one, at least not I, knew exactly what Johnson had in mind as he departed for Texas when Congress adjourned late in July. Did he know? Probably not. But he was clearly ready for something to happen. In that restless frame of mind, he was more unpredictable than ever.

Down in Texas, shortly before the convention was to open on August 13, Johnson replied to a reporter who again put the question about whether he was a serious candidate, "I'm always serious about everything I do." If the Democratic delegates in convention assembled should decide, he said, "that they would like me to be their standard-bearer, I will do my duty." And when he was asked whether he considered Stevenson or Averell Harriman, who had been endorsed by Truman, the better candidate, he came back snappily, "The best candidate at the moment is Lyndon Johnson."

He had an opportunity for a long talk with Rayburn when the two joined other congressional leaders in responding to a summons from President Eisenhower to fly to Washington for a briefing on problems caused by Egypt's seizure of the Suez Canal. The senator had become excited by the thought that his favorite son status possibly could be transformed into an actual drive to get the nomination. It might be done, he urged anxiously, if the Speaker would take the lead. If Truman was able to deadlock the

* *Lyndon B. Johnson: The Exercise of Power,* published by New American Library, 1966.

convention and stop Stevenson, who would be in a more advantageous position than Lyndon Johnson? Nobody, he thought.

Rayburn told me about this conversation—more of a typical LBJ monologue, apparently—the next day, after I was invited to be a passenger on the presidential plane flying the congressmen back to Chicago. He said he had just listened.

"I hate to see Lyndon get bit so hard by the presidential bug at this stage of the game," he observed morosely. "Stevenson's got it sewed up."

Incidentally, on the flight to Chicago, for a time I had Charles A. Halleck as my seatmate, the seasoned Indiana politician who had been a member of the House since 1935 and ranked high in the Republican leadership. The only thing standing out in my memory of our conversation is that I learned, incredulously, that the Indiana professional politician not only had never read Booth Tarkington's *The Gentleman from Indiana* but had never so much as heard of the novelist from the Hoosier state. I recommended the book to Halleck, but he did not promise to read it.

When we arrived at the Chicago airport I got off the plane in the company of Johnson and Rayburn. They were immediately descended on by a horde of reporters. One told Rayburn he was quoted in a wire service dispatch as having "passed the word" for Stevenson. "I haven't said I was for anybody but Lyndon, dammit," the Speaker growled. He kept walking toward a waiting automobile, with me tagging along, and the reporter fell back to join the group gathered around Johnson.

"I don't see why Lyndon lets those buzzards trap him like that," Rayburn said as we got in the car.

The week passed in a blur of confusion broken from time to time by periods of chaos. The Johnson people were doing the convention on the cheap, and Reedy and I and a perpetually clattering news ticker shared a room in the mammoth Conrad Hilton Hotel. An adjoining room was established as a press headquarters, so we were never lonely because reporters were always there seeking color stories about our candidate. We spent much of our time absorbing rumors and conveying them to LBJ, who stayed in his hotel suite with a telephone perpetually clamped to his ear. However, he did show up for caucuses of the Texas delegation, some eager members of which had allowed the excitement of the convention to convince them that their favorite son had a chance at the nomination.

If Johnson himself held such a glimmering notion, it was not for long. His hope that Truman's endorsement of Harriman would deadlock the convention proved illusory. Kefauver having withdrawn, with an eye on the vice-presidential nomination, there was no one left but the retread nominee, Adlai Stevenson.

On nominating day, Connally gave a riproaring, southern-politician-type speech (which he had rehearsed over and over in my and Reedy's room the night before) placing Johnson's name before the convention. An extended and wildly enthusiastic demonstration by delegates followed. Television commentators noted with some surprise—*had they missed something?*—that participants were by no means confined to the whooping Texans and their southern neighbors. It appeared that almost every state's banner was paraded around the hall. All such demonstrations are basically sham and this one was perhaps more so than most. The show for LBJ had been organized by several Texas congressmen who went around to their House colleagues in other delegations to remind them that Sam Rayburn would keep right on being Speaker. No doubt he would be watching with interest, and would remember, which states helped to add to the fervor of the convention demonstration for his friend.

It was a thrilling put-on. From their favored box seats, Mrs. Johnson and the two daughters beamed down happily at the banner-waving delegates. Johnson watched on television. At the Texas caucus the next morning, he expressed hearty thanks to the delegates. "You gave me the best demonstration any candidate had." Oh, boy, it even beats screwing.

But the demonstration signaled the end of the game. When

the balloting was over, only eighty votes could be counted for Johnson. All but two came from Texas and Mississippi. Stevenson was the overwhelming victor on the first and only ballot.

The nominee departed from the custom of designating his running mate, announcing that he would leave the selection up to the delegates. Kefauver, Gore, Kennedy, and Robert Wagner of New York were placed in nomination. The Texas delegation was led in caucus by Johnson and Rayburn to support Gore on the first ballot. Neither of them really liked the choice, but they considered him infinitely preferable to the other senator from Tennessee. On the initial roll call, however, Kefauver ran far ahead of Gore—and everybody else except Kennedy, who was a surprisingly strong second. Wagner and Humphrey trailed Gore.

Much of Kennedy's strength came from southern states, where Democratic leaders in general were violently opposed to Kefauver. Now the Texas leaders joined them. Johnson, delighted to be in a battle that he thought could be won, sent his emissaries fanning out over the convention hall with the word that Kefauver undoubtedly had polled his top strength on the first ballot. Kennedy was the man. On the second roll call, when Texas was reached, Johnson leaped to his feet and roared into the microphone, "Texas proudly casts its fifty-six votes for the fighting sailor who wears the scars of battle: Jack Kennedy!"

As the balloting neared its end, Kennedy seemed a certain winner. But delegations started switching votes and he was left behind.

So, for the time being, was LBJ. He had nothing to show for all the noise and frenzy of a convention in which there was every evidence that he had hoped at the very least to wield decisive influence. His first serious attempt at playing the political game on a national field had to be written off as a flop. This was not something he admitted. At a final press conference in Chicago, he greeted the attending reporters with a cheery "Good morning, fellows" and said the Democrats had named a winning ticket.

He campaigned for it, although not wholeheartedly. More

than once he told me, and undoubtedly other confidants, that he did not think the Democrats had a chance against Eisenhower. But he went through the motions expected of a party leader.

Johnson was depressed during much of that fall. His mood drifted over the telephone lines at the times he called me in Kentucky with his frequent queries about the Clements reelection campaign. He understood without saying so that, for whatever reason, things had not gone well for him in 1956. He received without joy my report that John F. Kennedy was campaigning in Kentucky for Stevenson-Kefauver and meeting with enthusiastic receptions, especially from the young. He predicted that Texas again would go for Eisenhower, which it did. He said nearly everything Stevenson was doing lost votes for the Democrats. He refrained from saying, but I felt he thought, that the outlook would be brighter if he were the candidate. Of course that was something he would never have said. Good things don't come easy, Booth.

By the time I left LBJ's staff in the fall of 1958, a growing number of political observers were thinking and talking of him as a serious contender for the presidential nomination in 1960. In retrospect, I believe this possibility was largely responsible for H. L. Hunt having engaged my services as, to use the term loosely, a public relations consultant. The seventy-year-old billionaire, to whom I was introduced by his righthand man, H. L. Williford, the father-in-law of a Texas newspaper publisher I had known for years, had never been, as he unnecessarily told me, a Johnson fan. Still, he said, he had to admit that the senator was right on the petroleum depletion allowance and Federal price control of natural gas. Besides, the old gentleman confided, Johnson was the man with the backbone needed to fight back against communist subversion inside the government.

"He's strong," Hunt said admiringly. "Look at the way he leads those Democratic and Republican senators around as though they had rings in their noses."

Hunt, known for his dedicated sponsorship of kooky right-wing causes and his fear that "they" would somehow wrest his money from him, was a strange supporter for Johnson to have. For that matter, a strange client for me to have. But the retainer he paid was sufficiently large to enable me to set up in business for myself and eventually, I hoped, get other clients. Our arrangement was satisfactory to me, despite my client's pronounced eccentricities.

So was his support satisfactory to Johnson, although it was not something he wished to advertise. Hunt felt the same way, saying candidly that an open endorsement by him probably would harm rather than help the senator, "since so many people who dislike my stand against communism oppose anybody I'm for." By implicit consent they avoided personal contact, even on the telephone they both loved so well. Hunt's advice on political issues, and it was extensive, came via a steady stream of letters and memoranda. He specifically stipulated that he neither expected nor desired replies, except orally through me. This role of go-between for the powerful politician and the inordinately rich man was rather stimulating to my ego.

Freed from the grinding routine and the pressure of Johnson's office, I found the relationship between him and me undergoing a subtle change. No longer the boss to be deferred to, he called on me when he felt he needed my services and flatteringly sought my counsel on matters about which he felt I possessed or could quickly acquire special knowledge. He asked me to keep up my ties with the press and act as his listening post—as, of course, he asked many others. Most days I went to the National Press Club for lunch, so I was in a position to report to him what the newspaper people were saying about his performance in the Senate and their gossip about the coming presidential campaign year.

The latter was the main subject of conversation at the Press Club, although there were many other happenings to talk about in 1959.

123

Fidel Castro, whose tatterdemalions had taken over Cuba, visited Washington and denied in a speech before the American Society of Newspaper Editors that any Communist influence existed in his government. John F. Kennedy, who saw Castro as "part of the legacy of Bolivar," thought Washington officialdom might have given "the fiery young rebel" a warmer welcome.

Illness forced the resignation of Secretary of State Dulles and he died soon after.

The nation went through its longest steel strike. It lasted 116 days and was ended only by an injunction brought under the Taft-Hartley Act.

Serious-minded elders worried about the upsurge of the apathetic beatnik philosophy among young people. Collegians played Telephone Squash Box, a game with the object of squeezing as many human bodies as possible into a telephone booth.

Such topics had their brief hour around the Press Club bar, but most of the habitues preferred to give their attention to politics. Almost daily I was asked if Johnson would make a serious effort to get the Democratic nomination for President—a matter on which he was frustratingly noncommittal.

Not alone with me either, as I learned from talking with other LBJ friends. There apparently was no way to induce him to say, "I am going to be a candidate for the Democratic nomination," although there was general agreement among those who knew him best that he dearly wanted to make a try for the biggest political job in the land.

Rayburn told me he was trying to get Johnson to let it be known quietly, without any public announcement, that he would seek the nomination. That was the only way, the Speaker said, to prevent the men of power in politics from lining up behind some other candidate. The Speaker spelled it out. Kennedy's campaign was already being well organized in the fall of 1959. A Humphrey-for-President organization had been established in Minnesota. Both men planned to enter presidential primaries in various states. Stevenson had a hard core of supporters who were hopeful that he would make one more effort. Symington wanted the nomination "so bad he can taste it." Rayburn said exasperatedly, "Lyndon listened when I told him all this, but he wouldn't say anything except that if he did decide to try he wouldn't enter any primaries."

The Speaker added, frank as always, "I'm going to assume that he'll run and that's what I advise you to do."

When I reported the conversation to Hunt, he said I should devote as much time as I could to following Rayburn's suggestion. I also told Jenkins about it. He said confidently, "He'll run all right. Just stay with us."

No such word came from Johnson. Speaking before a joint session of the Texas legislature, the senator declared, "I have no aspirations, no intentions, no ambitions for office other than that I hold." He did not, however, raise his voice to complain when that same legislature passed a law allowing a person to be a candidate for both statewide office and the presidency. He would be up for election for his third term in the Senate in 1960. The legislature also enacted a measure moving the Texas Democratic primary from July to May, which would enable Johnson to secure the Senate nomination prior to the national convention of the Democratic party. The state senator who sponsored the legislation remarked that it could be called "the Lyndon Johnson for President bill."

As he had done before, Rayburn finally moved ahead on his own. In October he held a press conference in Dallas, a rare occasion for the Speaker, and announced that he and Governor Daniel had formed a Johnson-for-President Committee and would open headquarters in the state capital. Johnson took no public notice.

But he was moving. After Congress adjourned, he filled a heavy speaking schedule, mostly in Texas to get his county organizations under assured control for his Senate reelection drive. But he also went into some other states, where he spoke not of next year's presidential campaign but of the Democratic Senate's accomplishments under his leadership.

One of his out-of-Texas appearances near the end of the year was in Des Moines. Asked once more at a news conference about the presidency, he said, "I am not a candidate and I do not intend to be."

I would have been more impressed by this statement, which I read in the papers, had I not just returned from a swing through Texas, undertaken at LBJ's request, to find out what some of the state's business and financial leaders were saying about his putative candidacy. He suggested that I try to make them understand that a worthwhile campaign for the nomination would be costly. Some of the men to whom I talked had never supported Johnson for senator, as I well knew, but all of them were ready to go with him for President. At least for the nomination. Several said cautiously that they "would see" what happened at the Democratic and Republican national conventions before deciding what to do in the fall. On the whole, the four-page typed report I submitted to Johnson was definitely encouraging. It was completely factual, giving the names of the men I had seen and brief resumes of our conversations.

Johnson read my memorandum intently as we were being driven in his car from somewhere to somewhere. When he finished he folded the pages and placed them carefully in the inside pocket of his jacket.

"It's a good report," he said, and that was all.

I find in my files a copy of a crisp memo directed from me to Jenkins. Dated February 19, 1960, it reads:

> These are things I would like to see done immediately, whether or not we have a campaign manager.
>
> 1. Locate suitable office space, subject to expansion, rent and furnish it.
>
> 2. Get a competent person with political savvy to manage the office. He need have no title. He could start off just by getting and keeping the work moving, then could make such contacts as is determined to be advisable.
>
> 3. Hire adequate stenographic help for the office and start

at once to funnel away from the Capitol some of the mail that is flooding all LBJ offices.

4. Have a place in the office where I can spend some time answering mail and doing whatever else I can.

5. Get together a dependable team of speechwriters.

6. As soon as we get a campaign manager, consider naming a campaign advisory board made up of persons really willing to give some time and effort to the cause.

I am ready *now* to help however I can to do any or all of the above.

None of these well-meant suggestions were followed at the time and some were never followed, although Jenkins telephoned to say that LBJ had read my memo and appreciated it. And keep in touch.

Johnson held to his determination not to enter any state presidential primaries. He gave as his reason that he felt he must stay in Washington to run things in the Senate. I suspected that he doubted his ability to win them. He was depending upon his friends in the Senate and Rayburn's in the House to line up delegate strength for him in their states, especially in the West and Midwest. His strategy gradually became clear. Again he was hoping for a deadlock. By spring it was generally recognized that Kennedy was the leading candidate. But he was far from having a clear majority. What if he and Humphrey and perhaps Stevenson, along with the predictable favorite son candidates, stymied one another on the first ballot? Then Johnson's opportunity would come. Rayburn thought this strategy might work. Anyway, he said, we would have to go along with it.

"I can't get Lyndon to do it any other way," he told me resignedly, adding, "Maybe there's not any other way."

Campaign money was being raised and presumably spent. Twice I personally carried packets of a hundred hundred-dollar bills, the common currency of politics, to Jenkins. This money came from Hunt, who said substantial contributions also were being sent to Washington by other oil men and business people in Dallas and Houston.

We opened what passed for a headquarters in Washington's Ambassador Hotel, not one of the city's best, for the Johnson-for-President Committee. Oscar Chapman, Secretary of the Interior in the Truman Administration, and India Edwards, a former women's chairman of the national committee, were co-chairmen. Connally and Marvin Watson, a young executive of the Lone Star Steel Company and a rising figure in the conservative wing of the Texas Democratic party, came up to take care of the mechanics. Connally brought along George Bevel, an experienced Fort Worth public relations man, to help out. I was able to add Tom Blake, a Washington friend with excellent political connections going back to FDR's latter years, to assist with press contacts. Bobby Baker sent down various functionaries. Some men were hired to go into the field and talk with state political leaders.

But it was on the whole a nothing operation, characterized by an element of paranoia. Johnson never came near the Ambassador, although he received daily reports about what went on there. Not much did go on. Connally and Baker somehow worked up a delegate count purporting to show that Johnson would have a first ballot strength of 502 votes. Chapman and Mrs. Edwards held a joint press conference and issued an optimistic statement. The 502 figure was received with marked skepticism by political writers, for which they could hardly be faulted.

Johnson's formal announcement that he would indeed go to the convention as a serious candidate for the nomination was withheld until July 5. Congress had recessed—not adjourned—until after the two national conventions were over. Organized groups pressing for special interest legislation would have a chance in Los Angeles to earn the support of the Senate majority leader when the session was resumed. It sounded like blackmail, I said to Jenkins. His reply was a short laugh.

The statement officially putting Johnson in the campaign

was written largely by Phil Graham, publisher of the Washington *Post*. Graham, a man who radiated charm and nervous energy, was a close friend of the senator and for months had been helping out, financially and otherwise, in the silent campaign. On announcement day he came up to the Capitol to put the final touches on the statement. Johnson had just begun wearing contact lenses and one of them fell out of an eye while he was going over the speech. The final moments before he appeared to make the much-heralded announcement were spent crawling around on his office floor looking for the lens.

The news conference was held in the theater of the recently completed new Senate Office Building. The audience of several hundred included not only reporters but also senatorial friends, a number of members of the House, a sprinkling of lobbyists, and quite a few faithful members of the Texas State Society. It was a sympathetic crowd, thrilled by the thought that the man standing on the stage at the front of the big room might actually become President of the United States.

The senator, who I thought seemed slightly ill at ease, had nothing especially remarkable to say. He chided Democrats who were talking about a first-ballot nomination at Los Angeles. It was not the Democratic way, he said, for the presidential nomination to be regarded as in the bag for anyone before the delegates voted. He hit at Kennedy, without mentioning him by name, in pointedly observing that his own duties in the Senate had made it impossible for him to devote the last six months to campaigning around the country. Privately, as I knew, he was more explicit: "Jack was out kissing babies while I was passing bills."

The next day I flew to Los Angeles. The jet was crowded with reporters on their way to cover the convention. As I talked and drank with them across the continent, I congratulated myself that I was not with a group of LBJ's staff members flying to California on a small prop plane, owned by a Johnson friend, with an overnight stay in El Paso.

At this convention, I had told Jenkins, I did not wish to find myself in a hotel room with Reedy and a news ticker. He assured me this would not happen. However, the accommodations assigned me turned out to be a room in a motel at Hollywood and Vine, which was packed with other LBJ workers. The place was miles and a fifteen-dollar taxi ride from the Biltmore Hotel, site of Johnson headquarters. Happily, I stayed there only one night before being instructed by Hunt to move into a suite he had at the Biltmore. He said he and his wife would go to another hotel, having forethoughtedly made reservations there as well as the Biltmore.

Except for a few hours in bed at night, I had little opportunity to enjoy my comfortable surroundings. For me, this convention was a constant repetitive rush from Johnson to Hunt to Rayburn and to the skimpy LBJ headquarters.

The first time I saw Hunt in Los Angeles, which was the day after my arrival, he told me with great glee of a scheme he had concocted and carried out which, he was absolutely certain, would kill off Kennedy for the nomination.

He had arranged to send to thousands of Protestant ministers throughout the country reprints of a sermon delivered by the Reverend W. A. Criswell, pastor of the First Baptist Church in Dallas. Criswell warned in apocalyptic terms of the disaster that would befall the United States if a Catholic should be elected President. It was a humdinger of a sermon, Hunt said, and preachers everywhere would be repeating Criswell's dire warning on the Sunday before the convention opened. The result was sure to be an avalanche of anti-Kennedy telegrams to convention delegates.

Swallowing my reaction of "Oh, my God!," I said hopefully that of course the sermon reprints were not identified in any way with the Johnson campaign?

"Oh, no," the old man chuckled. "I'm too smart for that. They're not identified at all except as a sermon by Criswell. Did you know that his church has the biggest congregation of any Baptist church in the world?"

130

The results were not what my client expected. By the time Johnson arrived in Los Angeles on July 8, the story of the sermon's distribution—but not, for the time being, Hunt's connection with it—had broken in the newspapers. Instead of a flood of telegrams to delegates, there ensued a wave of indignant newspaper editorial comment deploring such religious intolerance.

I felt I had no choice but to tell Johnson the whole story. "It doesn't matter," he said. "I know you can't hold that old man down. I just wish if he's going to throw his money around he'd give us some of it. We sure could use it."

LBJ also suggested that I keep Hunt away from his headquarters in the Biltmore. I said I would try. I was successful except for one evening when my client wandered in and stood around just long enough for a Los Angeles *Times* reporter to recognize him. But his appearance as a supporter of Johnson was worth only a paragraph in the paper.

When Rayburn arrived in the city, I met him by prearrangement to fend off reporters when he came to his quarters in the Biltmore. He said he absolutely did not wish to hold a press conference.

"I've got nothing to say right now that could help Lyndon," he explained. "Everybody knows I've refused to serve again as permanent chairman of the convention so I can be his floor manager, so that's not news any more."

The Speaker was not in an optimistic mood. He said delegates he and Lyndon thought were safely lined up, especially in the West, had slipped away to Kennedy.

"Looks like our only chance is if Stevenson does finally get in and helps hold off Kennedy from running away with it on the first ballot," he said.

When I reported this to Hunt, he said thoughtfully, "I think the senator should be prepared to take Vice-President."

It was not an idea that had occurred to me. Whether it had occurred to Johnson is still a matter of controversy among political aficionados.

Over the weekend, LBJ went about the city to speak before

caucuses of big state delegations, even those already committed to Kennedy—at least on the first ballot. He appeared relaxed and unworried, cracking jokes and addressing old political acquaintances as if he felt confident they were on his side.

A "debate" between Johnson and Kennedy before an audience composed of reporters and members of the Texas and Massachusetts delegations was staged on Sunday. Televised live and excitedly reported by the press, it provided a diversion but was of no importance. The high point for me was seing Bobby Kennedy act as an official taster for his brother. He was among the VIP's from both camps seated in a row of chairs with the candidates. Jake Jacobsen, a Johnson stalwart, was at one end. After a time he thoughtfully filled glasses with water and started passing them down the line. When a glass reached the younger Kennedy he took a cautious sip before handing it on to JFK.

"I wish it had been horse piss," exclaimed the usually gentle-talking Jacobsen when I laughingly told him what I had seen.

State delegations were scattered around in hotels throughout the sprawling city, but the Biltmore was the nerve center. Headquarters for all the major candidates and for the national committee were housed there. The television networks and hundreds of reporters were at the Biltmore. The "press bowl" was in the basement. Most of the convention news, except for the balloting that would come in mid-week, was made at the hotel where I was staying.

In the lobby, pretty girls passed out wide-mouthed smiles, California orange juice, miniature flags, striped walking canes, and—in the case of those working for Johnson—a thousand pounds of taffy candy flown up from Austin. Bands hired by the several candidates paraded noisily outside the hotel from early morning until late at night. The LBJ band consisted of the seventy-six trombones made famous in *The Music Man*. The trombonists, including three blacks hastily recruited at the last moment, blasted the air every morning in Pershing Square across from the Biltmore. Reporters hung around the press center exchanging rumors and predictions when they were not imbibing free drinks in one of the numerous hospitality rooms set up by American Airlines and other commercial enterprises.

The rumors were, to put it mildly, rife. And often contradictory. I listened to all that came my way in the press bowl and the hotel lobby, sifted them out as best I could, and passed on to Johnson and to Hunt—or Rayburn or Connally or Jenkins or Reedy—any that seemed to have some semblance of credibility. My activity was frenzied and probably meaningless for the most part. Still, it had the happy effect of causing me to feel fairly, if fleetingly, important.

Hunt, who had other persons than me moving among the delegates, was convinced by Tuesday morning that when the moment of truth came the next day Kennedy would get the nomination. He and I set to work composing a memorandum to Johnson urging that if this happened there was always the vice-presidential nomination to consider. Suddenly an unannounced visitor showed up in the hotel suite: Sargent Shriver, Kennedy's brother-in-law. He was accompanied by an oil man from Chicago who knew Hunt. Shriver said he had heard that Hunt was talking up LBJ for the second spot on the ticket. He wondered if there was any real likelihood that Johnson would accept it if offered. We added to our memo a note about Shriver's visit and I climbed the stairs to Johnson's quarters on another floor.

A cluster of reporters was standing in the hall near the doorway to his suite waiting for something to happen. I greeted them generally as I rushed by. An instant later an alarmed voice, which I recognized as belonging to my friend Bob Baskin of the Dallas *News,* shouted, "Look out, Booth!" I heard a loud thud behind me, but I was so intent on getting the memo to Johnson that I did not turn.

Juanita Roberts, who had been brought along from Washington, opened the door to my sure-admittance knock, closing it as soon as I entered. I thrust the sealed envelope into her hand.

"Juanita, please give this to the senator—as soon as you can and to nobody else," I murmured, looking around at the packed noisy room.

She said she would and I left. Outside, I saw the cause of Baskin's warning. A heavy standard holding television lights had crashed to the floor. It must have been nearly close enough to part my hair. At least the reporters said so when I stopped to chat with them, and I could only think how foolish I would have felt if I had been done in on the floor of a Biltmore Hotel corridor while delivering what was something less than a message to Garcia.

For years afterward Hunt boasted, and may even have believed, that he was more responsible than anyone else for Johnson's becoming Vice-President and, eventually, President.

Be that as it may, Johnson took the nomination.

I helped steady the chair on which he stood in the hallway outside his suite while he made his statement accepting Kennedy's invitation to become his running mate. As he stepped down from the chair he said, "Booth, come on inside. I want to see you for a minute."

Taking me by an arm, he shoved our way through the babbling crowd and into an adjoining room. It too was filled with people. He led me into an empty clothes closet and shut the door.

"This won't take long, Booth," he said urgently. "I just want to tell you we've got a lot of bills to pay here and other places. I have to raise a pile of money. Will you talk to Hunt and tell him he'll never regret it if he'll contribute ten or twenty to help us get square? If you think it's a good idea, let him think that memo he and you cooked up had a lot to do with causing me to take the nomination. Give it to him hard. Will you do that for me?"

"I'll talk to him," I agreed. "He doesn't much like to give away money."

"I know. Do what you can."

When I put the matter up to Hunt, he said in his dry, whispery voice that he believed he would decline the honor. LBJ never afterward mentioned our clothes closet conference.

No doubt the debts were paid off somehow. That they

existed was corroborated by Mary Rather, who acted as book-keeper and disbursing officer for the Johnson campaign during the convention. When I went to her room to say good-bye, I found her in tears. In response to my natural query as to the reason, she burst out, "These people! They're going off and leaving a stack of unpaid bills and I don't know where the money will come from. How can they be like that?"

Mary did not identify the "they," but I was sure she did not mean any member of the Johnson family. She would never have been guilty of that kind of treason.

Many of those people did indeed go away. During that last evening it became clear that some of Johnson's friends from Texas and other southerners felt he had made the greatest mistake of his life in accepting the vice-presidential nomination. Nor were they alone. On the lobby floor of the Biltmore, the Eliot Janeways of New York, long friends of Johnson, unending enemies of the Kennedys for what reason I did not know, grieved audibly. Economist Janeway cursed in a way of which I would hardly have thought him capable. Babs, his charming wife and popular novel-ist, clung to her husband's arm and mine and wept. "They've ruined Lyndon!" she cried. "The Kennedys are spoilers."

It was on this note that I went tiredly away from Los Angeles and the 1960 Democratic national convention.

Before my departure, however, I had the pleasure of learn-ing that Kennedy visited Hunt at his hotel and thanked him for his part in getting the right vice-presidential candidate on the ticket.

Also, just before I left, I encountered Senator Mike Mans-field, LBJ's assistant floor leader. "Well, Senator," I said jovially, "I guess you're going to be the majority leader." The senator pulled hard on an unlighted pipe. "I don't *want* to be majority leader," he said mournfully.

Nevertheless, he was given the job and held it longer than any other man in the history of the Senate.

Although some of LBJ's old political friends abandoned him

in anger when he ran with John F. Kennedy, I noted that all of them had come back by the time of the 1964 convention in Atlantic City. I was there too, at the direct request of the President, but for me the excitement was false and the proceedings too slickly planned. There was no suspense and not really much of anything for me to do. At the same time, it was fun to walk around the convention hall where so many Miss Americas had been crowned. I gaped at hugely blown-up photographs of LBJ and watched individuals I had known for years as they moved around carrying walkie-talkies on which they summoned one another to immediate conferences at this place or that.

"Some difference from 1960," I observed to a newspaper friend who also had been in Los Angeles.

"Yes, it is," he replied. "I have to keep pinching myself. Do you believe it's for real?"

I said I did, thinking long thoughts that went back over a time period of sixteen years. To 1948. In the heat of that year's campaign, many persons loathed Johnson and everything that he presumably stood for. Not a few of them had come over to him since then, either for selfish reasons as he grew in power or because they were true converts. Now he was at the top of the political heap, at the pinnacle where, he once told me, every born American politician hoped someday to be. I had been with him much of the time along the way and it was still a tossup in my thinking as to whether he was motivated solely by instinctive ambition or equally by a solid determination to make life better for the poor and striving. Something impelled him to run harder than the average man toward goals which may not always have been clear even in his incisive mind. Did anyone know for certain what that something was? Would anyone ever know? Could his mother have told me?

These were odd questions to be pondering in the mindless hubbub of a national political convention. They caused me to feel low, and I packed up and went home as soon as the nominee had made his acceptance speech.

In Austin, on election eve that year, when Johnson was running far ahead of his party to win a triumphant victory for a term of his own, he said on television it seemed to him that "I have spent my whole life getting ready for this moment." I considered it a reasonable statement of fact.

8

TROUBLES AND
TRIUMPH

Incredible as it may seem in retrospect, at times during his first few months in the presidency, Johnson saw, or thought he saw, serious obstacles in the way of his being elected to a term of his own. And there were at least moments in which he was not sure he should even try.

All his old insecurities rose up to bedevil his mind. It was impossible that he could escape the handicap of having been born in Texas. He was painfully aware of being an accidental President. He realized all too well that the Kennedy family and the John F. Kennedy idolators, including those who had heeded his emotional appeal to stay with him, regarded him as a crude interloper in the White House. And what of organized labor? What of the blacks? He felt he would have to fight hard and against odds to gain and hold their support, and he knew for certain he would never be acceptable to the highly vocal extremists of the right. The states of the Deep South, most of which he had carried for the Democratic ticket in 1960, could not be depended on for bloc support this time.

Along with everything else, the Johnson self-confidence had been somewhat eroded by his thousand days as Vice-President. In that job with perquisites but without power, the former majority leader of the Senate had considered himself submerged and unwanted. Drew Pearson, the newspaper columnist who for years carried on a running commentary on Johnson's political career, later summed up the situation: "You transpose a man from that [the LBJ type of Senate leadership] to the job of Vice-President where he has only one official duty, presiding over the Senate, which is very boring, and another unofficial duty, waiting for the President to die, which is disagreeable, and you have normally an unhappy man." In Johnson's case, the unhappiness was intensified in proportion to the distance he stood from what is generally regarded as normality.

His frustration began with an implicit defeat deeply wounding to his pride even before he assumed his new office. At a caucus of Democratic senators the day before the new Congress was to open its session, Mike Mansfield offered a motion that Johnson be authorized to continue to preside over such meetings. A shock wave moved through the big conference room in the Senate office building. The proposal was utterly without precedent and members of the United States Senate live by precedent.

Old Senate foes Clark and Gore promptly rose to express opposition to Mansfield's motion. The new majority leader himself may not have been wildly enthusiastic about it—but he was accustomed to doing whatever LBJ wished him to do. Neither the old nor the new leader expected what came next. Clinton Anderson, Olin Johnston, and A. Willis Robertson, each a power in the Senate, all of them dependable Johnson supporters in past years, stood up in turn to urge defeat of the proposal before the caucus. They made the point, painfully, that the constitutional doctrine of separation of powers would be violated if a member of the executive department should be permitted to preside over meetings of the legislative branch.

Johnson, still a senator, was present. He listened in still-faced silence to the grave protests from his old friends. The vote when it came was 46 to 17 in favor of the Mansfield motion, but the heavy majority made no difference to LBJ. He left the caucus room, not to return, feeling a deep hurt that the colleagues he had dominated for so long did not now consider him one of them. Nor was he cheered by newspaper accounts that on balance the Democratics senators were not unhappy to be relieved of his hard-nosed management.

As best he could Johnson eased the pains of rejection by holding onto his old suite in the Senate Office Building and the ornate quarters he had established in the Capitol for the majority leader. He also expanded into the vice-presidential offices set aside for him in the Executive Office Building across the way from the White House. He maintained a sizable staff, although not as large as he had commanded in his various Senate jobs. He held onto Jenkins and Reedy and several longtime secretaries. Bobby Baker still deferred to him and continued to relay gossip about the peccadillos of some senators, although the young secretary to the Senate majority turned increasingly to Senator Kerr as his new patron.

None of this was enough. An important element was missing. When friends importuned LBJ at the Los Angeles convention not to take the vice-presidential nomination because he would lose the authority of the majority leadership, he retorted defensively, "Power is where power goes." But power had not gone with him into the vice-presidency, nor could it.

The change in him quickly became discernible. At the very beginning of his vice-presidency during Inaugural Week, he had his own evening, a monster reception at the Statler-Hilton Hotel in downtown Washington. It was attended by approximately six thousand Texans and other well-wishers. The crowd was noisily enthusiastic, thirsty and hungry, an LBJ bunch through and through. The honor guest was in his element. He knew nearly everybody there and greeted most of them individually during the course of the long evening. Exuberant and vociferous, he grinned with pleasure when he was addressed as "Mr. Vice-President." He clapped male friends on the back and scattered kisses lavishly among the ladies.

A few weeks later my wife and I attended another reception, one given by the Vice-President and Mrs. Johnson for John Connally, who had been appointed Secretary of the Navy by President Kennedy. We saw here a different Johnson. He wore a fixed smile on his face as he stood in the receiving line. His demeanor was markedly restrained, almost painfully correct. He welcomed each guest in a low, uninflected voice, not hurrying anyone through the line but clearly not in the mood for prolonged chitchat. After we moved away, my wife observed that he had not so much shaken hands with her as engaged in a laying on of hands with a silent blessing from the summit.

"I wonder if he's on tranquilizers," she mused with female practicality.

LBJ frequently gave that impression in Washington when he appeared in public during this unsatisfying period of his life. The freewheeling days of old were gone, replaced by guarded caution when he was onstage. He could no longer be regarded as an important news source. Favored reporters who once had looked forward to rollicking, sometimes abrasive, off-the-record, inside-stuff sessions with the majority leader found the Vice-President singularly uncommunicative. A reporter who had covered LBJ for years told me he spent an hour with Johnson in his office one day and during that time not a single visitor appeared and the telephone sounded only once. Where was everybody?

He felt underused and neglected, but this is not to say he was sulking. He found himself in a new role, that was all. He told me, and repeatedly told members of his staff, that he was determined to be the kind of Vice-President he would want to have if he were President. He would not allow such loyal retainers as Jenkins and Reedy or his own faithful secretaries to criticize Kennedy, even by implication. Having been the boss of the Senate for so long, he fully understood who was boss in the executive department and he had no intention of being or seeming to be a recalcitrant subordinate.

Still, those who knew him best would not quarrel with the assessment of Chet Huntley, the NBC commentator, that Johnson was "not a completely happy man" as Vice-President.

President Kennedy undertook to deal with the situation. He was sufficiently perceptive—and enough of a practical politician—to realize that it was no Throttlebottom he had on his hands. Gratitude not being an essential ingredient of the usual political stew, the youthful President was understandably less inclined to dwell on favor shown him in the past by the Senate majority leader than he was to consider how he could now best make use of the Vice-President's abilities and keep him in harness. He had needed Johnson in 1960 and probably would need him again in 1964. So he tried.

In the Truman Administration provision was made for the Vice-President to be a member of the National Security Council. LBJ occupied that slot. Additionally, Kennedy designated him chairman of the Space Council, of the President's Equal Employment Opportunity Committee, and of the Peace Corps Advisory Council. These jobs gave him some things to do—although, of course, not nearly enough for a man who all his life was accustomed to stretching himself to the utmost limits of his considerable strength.

As a member of the National Security Council, he attended top-level meetings but, by all accounts, contributed little to their deliberations. If the President pressed him for an opinion, he was likely to say, in low monosyllables, that he lacked enough knowledge of the subject to speak with authority. During the Cuban missile crisis of 1962, Secretary of the Treasury C. Douglas Dillon later reported, the President always asked Johnson to speak his mind, "but he wasn't really called on in the same way the rest of us were." Also, Dillon said, "the Vice-President was rather careful not to take too strong a position there because I don't think he felt that he was representing a department with all this flow of information."

Was Johnson simply being careful to keep a low profile to avoid being shot at? Or did he feel that his scorned status as a Texan and a cornball politician—and only the Vice-President, for God's sake!—would cause other members of the group to attach no importance to anything he might say and therefore it would be better left unsaid? In his Senate days he often quoted with relish the old bromide that "Nobody ever learned anything while he was talking." But he had talked plenty then. Now he was a different and quieter man, one in whose face the creases had deepened perceptibly. Self-restraint came hard to the man from the Texas hill country.

The chairmanship of the Space Council was better. The investigator of the United States space effort in the 1950s and former chairman of the Senate Aeronautical and Space Sciences Committee operated in this area with a sure hand. At his suggestion, an old friend, James E. Webb, was appointed by Kennedy to run the National Aeronautical and Space Administration, which zoomed into importance as a top operating agency of the Federal Government. Johnson and Webb worked closely and happily together on all major decisions about NASA.

Because of internal dissension and the nature of its responsibilities, the Committee on Equal Employment Opportunity brought more headaches than joy to its chairman. But its objectives were close to Johnson's heart and he could be tough with employers when he felt the need. He bore in especially hard on Defense Department contractors, telling them firmly either to employ more blacks or they simply would not get future defense contracts. On the whole, however, he preferred his old conciliatory "Let us reason together" approach in dealing with employers. Then at times he would suddenly display a complete lack of interest in the body's work as he brooded over his cutoff from activity on Capitol Hill.

During his first year in the confining vice-presidency, he was a frequent visitor to the White House. Afterward his private conferences with the President became fewer, although not by his choice. He was humiliated and angry when his telephone calls to Kennedy were screened by Kenneth O'Donnell, the White House appointments secretary. Wry comments that Kennedy made privately about the necessity of continually massaging the Johnson ego ("It's easier to draft a message to General de Gaulle than to write a birthday telegram to Lyndon.") were leaked to favorite columnists by members of the presidential entourage. Some of the President's closest advisers, including in particular his brother Robert, the Attorney General, disliked Johnson and trusted him not at all. They derided what they saw as his provincial, old politician's inability to enter into the excitement of the New Frontier. "Whatever became of Lyndon Johnson?" they chuckled to one another at Georgetown cocktail parties.

All this was hard for the thin-skinned Texan to take. Nevertheless, take it he did. Relations between him and the President were cordial in private and eminently correct, almost excessively so on Johnson's part, in public. In the 1960 campaign the older man said repeatedly of the younger, "He is my leader and where he leads me I will follow." He was following now—and, inside himself, disliking it as much as any man could.

Only his travels abroad gave him respite. He made eleven trips to foreign countries for the President and then his personality irresistibly broke loose from the bonds he imposed on it in Washington. On these official journeys, *he* was the boss. *He* called the tunes. *He* gave the orders. Gone was the unnatural pose of humility. The rambunctious Texas politician emerged snorting and roaring in forays into countries in Europe, Asia, Africa, the Middle East.

In India, he handed out passes to the visitors' gallery of the United States Senate to children in the streets, instructing the bewildered youngsters, "Get your mama and daddy to bring you to the Senate and Congress and see how our government works." In

Pakistan, he impulsively invited an itinerant camel driver to come to America and visit Washington and Texas. In Athens, he ordered the chauffeur of his limousine to stop and pick up a woman pedestrian so she could ride to wherever she was going. He let out a joyously uninhibited cowboy yell in the Taj Mahal. He drove his State Department escorts and the personnel of most embassies up the wall by making sudden changes in travel plans and news conferences. In a throwback to the glory days of the Senate, he sometimes unmercifully bawled out aides in the presence not only of accompanying reporters but of heads of state as well. If a plentiful supply of his favorite scotch whiskey—Cutty Sark, if the bottlers wish to make something of it—was not on hand when he arrived at a city in a foreign land, he roared his voice around and ordered an Air Force plane to be dispatched somewhere to get some. At one post so much was flown in that embassy aides enjoyed free scotch for weeks.

State Department stiff-collars, at home and abroad, were dismayed by such goings on. They wished the President would keep his Vice-President in the United States. They passed among themselves with appreciative chuckles the statement of an assistant secretary in State that "Like some wines, Lyndon does not travel well." Certainly there was no doubt that he upset the routine of every American embassy he visited. Which could not have mattered less to him.

Johnson's running-loose activities on his travels abroad were well covered by the American press. Not always to the Vice-President's advantage. Most of the reporters on these trips, attuned to somewhat more sedate State Department ways, had never seen the real, the genuine, Johnson in action. He was hard for them to believe. Many of their stories made him look like a buffoon. Even his old friend Arthur Krock wrote a satiric column about his invitation to the camel driver, a witty piece that LBJ never forgave him for.

The newspaper people who went with him on his travels did

not know about the confidential reports—comprehensive, lucid, realistic—that he wrote for the President about his findings. He held a news conference, which I attended, after a trip to Asia in the spring of 1961 and said soberly that he believed hunger, ignorance, poverty, and disease constituted a greater threat on that continent than communism. Mrs. Johnson, who accompanied him to Asia, told me the only smiling children they saw anywhere on the journey were on Taiwan. In August of that year, after East Germany put up the Berlin Wall, Kennedy sent the Vice-President to West Berlin to pledge the support of the United States in keeping freedom alive in that city. It was a moment of high drama and LBJ relished it.

The euphoria induced during his foreign travels by being again the man in charge, if only temporarily, faded quickly when he came back to Washington. On a visit to one of his offices I found the Vice-President morosely flipping through a stack of newspaper clippings. He thrust a handful of them toward me as I placed myself in a chair in front of his desk.

"Look at them!" he exclaimed, scorn and anger in his voice. "These guys don't know any more about foreign relations than you do about running a whorehouse. They find a lot of chicken shit stuff to write about but they don't give a damn about substance."

He said he just about had a bellyful of traveling anyway, information I received with some skepticism. But he insisted that he really did want to stop going anywhere outside the United States unless absolutely ordered on a trip by the President.

"I get damned tired," he added, "of those State Department types looking down their noses at me through their invisible monocles." He grinned briefly. "I guess I do stir them up a little bit."

Johnson grew increasingly restless. The New Frontier programs were having hard sledding in Congress. Most of them were not widely popular in Texas, as he knew and I knew. The Vice-President defended the programs privately as well as publicly, but he felt that his influence in his home state was slipping away because he was part of the Kennedy Administration. He was deeply upset when Connally resigned as Secretary of the Navy to run for governor of Texas and for success found it expedient to disassociate himself as far as he could from the Administration and even from Johnson himself. He continued to have trouble, especially about Federal appointments, with Senator Yarborough and his faction of the Democratic party in Texas.

It was not Yarborough, however, but Robert Kennedy who refused to accept Johnson's urgent recommendation that a political and personal friend, Sarah Hughes of Dallas, be named to a Federal judgeship. She was too old, said young Kennedy. But while Johnson was on one of his trips abroad Sam Rayburn bluntly told the Attorney General that a legislative measure he was demanding would never get out of the House unless the appointment was made. When LBJ came back to Washington, he found that the Speaker had been able to accomplish what the Vice-President had not and Sarah Hughes was a Federal judge.* His anger at "that little snot nose" for bypassing him hit a new high even for him.

Of course the anger did not extend to Rayburn, who after all had done him a favor. Nothing could cause a rift between these two men. The old Speaker's death from cancer on November 18, 1961, was a severe blow to Johnson. "I miss him every day," he said to me more than a year later.

By the middle of 1963 LBJ was talking again, as he had sometimes talked in the Senate, about getting out of politics for good after one term as Vice-President and going back to Texas to stay.

His periods of gloom were intensified by the feeling that he and his wife were being socially slighted by all the Kennedys. The Johnsons gave a party one night at The Elms, the mansion they had bought from Washington hostess Perle Mesta, for Hollywood stars who had entertained at a Democratic fund-raising affair. At-

* It was she who administered the oath of office to the new President in the cabin of Air Force One on November 22, 1963.

147

torney General Kennedy and Senator Ted Kennedy had been invited, but neither made an appearance. Johnson thought and said it was a deliberate snub. He wondered aloud to friends if the President had lost confidence in him. "Why does the White House have it in for me?" he asked some.

On a trip to the ranch he took along a group of Texas correspondents, remarking that the President always carried favored reporters and columnists with him on unofficial trips and he might as well do the same. The Texans gained the impression that he was getting tired of being in government.

"You think," LBJ told them, "that I aspire to the presidency, that I am an extremely ambitious man, but what I really want to do is come back to Texas and teach political science at a university or college."

Even as he talked about quitting the political scene of his own volition, he was obsessed with the idea that the palace guard, if not President Kennedy himself, would welcome his absence from the national Democratic ticket in 1964. They were gunning for him, he felt sure. All right—maybe he would just pull out and leave it to them.

His instinct for political survival came quickly to the fore, however, when Bobby Baker, the young southerner who for years had meant so much to him, was charged with misusing his Senate position for personal gain. Johnson quickly concluded that Bobby Kennedy and the Department of Justice were determined to link him to the potential scandal. There was no evidence of this, but LBJ darkly suspected that the whole thing was part of a plot to drop him.

Some newspaper columnists speculated that Johnson might indeed be regarded as dispensable by the Kennedy people. Their speculation was encouraged by the not-for-attribution comments by reputed White House insiders. The President himself said firmly, in a news conference in early November, that he wanted LBJ to be on the ticket with him and expected him to be on it.

Still, Johnson wondered and worried and fumed.

Richard M. Scammon, the political scientist and analyst of voter attitudes, observed afterward that "some of the intellectuals who regarded Johnson as a sort of gauche, belly-scratching peasant," as well as being too conservative for their taste, might well have had dreams of a Kennedy-Somebody-Else ticket. The seasoned political observer gave his own view: "But I quite honestly can't imagine Jack Kennedy as President of the United States and leader of the Democratic party in the winter of 1963–64 as being in any serious way concerned with this kind of undertaking. Some of the people in the White House perhaps; some of the people on the fringe of the White House quite possibly; but not really the people that counted politically."

Scammon thought most of the talk about dumping Johnson came from the necessity of political columnists having to fill a certain quota of newsprint every week. He said unequivocally, in his interview for the oral history collection of the Johnson Library, he never came across any hard evidence during the last six months of Kennedy's tenure that there was serious thought of getting a new vice-presidential candidate.

The question became moot with the assassination of Kennedy and the succession of Johnson to the presidency. In a display of leadership that nobody could fault, the man from Texas moved swiftly and effectively to calm national fears that for some hours at least approached hysteria. He set the tone for his takeover Administration by entreating, "Let us continue," and the country responded.

"I have a feeling," the new President wrote a friend in a prophecy that was to become sadly ironical, "that the tragedy of November 22 marked a turning point in American history. The dissension in our land, hopefully, will give way to a new unity—a new reasonableness that will mark the beginning of a new era of progress."

His air of self-confidence, unmarred for once by any public

display of arrogance during his first weeks as President, reassured
the nation. But he still felt uneasy about his own situation and he
took a series of actions designed to shore it up. For three years he
had played second fiddle at best and often felt that he was not
even a member of the orchestra. That was over. What happened
now was up to him.

In those weeks Johnson must have thought at times of the
only political race he had ever lost, in 1941, and of the nerve-
shatteringly close victory of 1948. I recalled that at the 1956 state
convention in Dallas he had told his floor managers the night before, his voice suddenly shrill, "I know what it means to go to bed
thinking you've won and wake up the next morning to find you've
been counted out." Outside politics, he had seen family men back
in Blanco County, Texas, fall from relative affluence to poverty
because they did not do everything possible to watch out for themselves. A man had to be perpetually on guard.

Here he was: President by chance. He couldn't take any
chances. He *wouldn't* take any.

His first step was to persuade Kennedy staff members and
Kennedy appointees to carry on with him in his own Administration. In this endeavor he was largely successful.

Simultaneously, during his early days in the White House,
he tried hard to pull himself away from overt association with old
friends and political allies of a conservative coloration.

This policy, I quickly found out, reached so far down in the
pecking order as to encompass me. While I hardly considered myself a radical conservative, there was no getting around the fact
that I had as a client one H. L. Hunt and it was a fact that had
appeared in print once or twice. This did not mean I was automatically *persona non grata* at the White House, but I was not
surprised when Jenkins suggested a bit abashedly that I come in
by the East Gate to avoid the newspaper people in the West
Wing's press room. It made sense. What aspiring Democratic
politician would like to be linked, however tenuously, with a big-

rich Texas oil man who had often said that Calvin Coolidge was the last good President of the United States?

The revised edition of my LBJ biography had come out early in 1964 and it was no doubt somewhat of an embarrassment. Jack Anderson, at that time an assistant to Drew Pearson on the newspaper column he later was to take over, telephoned me to ask, disingenuously, how the book was doing and then proceeded to question me about my connection with Hunt. As soon as I could terminate the conversation I called Reedy, not yet the President's press secretary but installed in the White House, to suggest that he might find it worthwhile to get in touch with Pearson and say as directly as he considered feasible that no inside tips from 1600 Pennsylvania Avenue could be expected if Anderson wrote the kind of piece I thought he had in mind. Reedy gave me no subsequent report, but nothing appeared in "Washington Merry-Go-Round" about Hunt and me and my book on President Johnson.

It would be perhaps an exaggeration to say that Johnson was, in the old political term, running scared, but he was trying hard to cover all fronts. About this time a photograph of him appeared in the press showing only the back of his head as he sat in a big chair. It was, the President told reporters, a picture of "the loneliest man in the world," a phrase he had picked up about the presidency which appealed to him because of its dramatic, self-pitying quality. But he was far from lonely. He never gave himself a chance to be lonely. An ever-changing parade of representatives of organized labor, blacks, and other ethnic groups, and such liberal organizations as Americans for Democratic Action called on the President at his behest. Their support was essential to him and he was determined to have it.

His heavy hand was also felt in Texas. Joe Kilgore, an old friend who was rounding out his fifth term as a member of the United States House of Representatives from a South Texas district, announced that he would not run for reelection. It was generally understood in political circles that he would become a candidate for the United States Senate against incumbent Ralph Yarborough. That would have suited Johnson fine a little while earlier. One of the purposes of his journey to Texas in November was to find an opponent for Yarborough. But the situation had changed. Because Texas labor forces were strongly for Yarborough, the President virtually forced Kilgore not to announce for the Senate seat. He bluntly warned the congressman that expected financial support would not be forthcoming from the financial and political establishment of the Lone Star State. He would see to that, he said.

Governor Connally and former Governor Shivers, both of whom had gone into office with precisely that support, tried to get Johnson to change his mind. They engaged him in heated telephone calls from Austin, where Kilgore had gone with the intention of announcing his senatorial candidacy. Although in Washington, I was in on the Austin end of this minor but significant affray. Kilgore kept me informed by telephone about what was going on, which he found hard to credit.

Shivers said, recalling their talks with Johnson, "He told me he had promised George Meany [president of the AFL-CIO] he would support Yarborough and he was going to do it. I tried to tell him, and Connally did too, that he didn't need George Meany —George Meany needed him—and that Kilgore would make a much better senator than Yarborough and he could depend on Kilgore to really be of help to him and he knew he couldn't trust Yarborough."

Johnson was adamant. He kept telling the imploring men in Texas, "I told George Meany I was going to help him and I'm going to help him."

Connally, who was both a close friend of Kilgore and an unyielding enemy of Yarborough, finally said in resigned despair, "I knew Lyndon did it to everybody else, but I never thought he would do it to me."

In his relentless drive to clear all decks, Johnson also undertook to deal with the burgeoning Bobby Baker scandal as it affected him. The testimony before a Senate committee investigating Baker's activities was given behind closed doors, but enough of it was released to the press to put LBJ in a potentially bad light. Although he was not accused outright of being involved in Baker's get-rich-quick schemes, there was testimony about presents he had received and advertising time sold on his Austin television station after he bought life insurance from a Baker business associate in Maryland.

At a January news conference, the President told reporters that Baker had indeed given him and Mrs. Johnson a stereo set. He said the families often exchanged presents. "He was an employee of the public," Johnson added, "and had no business pending before me and was asking for nothing and, so far as I knew, expected nothing in return any more than I did when I presented him with gifts."

The reporters obviously would have liked to ask the President some questions about this evasive answer. Before they could do so, Johnson cut them off by saying, "That is all I have to say about it and all I know about it."

However, he did say more three weeks later on a national television program in response to a question about "your protégé and your friend." Johnson replied that Baker was an employee of the Senate and "no protégé of anyone." He continued, "He was there before I came to the Senate for ten years, doing a job substantially the same as he is doing now. He was elected by all the senators."

Knowing what I did about the close attachment between Johnson and Baker—"If I'd had a son, Bobby, I would want him to be just like you"—this statement made me distinctly uncomfortable. When I dug back into the files of the *Congressional Record,* I found that on August 30, 1957, in one of his statements praising Baker, the majority leader said he considered the young man "one of my most trusted, most loyal and most competent friends."

The subsequent disclaimer provided a prime example of

Johnson's firm conviction that people had to believe what he told them, no matter how outrageous it might be.

Bobby Baker kept his mouth shut not only during that election year but also later when he went to prison after being convicted on a number of charges. He served his term and when Johnson had left office, Baker told me, he visited the ex-President on his ranch and was warmly received.

But other problems confronted the new President during the early part of 1964.

One of them had to do with his money and how he had acquired it. The basis of the Johnson family fortune, estimated by the press at some nine million dollars, was radio and television properties in Austin and other Texas cities. Detailed stories in *The Wall Street Journal* and the Washington *Star* pointed out that during his first term in the Senate, Johnson was a member of the Commerce Committee. This panel had jurisdiction over the Federal Communications Commission, which regulated radio and television stations as well as granting licenses for their operation. The public records at the agency showed no evidence that Johnson ever sought or received preferential consideration there. The fact remained that his worldly goods, whatever their amount, were amassed principally after he began his rise to power with his election to the Senate. To be sure, the radio and television stations were held by a corporation controlled by Mrs. Johnson, not by him. She was reputed to be an astute businesswoman, but the investigating reporters found it hard to believe—as who, knowing LBJ, would not?—that her husband would be capable of refraining from keeping a hand alongside hers, and perhaps on top of hers, on the guiding wheel.

Johnson dealt with the innuendoes and implications in these and other articles on the subject only through Abe Fortas. This personal legal adviser explained that when Johnson became President the family gave up direct control of the communications company by placing the stock in a trust. It would remain in that status as long as Johnson was President. Fortas also denied that Johnson had ever used political influence in building up the family holdings. The President maintained a dignified silence on the subject.

Nevertheless, he worried about these and other attacks directed not only at his public record but at his personality as well. He was especially sensitive about recapitulations of the 1948 Senate campaign. After I returned from a trip to Dallas in the spring of 1964, I told him I had learned that a really scandalous book about him and that campaign was being prepared by J. Evetts Haley, a West Texas rancher and former University of Texas professor. Haley disliked everything about Johnson and was a virulent opponent of virtually all that had happened in the Federal government since 1932.

"Every charge ever made against me is going to be rehashed," the President said with gloomy resignation. "And when they throw so much dirt some of it's bound to stick."

Haley's book, *A Texan Looks at Lyndon,* came out in paperback form and was widely distributed. Johnson asked me to prepare a chapter-by-chapter analysis of it, which I did. The book was scandalous all right, but overstated Haley's case so baldly and was so scantily documented that I felt it could do little or no harm to its target.

A Washington-based outfit called Liberty Lobby, organized in 1955 as a self-described "pressure group for patriotism," published a twelve-page tabloid newspaper purporting to present a political biography of LBJ. It was an interesting document. The research into everything that might be considered detrimental to Johnson—from his dubious victory at the polls in 1948 to various scandals in Texas, from Bobby Baker to his alleged buying of votes through his presidential programs—was thorough, but the documentation was not. A special note in the publication explained why: "Due to limited space, it is not feasible to include the sources and verification of all the many facts contained in this edition." All the facts included a characterization of Abe Fortas as a "Communist front lawyer" and of Aubrey Williams as the "Communist-fronter who was LBJ's boss in the NYA." Liberty Lobby proclaimed that the tabloid was "the biggest bargain in TRUTH on the market today" and urged those who received it to buy extra copies at twenty-five cents each for distribution to members of unions and churches.

These were appeals to the conservative element among the voting populace. Ronnie Dugger, who as editor of the *Texas Observer* had been giving LBJ lumps for years, made a pitch to the liberals in an article in *The Progressive*. He professed to see great danger that the President would swing to the right after the election. Expressing distrust of the man in the White House, Dugger wrote, "We must take a chance with any President, and there is much guesswork in it, but if I had a free choice I would not choose Mr. Johnson."

Johnson expected and understood political attacks. He could shrug them off. But he was less equable about the constant snickering that he felt was going on about him in the salons of Georgetown as a hick from Texas who leaned his elbows on the table when he ate and was given to expressing corny thoughts in a corny idiom. So quick to mock others, it was almost more than he could bear to be himself the butt of ridicule.

At times during this period he thought, or anyway said, that he was half of a mind to let somebody else be nominated for President—"turn the whole business over to the Kennedys or the Goldwaters and let them see what *they* can get through Congress." As late as May 1964, he told a group of reporters that "maybe the country needs a new man as President, one who has fewer scars than I have." The reporters understandably refused to take the statement seriously.

When I visited Johnson at the ranch not long after he went out of office, he told me (well before he told Walter Cronkite and the nation on television) that he really had not wanted to run in

1964. He said he knew he would never have the wholehearted support of the "liberals" and their press, by which he meant primarily *The New York Times* and the Washington *Post*. He said he had told Mrs. Johnson he didn't think he would run and she subsequently wrote a memorandum to him making the following points: It would not be fair to the country for him to refuse to run and thus let the country fall into the hands of the Republicans; it would not be fair to the Democratic party, which had done so much for him; it would not be fair to himself, because people would think he was afraid to run.

"That last one was what got me," LBJ said, shifting in the seat of the car he was driving pell-mell over the ranch. "Nobody wants his wife to think he's a coward."

Certainly nobody who was born and bred in the Texas hill country.

I was stunned and literally said nothing at all in response to this confidence. LBJ at least prepared me for the future televised interview by Cronkite. Hardly anyone I talked to after that interview believed Johnson. To tell the truth, no one. But who knows?

In any case, by the late spring of 1964, regardless of his past or future thoughts about retiring from office, he no longer looked anything like a man running scared.

It now seemed fairly certain that the Republicans, giving way to the death wish that gripped their party from time to time, would nominate Barry Goldwater for President. Johnson planted stories with some newspaper columnists that this probability caused him definite unease, since the Arizona senator would be harder for him to beat than any other prospective candidate. Some columnists actually believed LBJ felt that way and put the misinformation into print as deep inside stuff. It was to laugh. If Johnson had been in a position single-handedly to select his opponent, his finger would have pointed straight at Goldwater.

He was giving some thought to his own running mate. After discussing various possibilities with his brother and other confidants, he turned to public opinion polls to determine which one of several Democrats would be most helpful to him as a vice-presidential candidate. The list included Humphrey, Robert Kennedy, Eugene McCarthy, Edmund Muskie, John Pastore. The surveys showed, as he proudly told a number of people, that any one of them would drag down his own standing by two or three percentage points. The only conclusion he could draw was that he was far and away the most popular Democratic politician in the country.

Goldwater's nomination made it easy for Johnson to put himself forward as the candidate of restraint. The presidential campaign as it developed had very little to do with troubles in Vietnam. Most Americans probably knew that the New York Yankees won the pennant that summer and many learned with astonished dismay that Liz Taylor and Eddie Fisher were splitting. But few were more than vaguely aware that a war was going on in Southeast Asia and still fewer appeared to care about it one way or the other.

Reedy told me he was urging the President not to conduct a campaign as such but to rest his case before the country on his amazing record in pushing long-stalled legislation through Congress. John Connally, who had quickly recovered from the trauma of the Kilgore episode, also thought Johnson should maintain an above-it-all attitude. The President himself appeared for a time to be inclined to follow their counsel. After all, by the time the Republican convention was held, Johnson had in his pocket and frequently displayed to visitors the results of a poll indicating that he probably would get seventy percent of the vote to Goldwater's thirty.

In the end, of course, the old pro could not resist the lure of the hustings. Johnson campaigned in 1964 as no incumbent President, including Truman, had ever campaigned before.

Once convinced that he could win, he was determined to win BIG. He would show them. He would show them all: the condescending Kennedyites and their lily-fingered, self-conscious intellectuals, the wiseacre political commentators who scoffed at the content of his speeches and sneered at the way he delivered them, the southern demagogues who said the states of the South would not go along with one of their own who had deserted and betrayed them. He would show the remaining old fogies in Blanco County who had predicted that the elder Johnson boy would never amount to a hill of beans. He would show everybody in the damndest campaign ever waged by any President.

Being LBJ, he took it for granted that his wife would also enter actively into the campaign. Being Lady Bird Johnson, she had no other thought.

One late afternoon, after a hard day, the campaigner and his entourage reached Inez, Kentucky, a hamlet in the Appalachians. The candidate was still going strong but Mrs. Johnson had approached the point of exhaustion. Haynes Johnson of the Washington *Post* reported that as her husband charged into a crowd of waiting people she remained in the car, holding a bouquet of roses that someone had thrust into her hands. In a minute or two the President became aware that she was not with him.

"Where's Bird?" he asked the Secret Service agent at his side.

The agent said she was waiting in the limousine.

"Tell her to get out here and walk with me," LBJ said, speaking in a low tone and continuing to move through the small sea of outstretched hands.

"Mr. President, she's very tired," the agent began to explain.

"Get Bird out here and tell her I want her to walk with me," the President ordered.

Shortly afterward, the *Post* man reported, Mrs. Johnson joined her husband, smiling faintly and still carrying the roses.

With and without her at his side, the President crisscrossed the country again and again between Labor Day and Election Day to make more than two hundred speeches. He rode through city streets bawling over a bullhorn to crowds alongside, "Y'all come to the speakin'." He kissed hundreds of babies and plunged exultantly into shouting, pushing masses of people to grasp every hand that was thrust in his direction. By the close of the campaign, his right arm was limp and he proudly displayed to reporters accompanying him his swollen and bleeding right hand.

"Have you ever seen anything like that?" he demanded. "The folks like me!"

His victory was the most one-sided presidential election since 1936. He showed them and it felt good.

9

JACKASS
IN A HAILSTORM

Outgoing President Lyndon Johnson in January 1969 offered incoming President Richard Nixon this suggestion about attacks from the press: "When those boys get after you there's nothing you can do but hunker down and take it like a jackass in a hailstorm."

LBJ did not consistently follow the advice he gave. He did little hunkering down. He was more likely to be found flailing about in all directions in the midst of the storm. He may have reeled under the full sting of the hailstones as they beat against his tender hide, but he in turn belabored individual reporters and commentators with harsh invective. Although at times he simply whined. And on occasion he took telephone in hand to deliver to their bosses searing blasts against writers he felt had dealt unfairly with him.

He did all these things as President, but he had been doing them for a long time before he moved into the White House. He was not a press agent's—or a press secretary's—dream.

During the years he held the majority leadership Johnson was unable to comprehend his failure to tame the press the way he had tamed the Senate. In fact, he never lost the illusion, if it was an illusion, that he could pull it off if he really put his mind to the task.

"Oh, I could charm them all right," he once told me after a press conference with Texas newspaper correspondents which had not turned out notably well because a couple of them pressed him with questions he did not wish to answer. "I could do it but I wonder if it's worth the trouble."

I indicated that I believed such an effort would be worthwhile, but he remained skeptical. "All you newspaper people hang together," he said impatiently. "Stop working for them and start working for me."

The idea that the press could be "charmed" into slanting their stories in his favor was one to which Johnson clung tenaciously. As Reedy wisely pointed out, he was unable to rid himself of the notion that newspapers were to a large extent scripted in much the same way as his in-house newsletter and radio programs were. It followed naturally, in his reasoning together with himself, that if he could cause a given writer to like him that person would also give him a hero's role even in factual news stories. LBJ really believed this. If the script he carefully placed before a reporter or columnist was not scrupulously followed, the Johnson reaction was a combination of bewilderment, hurt, and anger.

The majority leader met with reporters for five minutes every morning at his desk in the Senate chamber before the lawmakers went into session. His custom was to read several brief written statements on subjects of his choosing (usually current legislative matters) and Reedy's composition. There would be no time for questions. Nor any need for them, in Johnson's opinion. The majority leader of the Senate had given them a basis for their stories. What more could they ask?

He followed a similar practice in news conferences with

Texas correspondents, which I tried to set up once a week. I would prepare in advance four or five statements for him to make on matters of special interest to Texans. The senator would read the brief papers, usually in a hurried, disinterested fashion, and tell the reporters they could, if they wished, get copies of them from me—with the condition that "none of you put in your stories that I issued written statements."

"Just say Senator Johnson said this," he instructed the reporters, on at least one occasion adding, "If any of you say that anything came in a written statement, that's a good way of making sure that there won't be any more of these special Texas press conferences."

Whether dealing with state or national reporters, LBJ did not welcome questions unless they had been set up in advance to give him an opportunity to expound on a given subject. He made no effort to conceal his impatience and irritation over questions he dubbed as "silly." He gave tart, sarcastic, and often unresponsive answers to others.

He could not understand why the snake oil of the Johnson Treatment, so successful with most senators, did not sway the press. And he refused to believe that his attempts to apply it served only to annoy and alienate reporters. That was the case, however, as Reedy and I were told over and over by the news people.

Johnson was capable of directing his heavy sarcasm at the best of friends. William S. White of *The New York Times* was high in that category, he and LBJ having been on close terms for twenty years. Nobody would have guessed it from a telephone call White received at the *Times* office one morning. This call came at a time when Johnson was minority leader and Taft the majority leader, so the reporter understandably had been devoting more attention to the Republican senator than to his old friend. That was what the telephone call was about.

When White answered he heard a voice he knew very well

saying with exaggerated formality, "Is this Mr. William White?"

"Yes."

"Mr. White, this is Senator Johnson."

Since the two had been on a first-name basis for years, White braced himself and said, "Good morning, Senator Johnson."

"I realize, Mr. White, that in representing *The New York Times* in the Senate you are very busy with Senator Taft, but," said Johnson, "if an occasion comes on which you think you might see me, could I come and call on you?"

"Certainly, Senator," White deadpanned.

"Now, mind you, if it would be more convenient, I'd be glad to call on you in Senator Taft's office."

And the senator hung up.

White knew Johnson well enough to understand that he was not just trying to be funny. The call had a purpose, the reporter said in telling about it, and that purpose was to give him a not very subtle reminder that Johnson wanted and expected to get more space in the *Times*.

Bill White got off easy. Other news people were less fortunate. After LBJ graduated to majority leader it was not unusual for a byline reporter or a columnist to be summoned to his office after hours and addressed in injured tones about something he had written. How, Johnson wondered sorrowfully, could an old and trusted friend have done this to him? How could a man possibly operate in a responsible way in this terribly demanding job if somebody he had known ever since he came to Washington didn't stay with him? We have broken bread together, we have enjoyed drinks in good companionship, why can we not now think together? The majority leader was working sixteen, eighteen hours a day. Not just for the Democratic party, not just for the Senate, but for the country and for the whole people. Didn't he have a right to look for understanding from the press, in particular from such an intelligent and competent representative of the press as the one now sitting in front of his desk?

And so on. Sometimes, I was ruefully told by reporters thus singled out, for an hour or longer.

LBJ spent less time with someone who had written that what he was doing in the Senate approached the miraculous. A smile, a friendly squeeze of the shoulder, a muttered "That sure was a good piece you wrote," and that was likely to be that. The flatteringly autographed pictures, the birthday letters, the venison sausage at Christmas went to writers who were standoffish, for there was always a chance, Johnson reasoned, that he could win them over to his side if he tried hard enough.

The chance did exist. While his press conferences were not outstandingly successful, as Evans and Novak wrote, "Senate reporters and top columnists were captivated with Johnson in his office or at the LBJ Ranch." Nose to nose, the force of his personality was hard to resist.

He once had as a daytime guest at the ranch one Ronnie Dugger, editor of the *Texas Observer,* a weekly journal that was habitually at odds with the senator on almost everything he did. Johnson turned on the treatment as hard as he could. After several hours Dugger staggered away to indicate weakly in the next issue of the *Observer* that LBJ might have his good points after all. This hypnotic state soon wore off, however, and Dugger's paper was slamming Johnson as hard as ever.

Arthur Schlesinger, Jr., the liberal-minded historian from Harvard, had a similar experience, which I recall Johnson telling me about with great pleasure. The majority leader invited Schlesinger to come to see him in Washington and find out for himself what kind of man he was. Apparently the senator never gave the historian a chance. He answered questions before they could be asked, striding around his office and acting out the dramatics of passing a controversial bill through the Senate. He whipped out voting records to compare to his favor his own record with that of some of the liberals' Senate heroes.

The session lasted an hour and a half with Johnson doing

nearly all the talking. Schlesinger was definitely shaken when he left the office, Johnson gleefully reported. He may have been right, for the Harvard professor later observed that Johnson was "a good deal more attractive, more subtle, and more formidable than I had expected." But this impression also proved not to be permanent.

When Johnson was at his best with the press, he was very good. At his obstinate worst, he was terrible.

In those years in the Senate, what Reedy had to do and what I tried to do to whatever extent I could was to refrain from telling him outright he was awful when that happened while urging him with whatever gentleness we could muster to do better. That we were not always successful goes without saying.

The image was everything to LBJ. And his conviction that a desired image—of sincerity, of dedication, of standing above it all for the good of the country—could be imposed on the press was no less firm than his belief that newspapers were scripted. During the Senate space committee hearings, Reedy and I had the devil's own time in dissuading him from the mad idea of hiring Tex Mc-Crary, the flamboyant New York publicist, to "handle" him. We headed off that catastrophe, but it was a close call. The thought of LBJ and McCrary in tandem boggled the mind.

Sometimes the senator simply got carried away, as the old saw has it, with the exuberance of his own verbosity. Once he had a small group of reporters on the ranch and was taking them around the place, as he loved to do. He brought them up in front of a tumbledown shack, a sort of latterday version of the legendary log cabin as a politician's birthplace. He informed the reporters in a tone verging on the tremulous that this was the house in which he had grown up. His doting mother, who was along, listened until she could no longer stand such a reflection on the family's status in the community.

"Now, Lyndon," she said reproachfully, "you know we had a nice house over on the other side of the farm."

Her son, his face set, resumed the tour without any further implication that the shanty was the kind of home from which great men might spring. The reporters snickered among themselves but, being guests, offered no comment.

As majority leader, Johnson never let up in his efforts to manage the press. His passion for secrecy about his own plans and actions until he was ready to spring the news led him into frequent evasions and not-quite lies. When he decided the time had come to talk for publication, he tried hard to tell the reporters how to write their stories. As Drew Pearson, who had known LBJ since his service in the House, observed, "That's no more than a lot of other senators do." True, but Johnson did it with less finesse than some.

Even so, he was news. He saw more reporters than any other member of the Senate, either by choice or because he could not avoid them. They covered his press conferences and many of them wrote Second-Coming accounts of his achievements as the Democratic leader. But Chalmers Roberts, then national news bureau chief of the Washington *Post* and one of the best reporters in town, remarked some years afterward, "I don't think they loved him particularly."

They loved him still less, or anyway paid less attention to him, during the bleak years of his vice-presidency. Johnson was not much on the front pages then except during his trips abroad and the stories, as has been seen, were not always ego-bolstering. He missed the limelight and tried in various ways to get back into it without seeming to upstage the President. He wished very much to remain an important news source. He told one reporter for a leading newspaper, "If you'll cover me every day I'll leak to you like a dog on a hydrant." But even old friends among the press representatives, and he had some, could find little sustenance in the vice-presidency.

By the time of the Cuban missile crisis the jokes were going in Washington gossip columns about "Whatever became of——?"

and "Lyndon *who?*" They intensified his suspicion that the press was out to get him. During the conferences about the Cuban missile threat in 1962 a photographer got a shot of the Vice-President jumping out of a car in front of the White House—a man in motion in a worrisome time. Reedy thought his boss would be pleased. He was wrong.

"Is there malice in that?" Johnson demanded. "Look at how he caught me with my shoulders twisted, the way my jacket's awry. That son of a bitch did it on purpose."

Reedy tried to convince him that the picture was fine publicity because it showed the Vice-President being called on in an hour of need. Johnson was not buying that. He distrusted photographers even more than he did newspaper reporters and television cameramen. He suspected that they were in a conspiracy to picture him yawning or scratching his groin. For years he had been fighting with photographers to keep them from taking profile shots of the "wrong" side of his face. The sons of bitches did it on purpose, he knew that.

The tragic circumstances under which Johnson came to the presidency assured kind treatment of him by the press in the beginning. For days and weeks the print media and the airwaves were filled with accounts of the dignity and reassuring strength he displayed in assuming the duties of the office he had sought in vain, now thrust upon him through no choice or effort of his own. Touching stories appeared about his tender consideration of the Kennedy widow and her two small children. His long service in Congress was examined in detail and declared promising for the future. His family life was scrutinized from every angle and pronounced good.

The new President had no need to try to manage the news. Everything was going his way. For a time.

LBJ knew better than anybody else that this happy state of affairs had to be temporary. His problems with the press were basic and would always be with him. He and the media were not on the same wavelength. As Harry McPherson wrote in his splendid account entitled *A Political Education,** Johnson was "a high pressure salesman, always trying to get his foot in the door, frequently arousing—in professionally skeptical men who had spent their working hours listening to the apologies of statesmen—incredulous resistance."

The President once told a group of reporters about a recent conference with a high-ranking foreign statesman, "I had my hand halfway up his leg before he knew what was happening." Members of the press corps feared that he aimed to use the same tactics on them. Their fear was well grounded. Even before the official period of mourning for the assassinated President ended late in December 1963, LBJ was embarked on an intensive drive to make the kissing last as long as possible. He set about courting the press on a scale unprecedented in the history of the presidency and in a style that would have been considered overblown by any standards other than his.

Once again, as had happened before, a "new Johnson" was announced by the Washington press. The White House correspondents who crowded into the presidential office on December 18, 1963, for a news conference, not announced in advance, came away agreeing that Johnson was a changed man. For half an hour he answered their questions without showing impatience or any hint of irritation. There were no brush-offs, no biting replies. The President even smiled frequently. In reply to one question he made a statement that was to prove less than prophetic.

"We are going to maintain an adequate flow of information at all times," he solemnly assured the reporters. "We are determined to let you know as much about what goes on in your own house and your government as we can consistent with self-preservation."

Suddenly realizing the possible implications of his last

* Published by Little, Brown, 1972.

169

words, Johnson laughed and quickly added, "That's the nation's self-preservation, not mine."

A new Johnson?

It looked that way, even to some of the correspondents who had covered Johnson in the Senate and were now transferred to the White House by their employers in the hope that old acquaintance would enable them to come up first with the most about the President. Some of these, as Jack Bell, the Associated Press hand who knew LBJ well, wrote in his book *The Johnson Treatment,** "accepted him for what he was, a man who could be alternately aggravating and soothing, imperious and humble, demanding and understanding, petty and generous, humorous and solemn, fretful and calm, picayune and grandiose." Others knew him less well, if at all, and it was they and their bosses that the President wooed with ardor.

Courtships are best conducted in private. Informal and, later, formal televised news conferences might be all very well, but LBJ wished to make love to important opinion-molders face to face. I can charm them if I think it's worth the trouble. Now, in late 1963 and early 1964, it was worth the trouble. He would show them and show the nation that he was more than a cornball politician from Texas, not able, as he sarcastically said some of them believed, "to find my ass with both hands."

Person to person, that was the stuff. The President invited a long list of editors, columnists, newspaper correspondents, and television commentators to a series of luncheon interviews.

The guests included representatives of both the big United States wire services, the news magazines, all three television networks, and such papers as *The Wall Street Journal* and the New York *Herald-Tribune.* Air Force One flew him to New York for a long personal visit with the editors of the *Times.* He paid special court to Walter Lippmann, who at that time responded eagerly

* Published by Harper & Row, 1965.

to his overtures. He took executives of the television networks for skinny dips in the White House swimming pool. Hardly any visitor who boasted a byline in print or on the air could escape from the Oval Office without carrying away an inscribed photograph of the President. Writers and broadcasters were apt to find him on the telephone at any hour of the day and, sometimes, of the night.

To the regular White House correspondents, the people who were there every day, he held out a promise: "If you play along with me I'll play along with you. I'll make big men of you."

And a threat: "If you want to play it the other way I know how to play it both ways too. I know how to cut off the flow of news except in handouts."

No new Johnson.

The same tough pragmatist, believing in the efficacy of bribery and/or blackmail, who had been shaped in the hill country as a youth and in the cauldron of Texas politics as a man. Performing on a larger and more heavily spotlighted stage than ever before, that was the only difference.

Johnson was the same, but the press was quick to note that the social as well as the official ambiance in the White House changed radically. The French cuisine, as the wife of the soon-to-be-replaced ambassador from France publicly sneered, was replaced by what she called Bar-B-Ques. A bowling alley was installed in the basement for the benefit of the Johnson daughters and their high-spirited friends. Drawled howdys greeted guests and wide-brimmed hats were seen in the cloakrooms. What caught the particular attention of society reporters, however, were the parties that the new President and his wife started giving after the end of the month of mourning.

Some of these were state dinners, some were decorous affairs for members of Congress, others were late suppers with old friends. But the parties where LBJ flowered were great, steamy, crowded, music-laden get-togethers of men who kowtowed to him and attractive women who eagerly embraced the opportunity of

being jounced around the dance floor in the arms of the tall, exuberant, top-o'-the-heap man from Texas. He became tagged in
the society columns as the Dancing President. He was also the
Kissing President, reaching out to grab receptive females and
plant big wet busses on their unprotesting mouths while he called
them "Honey." He unabashedly felt and fondled his favorites and
no one said him nay. Nobody enjoyed the scene more than LBJ
when Christina Ford, the sultrily beautiful wife of the motor mag-
nate, partly fell out of her low-cut dress one evening and laughingly tucked herself back in. A woman of my acquaintance said,
not even acidly, that LBJ should really be known as the Porn
President. And he did at times give the impression of being, in
hill country language, as horny as a billy goat in the spring of the
year. He provided living proof of the accuracy of Henry Kissin-
ger's statement some years later that power is the "ultimate
aphrodisiac."

So far as the political press was concerned, Johnson worked
hard during his early presidency at trying to be one of the boys.
This course was against the advice of his friend Bill White, who
had left the *Times* and was writing a syndicated column of comment from Washington. Asked by Johnson about the best way to
handle the press, White said, "If I were you I'd deal frankly and
as fully with them as circumstances permit, but I'd never, never
get on a familiar basis nor would I have any pets." Johnson
nodded, the columnist said, and replied, "I quite agree with you."

Then, the next thing White knew, *Time* magazine was out
with a story telling how Johnson on a weekend trip to the ranch,
gathered up a few reporters in his Lincoln Continental, others in
other cars following behind, and roared down the road at ninety
miles an hour while sipping beer from a can. The news magazine
dressed up the story excitingly. It said the President gave the male
and female reporters a "graphic description of the sex life of a
bull." It reported that when one of the passengers exclaimed at the
speed of his driving Johnson removed his five-gallon hat and

slapped it on the dashboard to conceal the speedometer. Marianne Means of the Hearst newspapers, one of the passengers, was quoted as saying—or rather, *Time*wise, "cooing"—"Mr. President, you're cute."

Johnson was furious and on the telephone yelled about the story to Henry Luce, publisher of *Time*. He also spoke of it angrily to Bill White, who refrained from saying, "I told you so." White did, however, again mildly approach the point he had made earlier when Johnson asked his advice about dealing with the press.

"But, Bill, you don't understand," LBJ exclaimed. "They were my guests!"

In the hill country guests did not scoff at their host, especially in print for all the world to see.

Another of the President's attempts to get down among them was not reported in print. Rural folklore in Texas holds that the length of a man's penis bespeaks his prowess as a lover. Johnson, evidently more imbued than was usual even for him with the spirit of *machismo* one evening at the ranch, addressed himself to this subject in the company of a group of male reporters.

"I'll match mine against any of yours," he bragged like a country boy on a Saturday night.

Some of the newsmen gave perfunctory, coarse guffaws, but they were not really amused, according to Dickson Preston, who covered the President for Scripps-Howard. Preston, a friend of mine, reported the incident to me after the group returned to Washington.

"That's a pretty rough bunch, you know," he said, "but they were just a little bit shocked at hearing a President of the United States talk that way. Dammit," added Preston, who admired Johnson, "I wish he'd stop *playing* at being President."

I thought my friend's comment missed the point. Johnson was not really play-acting in the role of President, as shown by the steady march of his legislation through Congress. At the ranch, he was simply being his natural self in his natural surroundings.

The White House correspondents quickly came to detest Johnson's frequent trips to Texas. Only a favored few were invited to the ranch. Most had to stay in Austin—later in San Antonio— waiting for a press assistant to come up from the Texas White House in Blanco County with news handouts designed to show that the President was on top of his job there as in Washington.

To many people the cities of Austin and San Antonio are pleasant enough places, but the White House regulars had become accustomed to the more glamorous surroundings of Kennedy's "working vacations" on Cape Cod and in Palm Beach. They made sour comparisons in which LBJ and Texas came off a very poor second. Waiting in boredom for something to write about, they entertained each other with such witticisms as "Let's go down to the hotel barber shop and view the haircutting" and "Let's go out and watch them paint the stripe in the street." White House correspondents are inclined to have high opinions of themselves and they felt they had been banished to the backwaters. Not unnaturally, this feeling to some extent colored their attitude about the man who was the cause of their being there.

Johnson's credibility with the press was strained almost from the beginning of his presidency because he played a game of "You're it" with its representatives about the first Federal budget for which he was responsible. He let word get out that he hoped to hold expenditures for the upcoming fiscal year to something more than $100 billion. It would be hard, very hard, his story went. Some of his fiscal advisers were pressing for a budget of as much as $108 billion. But he was a frugal man, he said, and he was determined to get below that figure if he could. Which, he said, was doubtful.

The press gulped down the bait. Stories appeared nationwide warning the public to be prepared for the first $100 billion-plus budget ever in peacetime. LBJ was depicted as being locked in a Titanic struggle with the big spenders his Administration had inherited from Kennedy.

174

It was true that Johnson sent back to all the department heads the budgets they had submitted with instructions that they should review and reduce them. It was also true that he had a prior understanding with Senator Byrd, chairman of the Finance Committee, that the budget would be at least slightly below $100 billion. Otherwise, the tight-fisted senator from Virginia declared, the tax-cut measure the Administration was pushing would never emerge from his committee.

At a meeting of the Council of Economic Advisers, according to Secretary of the Treasury Dillon, there was some dissension. But when the discussion was over, Johnson made it clear that the budget would be under $100 billion because, in Dillon's words, "of the simple fact that the chief thing was to pass the tax bill and you couldn't pass it otherwise."

The budget as finally presented was indeed below $100 billion. The press had copied the picture Johnson put forward of himself as a prudent man wrestling against odds to save the taxpayers' dollars. And when all the facts emerged the press people responsible felt they had been bamboozled. Their confidence in anything Johnson said was badly undermined.

Their skepticism soon extended to the handouts issued by the White House press office about the accomplishments of the various Federal departments. They were *his* departments, Johnson felt, and he should get credit for any newsworthy actions they took.

Not long after he assumed the presidency, he made a personal appearance at a meeting of departmental public affairs advisers called at the White House by Pierre Salinger, the holdover press secretary. The President lectured the presumed public relations experts about the nature of their job and said he expected a great deal from them. Also, he was unable to refrain from adding, "I could go to Dallas and get some high school seniors and they could do a much better job than some of you folks do."

The public affairs advisers left the meeting feeling somewhat chagrined, according to Dixon Donnelley, who was present as the information man for the Treasury Department. Whatever their disgruntlement, they had received word from the top that they were expected to produce on demand stories for the greater good of the Johnson Administration.

Whenever Johnson planned to go to the ranch for a few days, the public information specialists received telephone calls from the White House alerting them to the need for providing some affirmative news to be released in Texas. LBJ was not going to permit the American people to get the impression that the government ground to a halt when the President was away from Washington. The stories were turned loose from the ranch to prove that a "can-do" man was on the job.

Once again, Johnson overdid a good thing. Donnelley, in an interview for the LBJ Library oral history collection, explained that the system came a cropper because one day at the ranch an assistant press secretary released nineteen separate items.

"This was too much for the press," Donnelley said. "And this helped to start a lot of the news management accusations because there was more appearance of activity than could be justified by the realities. Perhaps half of these items could have been more logically given out by Interior or Agriculture rather than by the White House."

Thus in many ways, some trifling, some to assume major proportions, the groundwork was laid early for the swift and ultimately disastrous deterioration in the relationship between the President and the press.

At his first informal news conference Johnson had been asked if the same format would be used for future sessions with the press. He replied, "I don't think we should be too rigid. Maybe one day we can do this, the next we can have coffee together and the next day we can have a television meeting."

Eventually he tried them all and more.

One day he suddenly appeared at a news briefing being given by the press secretary and took over. He led reporters on long, fast walks around the White House gardens, talking all the time as they trotted along to keep up with him. Once he stood on the balcony of the White House, Carl Sandburg at his side, and bawled down answers to questions from reporters gathered on the lawn below. On one occasion he invited correspondents to bring their wives and children to a meeting, held on the South Lawn, complete with music by the Marine Band and, of course, cookies and lemonade for the youngsters. He also held mass television news conferences, although he hated them and fretted constantly that the reporters would compare his painfully staged perform-ances with Kennedy's greater skill under similar circumstances.

Nothing worked for long. Even in 1964 when Congress, responding to Johnson's incessant prodding, set an amazing legis-lative record and the public opinion polls were giving gratifying reports of the President's popularity, many reporters and col-umnists and television pundits were writing and speaking of what they regarded as LBJ's dark side.

Much of the trouble lay in his style, which was the same as always but magnified as everything is in the White House. If he was feeling on top of the world his ebullience often caused him to behave like an adolescent exhibitionist. If his mood was low he snapped at questioners and indulged in heavy irony at their ex-pense. He talked overmuch about "the awesome responsibility" that rested on his shoulders. He was addicted to the use of the imperial "we" in speaking of himself. He reacted bitterly to criti-cism, stated or implied, a reaction that as a matter of course gave birth to further criticism.

At the end of his first hundred days in office, the traditional honeymoon period for any new President, *Life* magazine pub-lished an editorial giving mixed praise to Johnson. The editorial accorded him high marks for his "earnest and honest readiness to work out all problems by 'reasoning together,' " but was more concerned with his political vulnerabilities. High among them, the editorialist thought, was "his own wheeler-dealer personality." The writer also saw disagreement among White House correspondents with Adlai Stevenson's observation that Johnson "would rather be judged by what he does than what he says."

The editorial continued:

"Instead of letting his deeds speak for him, Johnson has released four to 10 press releases a day about his own whirlwind activities. In addition, he has done more formal cultivating of the press, clocking the results and studying the polls more than any President should have time for. Johnson is not only thin-skinned toward criticism but heavy-handed in reacting to it. In two speeches last fortnight he denounced critics of his foreign policy as 'bellyachers' and 'alarmists' who 'like to jump on their government' and are 'almost as much of a problem as some of our other enemies.' Johnson holds that politics stops at the water's edge, but if this means that criticism of his Cuba, Panama or NATO policy is an attack on the nation, then Johnson's version of nationalism is pretty parochial after all."

This kind of thing was bad enough in Johnson's eyes, but still worse were articles in the press contrasting his mode of operation with that of his predecessor. He raged when James Reston, writing in *The New York Times,* commented that this President, unlike Kennedy, "grants nothing in an argument, not even equal time. He is not detached or objective but highly subjective: Ask not what you have done for Lyndon Johnson, but what have you done for him lately."

Despite his sensitivity to such comparisons, Johnson, like a tongue seeking an aching tooth, could not stay away from them himself. Boasting to reporters one day that he had successfully dealt with every international problem that faced him, he chided his listeners for jeering at him as the "cornpone bumbler" who had come into the presidency "after that shrewd, sophisticated man with style and grace." He was stung by commentaries that he unquestionably was much more conservative than Kennedy and that he might or might not be able to hold the support of liberal Democrats.

Watching all this from the outside but staying in touch with what went on in the White House press room through friends there and in the Administration, I expected that matters might improve after Reedy took over as press secretary. In the first place, he was sorely aware that improvement was needed. In the second, I knew that Johnson had often heeded his counsel in the Senate.

But there was no real improvement. Reedy never could convince LBJ that a press secretary should be exactly that, not a public relations agent. He did his best to keep currently informed about what Johnson was thinking—in contrast all too often with what he was saying—and to pass on to the press as much of it he felt was feasible without subjecting the President to accelerated charges that he was evasive most of the time and a liar at least part of the time. Reedy was forced to develop to a fine art the avoidance of direct questions by saying at his twice daily press briefings that he didn't know or had no comment. Soon the press, including some old friends, distrusted him only a little less than they distrusted his boss. Unfair, but there it was.

Most of the responsibility for this state of affairs rested with Johnson. Reedy's value was lessened by LBJ's misuse of him. He never gave this important aide anything approaching a free hand. How could he? Giving anyone a free hand to speak in his name had never been possible for him. At times in his office he monitored Reedy's briefings of the press and on at least one occasion summoned the press secretary to the telephone in the middle of such a session to upbraid him for what he was saying. This was hardly calculated to upgrade Reedy's standing with the correspondents. In rattling off to one group of reporters, Johnson said mockingly that Reedy "carries more useless information around in his head than any man I ever saw." He complained constantly that this conscientious and able man was working for the press instead of the President, an old imaginary grievance of his against almost every employee at one time or another.

After he was no longer on the job, Reedy astutely observed

that Johnson regarded the press largely as a disturbing factor in the transaction of business. In LBJ's view, the press was valuable to the President—or to any political leader—only to the extent that it created a favorable image of him. In fact, though, as Reedy said, that was irrelevant: "It doesn't matter whether the press likes you or dislikes you. It does matter whether they respect you, but not whether they like or dislike you. They're still going to report what you do, and what you do is what's going to make public opinion."

The press gave Johnson full marks for accomplishment. Nevertheless, the relationship between him and the working press suffered a steady erosion. By the time he was inaugurated for his full term on January 20, 1965, the reservoir of goodwill with which he had begun his presidency was pretty well exhausted. When things began to fall apart in that year, few news people were willing to give him the benefit of any doubt. As a result, Americans in general, readers of newspapers, and viewers of television soon began to blame the President for the political fires that started to blaze at home and abroad.

During his campaign Johnson had talked soothingly about difficulties in foreign lands, in particular downplaying the seriousness of the situation in Vietnam. He had pledged that American boys would not be sent "nine or ten thousand miles away from home to do what Asian boys ought to be doing for themselves." But United States involvement in Vietnam escalated, as the popular word had it in those days. Misled by stupid or self-serving military advisers and ill-founded intelligence reports, driven by his stated determination not to be the first President under whom the nation was defeated in war, Johnson took a hard-line attitude toward his critics. He faulted television for its coverage of bloody battlefields that brought the faraway war into the homes of horrified Americans. Questions raised by the Senate Foreign Relations Committee made headlines not welcomed by the President.

Closer to home, an uprising in Santo Domingo brought the

dispatch of United States forces into the Caribbean for the first time since 1927. The initial popular approval of this move soon turned into general dismay, deepened by "interpretive" news accounts and editorial comment that portrayed the President as either foolishly flamboyant or a deliberate liar.

Right at home, the civil rights movement in the nation came to a crisis point. In Selma, Alabama, blacks and many whites joined in a massive protest. The Watts riots in California showed an ominous change in the racial picture. Other riots scarred other cities.

Dissent on college campuses reached a crescendo over the ever-increasing bloodshed in Vietnam. A cruel chant was born: "Hey, hey, LBJ, how many kids did you kill today?" Placards bearing this sentiment and others almost as biting were carried in youth demonstrations and pictured on television and in the newspapers.

Although the public opinion polls placed Johnson's popularity still high in mid-1965, even in that year a security report showed that the White House was the object of more than 51,000 "unfriendly contacts." They ranged all the way from abusive telephone calls and threatening letters to 166 instances of picketing. More than 300 "unwelcomed visitors" were encountered at the Main Gate, 112 of whom were arrested or committed for mental observation. Seven persons were apprehended in the act of climbing the wire fence enclosing the White House.

Most of the dissidents stayed their distance, but other people who saw the President close up were becoming more and more unhappy about him. Anti-Johnson jokes, usually based on his personal characteristics, made the rounds of cocktail parties. A typical one told of a white Lincoln Continental rocketing down a Texas highway when it was overtaken by a motorcycle cop. The officer waved the driver to the side of the road and, ticket book in hand, walked back to the car. He looked at the driver's unmistakable profile and gasped, "Oh, my God!"

"Yes," growled a voice from inside the car, "and don't you forget it again."

Alan L. Otten of *The Wall Street Journal*'s Washington Bureau related this story in a long editorial page article and went on to recount some of the most-often heard complaints about Johnson: "That the President drives people too hard, is too high-handed and arrogant, doesn't really want argument and independent point of view. That he is too preoccupied with his popular image, is too sensitive to criticism, spends too much of his time answering attacks he should ignore. That he tends to whine over his troubles and blame others for his mistakes. That when things go wrong he frequently turns nasty."

The same old litany, over and over.

In Johnson's view, the obvious cure for such bad publicity was not to change his ways but to get a new press secretary. So out went Reedy from that post and in came young and aggressive Bill Moyers, the first ordained Baptist minister ever to serve in the job.

This Texan had worked one summer for Johnson in the Senate, under my supervision as it happened, when he was twenty. After completing his education, he again joined the senator's staff, participated in his campaign for Vice-President, and in the Kennedy Administration was named assistant director of the Peace Corps. Moyers was in Austin the day Kennedy was assassinated. Not a fellow to miss the main chance, he chartered a plane as soon as he heard the news and flew to Dallas to place himself at LBJ's side. Johnson brought him into the White House as one of his speechwriters and a general handyman. Moyers had been shopping for the press secretary's job—as a youth he had worked for a few months on the Marshall, Texas, *News-Messenger*—and he entered into his duties with gusto.

Most of the White House correspondents welcomed the change, all the more so since Moyers played up to them to the extent of sometimes ridiculing LBJ and making it clear that he at least was on their side. Soon the press was hailing Moyers and giving him a vast amount of favorable publicity, while continuing to slam the President with growing rancor.

A veteran member of the Washington press corps told Willie Day Taylor, Reedy's faithful assistant in the White House as she had been in the Senate, "The trouble is that George always made himself look like a fool while making Johnson look ten feet tall, while Bill makes himself look ten feet tall and causes the President to appear a fool."

In any event, the change brought no lasting betterment of LBJ's relationship with the press, resulted in no brightening of the colors in which they painted him. Eric Goldman, the professor from Princeton who for a time represented LBJ's effort to set up a bridge to the cultural world, quoted the President as demanding in anger and frustration, "What do they want—what *really* do they want? I'm giving them boom times and more good legislation than anybody else, and what do they do—attack and sneer! Could FDR do better? Could anybody do better? What *do* they want?"*

Johnson could not or would not understand that his own personality had become an issue in itself—to many observers, the overriding issue. His vanity, his instant rages, his excessive use of four-letter words, his flagellation of loyal and hardworking employees had become legendary in Washington. None of these qualities really had anything to do with the major war going on in Asia or the major revolution under way in the United States. But they were idiosyncrasies, to put it mildly, that did nothing to endear LBJ to the men and women of the press—and, just as Reedy said, what they wrote formed public opinion.

George Christian, the President's last press secretary, said one fundamental difficulty was that the press people sensed Johnson had no feeling at all about them as individuals. "They were

* *The Tragedy of Lyndon Johnson,* Alfred A. Knopf, 1969.

unimportant to him as people," Christian observed, and since he showed them no consideration they felt no obligation to be considerate of him. *I hate the son of a bitch,* my new acquaintance had said to me years before in the National Press Club.

"We created problems that we didn't have to have," Christian remarked after he was back with his public relations firm in Austin. "We had a reputation for never knowing whether we were going to do something or not, and the press never did believe our reasons for keeping these options open."

The press did believe, however, and joyously gave circulation to stories showing Johnson as a calculating, domineering, boorish Texan who had little regard for the truth when it did not serve his purposes.

Newsweek reported that when Fulbright refused to guide the President's foreign aid bill through the Senate, Johnson spoke his sentiments to a friend: "You know, when you're milking a cow and you have all that foamy white milk in the bucket and you're just about through when all of a sudden the cow switches her tail through a pile of manure and slaps it into that foamy white milk. That's Bill Fulbright."

The reporters talked among themselves about Johnson, on holiday at the ranch, asking an assistant if any additional reporters had shown up. The aide replied he had been told columnist Bob Novak was there, "but I haven't seen him."

"See him?" snapped the President. "You don't have to see him—you can smell him."

This story did not surprise me. I knew why Johnson was down on Novak. When he was Vice-President one of his secretaries, Geraldine Williams, married Novak and Johnson gave an elaborate reception for them in his home. When Novak wrote critically of him in after years it proved to LBJ that the columnist was an ingrate. *You don't understand—he was my guest!*

When he found fault with a telecast by CBS correspondent Daniel Schorr, as later reported by Thomas Whiteside in *The New*

Yorker, he called the commentator one midnight and exclaimed, "Schorr, you're a prize son of a bitch." Schorr told Whiteside that he had also been bawled out by Kennedy for some of his comments about that President. "I've always found that sort of reaction understandably human," he said forgivingly.

Others were less tolerant. However, Malcolm Kilduff, an assistant White House press secretary, could laugh as he told of LBJ walking into his office one day, looking at his neat desktop, and remarking acidly, "Kilduff, I hope your mind is not as empty as your desk." A few days later he again came into the office and this time papers were spread out on the working surface. "Kilduff, clean up your desk!" Johnson barked and strode out of the room.

The significance of such gossipy stories, wholly unimportant in themselves, was that they reflected the nearly complete disenchantment of most press people with the President. They were ready to believe anything that made him look like an unfeeling clod. Johnson being Johnson, the more they jabbed at him the more he opened up additional targets for their sneers.

George Christian believed that, in spite of the President's penchant for secrecy, his relations with the press were unwholesomely close and familiar. LBJ said near the end of his term that he and Congress knew each other better than was good for either side. He claimed they were like an old man and an old woman who had been married too long. Christian thought this concept, rather unflattering to the institution of marriage, applied to Johnson and the press. "He was in the arena a little too much with the reporters," he remarked.

Katharine Graham of the *Post* took the view that the President believed the press kept him from getting his opinions across to the American people. His idea of a free press, she observed, "is one that prints what he wants to be printed." She added, "He thinks that if he sees things from one point of view that is what happened." The result was, Mrs. Graham said, that "when he read something in the paper that wasn't what he conceived of as happening or, in fact, wasn't what he wanted the public to know about what happened, he would get tremendously angry." The publisher of the *Post* was in a position to know about this, for LBJ often became tremendously angry at her paper.

Once, Mrs. Graham recalled some time after the event, she was at the White House and LBJ called her into his bedroom. While giving her unshirted hell for a *Post* headline that had displeased him, he removed his clothes and clambered into bed. Supreme Court Justice Fortas was also present, so Johnson probably saw nothing untoward in this minor happening.

"He was liberated before his time," Mrs. Graham commented tolerantly on NBC's "Today" show.

Chet Huntley, the NBC commentator, said that at private dinners he had in the White House on two occasions Johnson vigorously denounced what he called "the Georgetown press." He ticked off a list of newsmen he "utterly loathed and detested" who presumably lived in that self-conscious area of Washington.

In an interview for the oral history collection, Huntley went on to say, "There is no such thing as a Georgetown press. But there is a group in Washington that—well, it does feed on each other—I think that part of it is true. They borrow from one another. It's a vast dialogue which most of the time, I think, is healthy. But a number of these people were rather vigorous in their criticism of him and he just did not respond to it entirely graciously."

Johnson was so vulnerable because of his obsession with everything that was written in the newspapers or said on the air about him. He missed none of it, no matter how sorely he was wounded. Christian explained: "Exposure to that much news copy became sort of an albatross, because the press knew it could antagonize him if it wanted to. A guy knew he could twit him. All he would have to do was write just a little line and he would get a reaction."

The reactions were very much in evidence during Johnson's

last two or three years in the White House. His vaunted consensus was gone by the latter part of 1966. Republicans marked up substantial gains in the fall congressional elections. The music and dancing had stopped.

Johnson did not campaign, although an itinerary had been released, showing that he planned to go here and there over the country to try to help elect Democrats. He publicly repudiated the whole plan, saying it had been drawn up without his knowledge or consent and he never intended to try to tell the voters what they should do. This did not go down well with the press. Most writers and commentators believed he had foreseen the election results and pulled out of the campaign to avoid what inevitably would be taken as a widespread repudiation of him personally. The credibility gap grew wider, assuming chasmlike proportions.

Loyal Bill White, looking back, stoutly declared this widely heralded gap was a fabrication "in the sense that it was supposed to imply genuine untruthfulness on things that mattered." White thought many political writers became upset because the President did not act in specific instances as they had confidently predicted he would. When that happened, they concluded that somebody had misled them and it must be the President.

Remarking that "he never told the truth all the time, nor did any President, because that would be idiotic," this old friend further conceded that LBJ did at times have "a certain undue regard" for secrecy as such.

"There were times," White said, "when he would not let people know things that were quite unimportant because he had the strong feeling that he must keep things to himself. It was one of his working habits and it caused him a great deal of unnecessary trouble."

Everything combined to cause trouble for Johnson in the end. He believed wholeheartedly that the press was mainly responsible. Flying back from a Chicago speech the day after his announcement that he would not be a candidate for reelection, he turned his venom loose on the small group of reporters accompanying him. "You fellows won't have me to pick on any more," he said bitterly. "You can find someone else to flog and insult. The press can bring a man to his knees in a moment, but you can't bring me to my knees because I don't depend on you any more."

It had been a long, long time since he had read anything like the sentence *Newsweek* published about him at the end of his third year in the Senate: "His manner is quiet and gentle, and everything he does, he does with deliberation and care."

Conflict between the President of the United States and the press is not new, of course. Press attacks on George Washington caused the first President to reflect that "I have brought upon myself a torrent of abuse from the factious papers in this country." The Virginia squire was too proud to complain publicly, but in private correspondence he denounced his critics "as indecent as they are devoid of truth and fairness."

John Adams did not specifically seek passage of the Alien and Sedition Acts of 1798 as a means of dealing with political opposition in the press, but he did not oppose them and signed them after they were passed by Congress. He instructed his attorney general to persecute several editors under the controversial laws.

Thomas Jefferson said, "Nothing can be believed which is seen in a newspaper. Truth itself becomes suspicious by being put into that polluted vehicle." Madison, Monroe, and John Quincy Adams had serious difficulties with newspapers. Relations between the press and the presidency reached a peak of acrimony with the election of Jackson, who symbolized to the East a new and alarming kind of aggressive participatory democracy.

Lincoln was constantly harassed by Greeley, Bennett, and other editors. After one particularly vicious attack he cried, "If the scoundrel who wrote that don't boil hereafter, it will be because the devil has not got enough iron to make gridirons." Editors of southern papers freely referred to the Civil War President as "the Illinois ape," a baboon, a satyr, a buffoon, a monster, an idiot. Even Union newspapers were bitterly critical of his conduct of the war. Several papers were suppressed for varying periods of time.

Grant suffered from a bad press during most of his eight years in the White House. No doubt he brought much of the opprobrium upon himself, having a genius for getting into trouble, but he hardly deserved the portrait *Harper's Weekly* painted of him as "the drunken Democrat whom the Republicans dragged out of the Galena gutter, besmeared with the blood of his countrymen slain in domestic brawl, and lifted to a high pedestal as the Moloch of their worship." Grant said, "I have been the subject of abuse and slander scarcely ever equaled in political history."

Cleveland publicly blasted "the silly, mean and cowardly lies that are every day found in the columns of certain newspapers." Theodore Roosevelt wrote his sister that the New York *Sun* "is frankly the organ of the criminal rich, quite as much as the *Journal* is the organ of the criminal poor." Taft once instructed his secretary not to show him any more clippings from *The New York Times* because they only provoked his "anger and contemptuous feeling."

Wilson, although he maintained that he believed firmly in "pitiless publicity" for public business, had little confidence in newspaper publishers and little rapport with the Washington reporters, once exclaiming, "Their lying is shameless and colossal!" Coolidge saw few reporters but lectured the press in speeches, saying in one that no truly American newspaper would hamstring the Administration by being critical of its conduct of foreign affairs. The Hoover Administration, beset by the depression, was charged by *Editor & Publisher* with creating "a wall of official silence on public questions" and being guilty of "evasion, misrepresentation and, sad to say, in some cases of downright lying by public officials."

Franklin D. Roosevelt frequently said newspaper owners—

as distinguished from most reporters—misrepresented the facts. In one news conference he accused publishers of "appealing to the ignorance, the prejudices and the fears of Americans and acting in an un-American way." Arthur Krock wrote in the *Times* that the President "lost few opportunities to weaken public faith in the integrity of the news columns and the humanity, fairness or intelligence of the comment columns."

Truman often spoke acidulously of "the kept press" and fought scrappily with reporters. Eisenhower and the White House correspondents never had any mutual understanding, although the skill of Jim Hagerty as press secretary kept things going smoothly most of the time. While Kennedy worked hard and successfully at charming the correspondents, in the months before his death, resentment was growing over what some of them considered his evasiveness and worse.

So there could be found ample precedent in American political history for the antagonism that developed between Johnson and the press. It was an old story.

Only, as things turned out, Richard M. Nixon was to make LBJ look good and to cause more than one nostalgic White House correspondent to think with longing of the days when the big, brawling, lusty Texan with the thin skin was leading them on walks over the White House grounds while talking a blue streak.

10
HIS BROTHER'S KEEPER

One day in the spring of 1949, I was having lunch in Austin with Pierce Stevenson, brother to Coke Stevenson, my candidate in the preceding year's Texas senatorial campaign, and a mutual friend. Pierce Stevenson told us about a visit recently made by a lawyer he knew to Senator Johnson's Washington office.

"When he walked in, who do you think was the first man he saw sitting behind a desk and looking important? Old Sam!"

His voice was so filled with scorn and he and my friend laughed so knowingly that I naturally had to ask who "Old Sam" might be.

Sam Houston Johnson, they told me. Lyndon Johnson's younger brother—his only brother. A no-good. A periodic drunk, a gambler, a chaser after loose women. A man who all his life had been doing his brother's dirty work in politics. Bad news from the word go.

"Even old Lyndon don't deserve a brother like him," said Pierce Stevenson.

The words came back to me on my first day on the job with Johnson when a thin-faced man with a crooked, rather engaging smile ambled into my office and said he thought we might have a little visit. He did not bother to introduce himself, but he looked so much like a shrunken version of the senator that I would have known who he was even if he had not referred early and often in that initial conversation to "my brother."

As I scrutinized him I could not see the scamp that had been described to me. Sam Houston came closer to being handsome than his brother, was not as tall, had nothing of his brother's hustle and bustle. His manner was mild almost to the point of self-effacement, and while he was loquacious enough his way of speaking was more hesitant than glib. Even the frequent "goddams" came out soft and easy. A tinge of irony and something approaching self-mockery colored everything he said. Perching on the edge of my desk and smoking one cigarette after another, he told a few slightly ribald political tales, said he had no particular duties in the office but was just around to help his brother however he could, and assured me of his readiness to assist me in any way possible while I was settling into my job in "this insane asylum."

"Glad to have you with us," he said as he departed.

This innocuous statement, as I learned after we became friends, was a lie.

Sam Houston had vigorously opposed my employment. "I figured we'd be asking for trouble if we went into the Coke Stevenson camp to hire a writer and publicity man," he explained to me a few months later. "Lyndon overruled me, but," he added with a grin, "he told me to keep an eye on you at first to make sure you were working for him and not anybody else."

Keeping an eye on matters of concern to his brother was Sam Houston's principal role in life. That was the way things had been for a long time.

Worship is not too strong a word for the feeling the younger man had for the older. It was not a case of his believing his big brother could do no wrong. On the contrary, he recognized, readily admitted to intimates, and laughed at LBJ's foibles and flaws. But they did not matter to him and really, he felt, should not matter to anyone. Lyndon Johnson was a great man, a truly great American. That was Sam Houston's faith and it never became dulled. He was completely convinced that as early as the beginning of Franklin D. Roosevelt's second term as President in 1941, Lyndon Johnson was the most influential man in Congress—a high estimate of a young man who had been in the House of Representatives less than four years. Years later, when I was on Johnson's staff, Sam Houston felt only irritation when the majority leader was hailed in newspaper stories as the *second* most powerful man in Washington. He knew better.

From the time he was a little boy Sam Houston had walked in his brother's shadow. Although he obtained a law degree, he never hung out his shingle. When LBJ left his position with Representative Kleberg, he was succeeded by Sam Houston. The younger brother tried, but failed, to follow his brother as Speaker of "the Little Congress" composed of congressional staff members. At times he was on retainer as a consultant to one or another private business concerns. Through the years he sometimes held jobs in various government departments and agencies. But mostly he worked for his brother as an administrative aide, adviser, and political troubleshooter.

After LBJ was elected to Congress, he insisted that Sam Houston move into the spare room in the rather modest house where he and Mrs. Johnson lived at the time. Thereafter the younger brother was in residence at various increasingly large Johnson homes—including the White House. Sam Houston was married twice and divorced twice, but before, between, and after the marriages, LBJ usually had him at hand day and night.

"I guess Lyndon wanted me close by," Sam Houston wrote in his book *My Brother Lyndon,** "so that he could keep a big-brotherly eye on all my extracurricular activities."

* Cowles Book Co., 1970.

No doubt that was a factor. Sam Houston's behavior was not uniformly all that could be desired by an older brother who, as an ambitious politician, wanted no skeletons popping out of closets. The two men could and usually did see eye to eye on political matters, especially the importance of getting elected, but there were glaring differences in the style of their personal lives.

In contrast to LBJ's relentless, endless reaching out for power, Sam Houston was a cheerful rogue, convivial and cynical, who liked to set up elaborate practical jokes and in his younger days had a great fondness for parties and girls and liquor. He was deadly serious about anything affecting his brother's career but about hardly anything else.

A prime example of their different attitudes was provided by their respective experiences as members of the Little Congress. When eager-beaver LBJ entered the Washington scene as a congressional secretary, he found that organization in the hands of a small, self-perpetuating group of lackluster congressional employees who ran it more or less as a gossip and entertainment club. Young Johnson proceeded to conduct an intensive recruiting campaign among Capitol Hill aides who had not bothered to join the Little Congress. He signed them up in such numbers, making sure they pledged fealty to him, that he was able to overthrow the entrenched old guard and get elected Speaker. It was perhaps a minor triumph, but it was his first one in this new milieu and he treasured it. Also, he proceeded to transform the Little Congress into an organization that heard serious discussions by guest speakers of issues that concerned its members' bosses.

Sam Houston, on the other hand, having been defeated when he ran for Speaker of the Little Congress, maneuvered to be named chairman of the entertainment committee. One of the highlights of his tenure, as described in *My Brother Lyndon,* was a fun-laden weekend trip to New York City by party-minded members of the Little Congress.

Sam Houston organized a thorough shakedown of lobbyists

to make the jaunt a hedonistic success. An employee of a Georgia congressman wangled free tickets for the group from the Pennsylvania Railroad. A member from Tennessee arranged for a supply of liquor from a major distiller. Still another used his congressman's office to get free theater tickets. Sam Houston himself pulled strings to secure complimentary accommodations for the group in a Manhattan hotel. In New York, along with all the other festivities, the junketeers were guests at a ceremony in City Hall at which Mayor LaGuardia presented them with a huge wooden key to the city.

"I reckon the trip I organized was one of the social highlights of that decade," Sam Houston reported modestly.

By the time I knew him, the parties and girls were largely in the past. Moreover, he was strictly on the wagon. This was a sometime thing with him, however, and I soon came to understand that an extended absence from the office meant he had kicked loose from the traces and was off somewhere drinking more than he should. It was one segment of Sam Houston's life that his big brother could never fully control, although he tried. Drink was the sole escape, and that one temporary, from LBJ's domination. But he always came back.

When he was functioning properly, Sam Houston provided invaluable assistance to the senator. More than any other man I have known he loved politics for its own sake. His greatest pleasure was to set up intricate, devious schemes for bringing about the discomfiture of any Texas or Washington politician who dared to oppose his brother. He developed to a fine point the art of leaking to a few favored press correspondents the raw material for stories—which must never, never be attributed to him—he hoped would damage the enemy and uplift his brother. He spent hours on the telephone with Texas politicians to ensure that any brush fires springing up down there would be promptly extinguished. He dictated cogent, succinct memos to LBJ about political issues and how he thought they should be met.

195

One of Sam Houston's great values to the senator was his feeling for people as individuals rather than as masses of voters. LBJ's compassion for the oppressed and disadvantaged was on a broad, sweeping scale. Sam Houston's empathy with the underdog was direct and personal. He might not know what it meant to go to bed hungry, but he knew all too well what it meant to wake up with a ferocious hangover. He instinctively put himself in the shoes of the feckless and fearful.

Sam Houston liked to tell a story about a country judge who, emerging from the courthouse one noon, encountered near the entrance the town derelict, a man aged beyond his years by drink and destitution. The ne'er-do-well tremulously asked the judge for a dime for a cup of coffee. The judge looked him up and down before reaching in his pocket. "A cup of coffee won't do you any good, Ben," he said judicially. "What you need is a pick-me-up and then a dish of ham and eggs, and that's what I'm telling you to get." He handed the man a dollar bill. The old fellow gazed at it unbelievingly before turning a grateful, if bleary, eye on his benefactor. "Judge," he said with feeling, "you've *been* there, ain't you?"

Sam Houston, who had been there often, figured that anybody on his brother's staff who took his job seriously and tried to work as hard as LBJ demanded was an underdog and therefore deserving of sympathy and assistance. He extended both on an individual basis.

The sympathy was likely to take the form of his inviting a down-in-the-mouth staffer out for a cup of coffee and "a little talk." His usual tactic was to explain that he knew his brother often acted like an unfeeling bastard but wasn't really one and had a full understanding of the great worth of that particular staff member. He would even go so far as to invent complimentary remarks about the employee's work which he attributed to his brother. He was as skilled as LBJ at laying on flattery with a heavy hand.

"Just let it slide off your back when he bawls you out," was Sam Houston's refrain on such occasions. "He forgets all about it in three minutes if you're doing a good job—and you damn sure are. Hell, you know he cusses me out worse than he does anybody else."

There was truth in what he said, although I had a feeling that the excoriations Sam Houston received from LBJ were window dressing for the most part. If the senator castigated his own brother, why should any lesser member of the staff feel hurt or angry if he was accorded the same kind of treatment? When I taxed Sam Houston with this reasoning, he conceded with a sly grin that the thrust of my question was sound.

"My brother's so busy doing his job that he doesn't have time to think about people's feelings," he said defensively. "I figure it's up to me to do anything I can to keep things smooth."

Anyway, his method worked most of the time. Sam Houston deserved high marks as a staff morale booster.

He did it in other ways too. He was consistently giving me, after he grew to trust me, and other Johnson employees he liked tips for suggestions we might offer the senator that would make him look good in the Senate, in the press, and in Texas. More than one action memo proudly presented to LBJ by one or another of us had its genesis in a conversation with Sam Houston. An amusing aspect of this procedure was that the senator almost invariably would take up such a suggestion with his brother, who would solemnly state that it was a very good idea indeed and should be acted on forthwith.

Johnson told me repeatedly that Sam Houston knew more about politics than he did, and I think that in a way and to some uncertain extent this was true. Certainly he showed uncanny accuracy in predicting the political effects of actions taken by the majority leader. LBJ was once quoted by John Cameron Swazey in a national telecast as saying that Sam Houston was his chief political adviser and "always has been."

He was, of course, more than that. The implications of their blood relationship were inescapable. Johnson raged to others when Sam Houston went off on a spree, spitting out dire threats of dismissal from the staff and permanent exile from the family. But then the younger brother would turn up, showing no signs of contrition, and again slip easily into his role of confidant, adviser, and morale builder. He flattered the senator without shame or stint, excusing himself laughingly by telling me he had learned that the application of lots of soft soap made it easier for him to get LBJ to do what he should do for his own sake. He could get Johnson out of his occasional black moods quicker than anyone else around the place.

After LBJ's heart attack Sam Houston came to the hospital one day and found his brother blubbering with tears in his eyes. "I'll never get a chance to be President now," he mumbled. Sam Houston, shaken and depressed, went back to the Capitol and described the scene to Grace Tully, Franklin D. Roosevelt's longtime secretary, whom Johnson had placed on the Democratic Policy Committee staff.

Miss Tully, undertaking to cheer him up, told Sam Houston she saw a marked similarity between FDR's polio attack in 1921 and LBJ's heart attack in 1955. She pointed out, in her cheery Irish way, that her former employer's illness had proved not to be the finish of his career but a prelude to his great triumphs. So why, she asked, shouldn't her present employer's illness also signalize a new start?

Sam Houston took the idea and worked with it. He persuaded Holmes Alexander, a syndicated newspaper columnist with whom he was friendly, to write a piece on the subject. Alexander's column began, "Senator Lyndon B. Johnson's career, far from being ended by his illness, has been given a new beginning."

Sam Houston took a copy of a newspaper containing the column out to his brother. It proved to be excellent medicine for the patient, all the more so because FDR was his great hero.

Johnson had his own opportunity to administer therapy a couple of years later. Sam Houston was married again in the fall of 1957—to a former LBJ secretary—and living with his wife in an apartment. He told me he was drinking only sherry, "and for me," he joked, "that's practically being on the wagon." He did not say how much of it he was drinking. Whatever the cause, he fell one day in the kitchen of the apartment and broke his leg.

It became Walter Jenkins' lot to give the senator word of the accident. He told me he dreaded doing so because he expected that Johnson would erupt all over the place. But LBJ took the news with the utmost calm, remarking thoughtfully, Walter told me, that "Sam Houston always did have brittle bones."

He was less casual as it became evident over a period of several months that the fractured leg was not mending properly. Sam Houston was in constant excruciating pain. LBJ finally ordered him to Johns Hopkins Medical Center, where a bone specialist diagnosed osteomyelitis and recommended immediate surgery. A section of Sam Houston's hip was removed to replace the diseased bone in his leg. The eight hours of surgery left him with his right leg five inches shorter than the left.

When LBJ visited the hospital, Sam Houston reported in his book, to find his brother in a complete body cast from his neck to his toes, he choked up in shock and could only mutter, "Sam Houston." The man in the hospital bed typically attempted a feeble joke to lighten the atmosphere, but his effort was not successful.

The senator started his treatment soon after Sam Houston was moved to his apartment.

"Sam Houston's got to have something to occupy his mind," he declared at the office. "He'll go crazy lying out there and thinking about how he's crippled for life."

His solution was simple. He would put his brother to work. Sam Houston had nothing to do but read the newspapers and news magazines and look at television. He was in an ideal position to keep Johnson informed on what editorial writers and political commentators were saying about events that might have a bearing on the majority leader's job. Sam Houston should look and listen and send him a memorandum every day, he instructed, giving him that kind of communications rundown along with his recommendations for appropriate action.

Every morning thereafter, beginning at five o'clock for several months Sam Houston dictated to his wife a memo to report and suggest. By eight-thirty she would have the memo typed. A messenger would pick it up and place it on the majority leader's desk before his arrival at the office. By mid-morning Johnson was on the phone to discuss the memo's content and often to ask Sam Houston to elaborate on some point he had made.

This was good medicine for the bedridden man, no question about that, and LBJ felt he was getting value received. He showed me many of the memos and, in talking them over, was apt to say—accusingly, it seemed to me—that the best ideas he got came from Sam Houston, crippled and sick though he was.

One idea the senator did not like was his brother's insistence that John F. Kennedy had his eyes fixed on 1960 and already had started a campaign for the presidency. LBJ simply did not believe Kennedy could have set his goal so high so soon. He was too young, too inexperienced in government. Perhaps, he told me, the Massachusetts senator would make another try for the vice-presidential nomination. If he did so and won and served two terms with a Democratic President (and LBJ did not speculate as to his identity), he probably would be ready for the top job in 1968.

After Kennedy was nominated and elected, proving at least in this instance the validity of LBJ's often-repeated declaration that his brother knew more about politics than he did, Sam Houston pulled out of the game. He was back on his feet, in a manner of speaking, but he got around only with the utmost difficulty, so he decided to retire on a disability pension. His marriage was breaking up. He left Washington for Austin, moving into the home of his sister Rebekah and her husband Oscar Bobbitt, who worked for the Johnson television station.

Sam Houston spent the next three years there, broken only by rare visits to Washington and occasional forays with old drinking companions. In addition to suffering continual physical discomfort, his formerly irrepressible spirit was worn down by what he considered the humiliation imposed upon his brother by Kennedy's high-riding New Frontiersmen.

On the phone to me from time to time, he complained that "Bobby Kennedy and his gang" were afraid to permit LBJ to get into the limelight. They had persuaded the President not to make use of his brother's legislative genius. They snubbed him socially. They encouraged newspaper people to publish snide stories about him. The whole trouble was, Sam Houston said again and again, that they knew his brother was better qualified than their hero to be President and were afraid the American people would become aware of this truth.

Sometimes my caller was almost maudlin and I wondered about his drinking. Not that I could blame him if he got at least mildly drunk every day. He had reason enough. He was disabled and his life's work had been shot out from under him. I tried to cheer him up and to be as patient with him as was in my nature.

One night when I was aroused from sleep by the telephone it was not Sam Houston on the other end of the line, but the call was about him. An old friend on Capitol Hill told me he had just finished listening to a long monologue from, he said cautiously, "our friend in Austin, you know who I mean." Sam Houston had escaped from the Bobbitt house and, holed up in an Austin motel, was drunk and promised to get drunker. He announced his intention of calling several prominent Washington newspaper columnists, whom he named, to give them the lowdown on what was happening to his brother at the hands of "those damn Kennedys."

My friend had managed to get from Sam Houston the name

of the motel where he had checked in. He gave it to me and said he hoped I could think of a way to deal with the situation.

I could and did, although not without a guilty sense of betraying Sam Houston. Late as it was, I called Walter Jenkins at home and relayed the information to him. He was instantly alert to the danger of publicity that would infuriate LBJ and do no one any good.

"All right, thanks," Jenkins said. "I'll call Bobbitt and have him go to the motel and see if he can put a stop to this foolishness."

Bobbitt evidently accepted and carried out what must have been an unwelcome assignment. At any rate, no columns appeared in print about a midnight telephone call from the Vice-President's brother.

When Kennedy was assassinated, Sam Houston wrote in *My Brother Lyndon*, "In spite of all my resentment against the Kennedys, I broke down and wept for the President and his family." His grief was not alone for Kennedy, he said, but also for his brother, "who had just taken over the most thankless job in the world."

His brother was uppermost in his mind when he telephoned me a few days later. One of the wild rumors that got into print named me as a possibility for press secretary in the Johnson Administration. Sam Houston seemed his old self as he congratulated me and said it was a smart move on Lyndon's part. I assured him the rumor was completely without any foundation and told him, truthfully, it had not originated with me. There was no chance, I added, that I would join the White House staff in any capacity even if I were asked, which I was certain would not happen.

"But you'll be helping him any way you can from the outside, won't you?" Sam Houston immediately demanded. "Lyndon will need all his old friends."

"Sure, Sam," I said, flattered but not overwhelmed. "You know I will."

Sam Houston called me frequently during the next few days. Once it was to say with good-natured scorn that he and every other member of the Johnson family suddenly had become very important and reporters were swarming all over the Bobbitt home. "I won't talk to them," he snorted. Another call was to tell me in a pleased way that LBJ had asked him to round up all the Johnson and Baines relatives for a huge Christmas dinner celebration at the ranch. "It's a job," he said. "Must be sixty or seventy in all." Then he added that his brother wanted him to come to the White House to live after New Year's.

"Are you going to do it?" I asked.

"Aw, hell, I don't know," he said. "Don't even know if I want to. I told him we could talk about it while he's down here for Christmas."

There could be but one outcome to that talk. Sam Houston came back to Washington after New Year's and most of the time for the next five years occupied a room in the family quarters of the White House. He usually joined the President and Mrs. Johnson for breakfast and dinner, during which, he reported, they had "wonderful conversations." Again, as in the past, he was not held down to any specifically assigned duties. A tape recorder was installed in his room and a secretary placed at his disposal to type memos to his brother. It was like old times. Only the stakes were bigger than ever before.

Sam Houston worried about the strains the presidency placed on his brother. He tried to divert him by engaging the President in their favorite game of dominoes when there was a free hour, usually late at night. He was always ready to listen to talk about the burdens of the presidency. Still a sounding board. All his life he had looked up to his big brother. Now he confessed that he could not help regarding the President of the United States with a certain amount of awe. But for the first time, as the country's problems proliferated and the President's troubles grew in proportion, he actually found himself feeling sorry for the older man.

Such a sobering emotion could never be permanent with Sam Houston so far as his actions were concerned. His nature demanded that he have some fun.

He told me one day in 1965, speaking with his habitual air of ironic self-mockery, that he might as well be in the penitentiary. He realized that the President had him in the White House for more than one reason. True, he said, he could talk up to his brother and give him counsel that no one else might dare to offer. That probably had a certain value. But also, Sam Houston added with his twisted grin, "Lyndon's got me confined so he can be sure I don't do anything that would disgrace the President."

A Secret Service man was assigned to stay with him at all times—"especially," said Sam Houston, "at night." This agent, a very pleasant fellow, never did anything to interfere with or curtail his activities; but he was always there. And, of course, always subject to grilling by LBJ about what Sam Houston was doing, where he was going, whom he was seeing, how much he was drinking.

I met the agent, who also served as a chauffeur, one day when Sam Houston invited me to have lunch with him. The White House car picked me up on the street in front of the building where I had an office. Sam Houston told the agent-driver to take us to a Marriott Inn across the river in Virginia. When we arrived it was not the place Sam Houston had in mind. He asked the agent with some asperity where the other Marriott Inn was—the one he had been to before. The Secret Service man said equably, "Oh, that one" and drove us to another restaurant that, so far as I could see, was little different from the first. But Sam Houston said with satisfaction, "They know me here." Inside, we were indeed greeted with warmth by the manager and the waitress assigned to our table. We had two martinis each and an excellent lunch while the agent waited outside.

"Oh, he'll tell Lyndon where we went and what we did," Sam Houston said. "But this time it won't matter. Lyndon approves of you."

At other times it did matter. Occasionally Sam Houston would give his Secret Service agent the slip. At least once his escape was so thorough that several days passed before he was tracked down and placed in a hospital to dry out. Although registered under another name, soon he was heatedly informing attendants that he was the President's brother and loudly demanding better service. So I was told by a friend who had a relative in the hospital at the same time.

Most of his lapses were more innocent. Sometimes he would go away and spend a night in a Washington hotel just to get away from the feeling of being a prisoner. He might drop in on his friends Glen and Marie Wilson, of whom his brother also approved, and end up by sleeping on a couch in their living room. One Saturday night when LBJ and Mrs. Johnson were out of town for the weekend, he invited this couple—invited me and my wife too, but we had a previous engagement—to the White House for dinner. In a great gesture of defiance, he ordered all blazing lights turned on in the dining room as the three of them were formally served. Sam Houston loved it.

"Had Lyndon seen his home shining in a blaze of glory with that shameful waste of electricity, he would have blown his stack," he joyfully wrote in recalling that evening. "I'm sorry I didn't take a picture of it. Had he been disposed to poke fun at himself, it would have made a nice Christmas card."*

Before long the fun and games appeared to be all over as the Johnson family made a final exit from the White House. But the taste of glory was not over for Sam Houston.

Early in 1969, he telephoned me from New York to give me the news that he had signed a contract to write a book about his brother. He said he was dictating into a tape recorder for hours every day. He explained that he had a fine editor, who was helping him put things together. He gloated that his contract

* My Brother Lyndon

called for him to receive an advance of fifty thousand dollars—
"the same as the papers say Liz Carpenter is getting for her book
about Lyndon and I damned sure wasn't going to take any less."
He told me one of the main purposes he had in mind was to "get
even with the Kennedys."

Publication of *My Brother Lyndon* created something of a
stir, although I, reading it with care, could find nothing especially
sensational. Sam Houston did not begin to "tell all" about his
brother's political career or personal life. In fact, I considered it
on the whole almost excessively protective.

The book was made up largely of a compendium of anecdotes about the Johnson boys' childhood and youth, a running
account of LBJ's ascent to power, and stories about an array of
national politicians. A good many private conversations between
LBJ and Sam Houston were set down. A few of these threw more
light on the private Johnson than, I could see at once, he would
like. Some of the stories in the book were malicious on their
face, but no malice was directed toward the big brother. Sam
Houston also indulged in some of his own variety of political
philosophizing.

My Brother Lyndon hardly justified the jacket blurb that "It
adds up to a powerful, revealing document of personal and political history, illuminated by moments of high drama, humor, and
tragedy." Still, the book contained much of interest. And it did
prove beyond any doubt that Sam Houston really knew his brother
—"a lot better than he knows me because he's been too damned
busy with other matters to think about me, while I've had practically nothing to do but study him."

Two unsurprising facets of Sam Houston's thinking were
made clear. He hated the Kennedys, especially Bob Kennedy. He
adored his brother. Five years later, in speaking of the book, Sam
Houston said he wrote it to "bring out the greatness" of Lyndon
Johnson and to "get back at those who hurt my brother."

No doubt. At the same time, Sam Houston frankly liked the

money and enjoyed the notoriety that his book brought him. After years of obscurity, he was a public figure in his own right. He gave interviews to the press, appeared on television talk shows, autographed copies of *My Brother Lyndon* in department stores. It was exhilarating to speak his own piece after a lifetime of operating behind the scenes. The Johnson ego evidently had been lurking beneath the surface all along. Now there was an opportunity, even though of brief duration, for it to flower. Sam Houston Johnson was a book author!

"No one knows more," he ended his book, "about the government of the United States than Lyndon Johnson, no one has a deeper concern for his country. And since he is not a naturally reticent man, it would be most uncharacteristic for him to remain silent.

"We haven't heard the last of LBJ."

Sam Houston had heard the last, however, *from* his brother.

LBJ made that clear to me when I visited him at the ranch shortly before the book was published (although he had managed somehow to see a copy of the manuscript) but after a long excerpt from it appeared in *Look* magazine. He was through with Sam Houston, he said with more deep-seated bitterness than I had ever before heard in his voice.

The book, he declared venomously, was filled with betrayed confidences and "psychopathic lies." Sam Houston had shown himself to be ungrateful, disloyal, and probably not wholly sane. He said doctors at the Scott-White Clinic in Temple, Texas, would testify that his brother appeared mentally unbalanced the last time he was there.

"I don't see how Sam Houston could do it just for the money," he said. "He won't use the money anyway to pay up his bills or cover the hot checks he's given to everybody who would take them. How could he have done this to me and the family?"

The former President turned sideways in the seat of the car he was driving to peer at me from beneath the absurdly long bill of the golf cap he wore. His mouth was a thin line, turned down sharply at the corners. I was saddened by his expression of angry resignation and tried to tell him, as I had promised Mrs. Johnson earlier in the day I would do, that I could not believe Sam Houston's book was so earthshakingly important. It would do no lasting harm, I argued. LBJ was not impressed. He went off again about Sam Houston.

"I wanted to give him up that time he got drunk at home and broke his leg when I was in the Senate," he said. "But Bird—she's always so gentle and forgiving—hoped we could do something with him. I tried, but it didn't work. Now he's done this to me."

He added a denial of newspaper stories that he had tried to stop publication of the book. He had never given any comment to the press about it and never would. He understood, he said, that the Kennedy Foundation "owned a piece" of *Look* magazine and no doubt had arranged for publication of the excerpt to damage him. This seemed irrational to me, but I refrained from saying so. I was glad when he turned to other subjects I had come to discuss with him.

Nothing about his remarks concerning his brother made me feel good as I recalled years past. But there was not, I realized, anything I could do. As LBJ and Sam Houston probably would have agreed, it was a family affair.

Sam Houston had said many times to many persons, when for one reason or another he was in disfavor with LBJ, "After all, he can't fire me from being his brother."

But that was what happened in the end. There was no reconciliation. When LBJ died his will contemptuously bequeathed the sum of five thousand dollars to Sam Houston.

Some two years after his brother's death, Sam Houston was interviewed by a reporter for the Austin *American-Statesman*. At the end of the interview, he said fiercely, "I don't want anything written that would hurt Lyndon."

11

GREAT CAESAR'S GHOSTS

LBJ was a man perpetually surrounded by ghosts moaning in anguish and rattling their chains most of the time but occasionally giving way to bursts of manic laughter when their efforts met with the approval of the master.

Probably few men have been credited with so many millions of words strung together by other persons. Like most public officials, Johnson depended heavily upon ghostwriters to produce the unending stream of prose that flowed, sometimes ripplingly, sometimes turgidly, out of whatever office he currently occupied. Big corporation executives, television's famous funnymen, senators, and Presidents have too many other things to do to permit themselves to sit down at a desk and address themselves to the essentially grubby task of setting down one word after another.

In Johnson's case, judging by my own experience and stories I heard from and about other LBJ ghosts, he was far above the average in furnishing the key ideas for his public utterances. He would snap out one-two-three orders about what he wished to get across in a speech. ("Dammit, aren't you going to take notes? How can you expect to remember what I want to say unless you write it down?") He could create a skeleton in five minutes. The longer task of filling it out with flesh, puffy or firm, was up to the writer.

In the Senate days, ghostwriting for Johnson was a relatively simple matter. Insofar, that is, as any operation involving him could be simple. On a regular basis, Reedy and I did most of it. Between us, we turned out a wide variety of speeches, short statements for the *Congressional Record,* messages from the senator to be read at meetings to which he had been invited but could not attend, memos to other senators and to newspaper columnists whose favor he was especially anxious to gain.

Reedy was singlehandedly responsible for Johnson's use, with good results, of the biblical admonition, "Come now, and let us reason together." The big slow-talking, keen-thinking former newspaper reporter had a genius for putting the right words in the majority leader's mouth. LBJ leaned heavily on him but at times grew dissatisfied and called for outside help. Horace Busby, who had been on Johnson's staff in the past and would be again in the future, during this period ran a public relations firm and published a business newsletter in Texas. Nevertheless, he occasionally was summoned to Washington to put his way with words to work on a special project. Lawyer Jim Rowe sometimes contributed speeches. Johnson was forever impulsively asking various reporters and even aides to other senators to give him "a paragraph or two" on subjects they knew something about. Still, it would be fair to say that Reedy, with assistance at times from Siegel, McPherson, and, during one year, Jim Wilson, a very bright young lawyer from Austin, wrote most of Johnson's pronouncements.

These included not only the day-to-day statements expected from the Senate's majority leader but also what the newspapers termed "major speeches." This was a term Johnson himself did not care for. Once a reporter asked him if a forthcoming address was to be "major." LBJ retorted snappishly, "All my speeches are major."

My own ghosting efforts, in addition to the newsletter and the radio scripts, included articles for magazines. I wrote for LBJ's byline a story for *Progressive Farmer* about his determination as a young congressman to get rural electrification projects going in his district. *American Magazine* published an article in which the senator explained how his heart attack changed his outlook on life. When legislation removing Federal price control of natural gas was on the agenda, I composed for his signature what turned out to be a rather prophetic essay on the subject for *Public Utilities Fortnightly*. Payments for this kind of writing provided a pleasing supplement to my salary. It apparently never occurred to Johnson to demand a share of the proceeds. Both of us were happy with the arrangement of credit to him and cash to me.

He was less happy about a particular newsletter I presented to him during one of the Eisenhower recessions. LBJ talked frequently in the Senate and had me write frequently in the newsletter about the terrible state of the economy. He made a trip to Texas and during his absence I dashed off still another piece deploring the recession and the policies that had caused and were prolonging it. On the senator's return, I confidently handed over my copy for his approval. He read only the first two or three sentences before flinging the pages back across the desk at me. "Recession!" he snarled. "Recession! I'm so damned sick of hearing about the recession I could puke." I sensed that business was turning upward, at least in Texas, so I went away to write on another subject.

A ghostwriting assignment I would have liked but which stood beyond my grasp grew out of a trip Vice-President Johnson made to the Scandinavian countries. Included in the party was Bart McDowell, a senior editor of *National Geographic*. Recognized around the magazine as a man of unusual writing skill,

McDowell was often called on to put words together for Melville Grosvenor, head man of the National Geographic Society. This time he was putting them together for the Vice-President in an article to be published in the magazine.

In the same month of 1963 that the first-person story of Johnson's journey appeared in print, the Society's magnificent new building in Washington was officially dedicated with Grosvenor presiding over the ceremonies. Vice-President Johnson (in remarks prepared by Busby) accepted the building more or less on behalf of the nation.

When it was all over, with the ghost standing by, LBJ said graciously to Grosvenor, "Bart has certainly been a great help to me." "He's a help to me too," said the Geographic Society chief, and the two men beamed approvingly at their helper.

"I felt like a shared toothbrush," McDowell later commented to his wife.

Johnson's speeches were the most important outlet for his views and programs, and for these he really stood in need of ghostwriters. Without a script in front of him, his performance as a speaker was as unpredictable as the behavior of the little girl with the curl in the middle of her forehead. Under such circumstances, if the occasion was right, he might give a shouted political oration off the cuff that would have a partisan audience roaring its approval. Or he could deliver an unscripted lecture crammed with bromides, as I heard him do as the commencement speaker at a college in Brownwood, Texas. For nearly an hour the senator exhorted the graduates in so many words to do right, work hard, observe the Golden Rule, be nice to others, keep smiling. And he was so urgently earnest about what he was saying! I wished I could have been somewhere else, a sentiment I felt sure was shared by most of the audience.

Even when he was armed with a script, which might have been worked over half a dozen times before Johnson approved it, there was no way of foretelling how the speech would come out.

So much depended upon the LBJ mood of the moment. If something had gone wrong during the day to cast him down, he might well read the speech in a dead monotone, get it over with as quickly as possible, note that he was not being wildly applauded, then depart to berate his unfortunate speechwriter for letting him down.

He was forever laying down the law about the importance of using short words in short sentences and short paragraphs. "No word with more than seven letters! No sentence with more than six words! No paragraph with more than three sentences!" If I heard such an admonition once I heard it a hundred times. Whenever a writer followed the order literally, the end product could sound exceedingly choppy. One speech published in full in the Washington *Post* looked and read like an overly ambitious attempt at a free verse epic by a high school sophomore.

A word could be short and still be considered unsuitable if LBJ thought his audience might not readily understand it. After giving one speech Reedy wrote for him, he said peevishly, "George, don't ever again use 'eon' in a speech of mine. Hell, you know I don't know what it means and if I don't know how's that farmer sitting in the front row going to know?"

On the other hand, he liked to dress up his speeches by quoting striking thoughts expressed by great men of the past. He told me one day during his vice-presidency, "I've got to improve my speeches because every time Kennedy gives one of his he makes me look sick. It's all those famous sayings he uses from Lincoln and Shakespeare and people like that. I want you to find me a lot of new trite sayings I can use in my speeches."

I duly found some at the time and even continued my quest to send a few to the White House after he became President.

By then, of course, the entire process of preparing material for him had undergone a radical change. Putting together a major presidential speech was an extensive engineering operation. It called for the sweaty efforts of not one person, not two persons, but of a team some of whose members at any given time were almost certain not to be speaking to one another. Although the President was the top prima donna working in the White House, he was by no stretch of the imagination the only one. The atmosphere begat temperament. Competition to get one's own words into a presidential speech was intense and sometimes bitter. And, to a detached onlooker, often quite funny.

A Texas lady remarked after hearing an early speech by President Johnson on television that she enjoyed listening to a President "who speaks without an accent." It takes one to know one, of course, but this admirer of the presidential diction might have been taken aback if she had heard the various accents of the numerous persons who participated in erecting LBJ's speeches. They had differing ideas too. The struggle among the speechwriters to get to the Oval Office first with the most went on unceasingly.

One way for a speechwriter to influence the course of government, said Richard N. Goodwin, a Kennedy hand who had been brought into the Johnson White House mainly through Moyers' efforts, was to wait until the last possible moment before submitting a draft. This strategy, Goodwin knowingly explained to McPherson, gave the President and his advisers little time to get somebody else to write another draft. "They must bargain with you," McPherson reported Goodwin as saying, "to temper what you've written."

This young man, looked upon by some of his colleagues as an abrasive adventurer strictly devoted to advancing his own interests, for a time was regarded by Johnson as one of his best speechwriters. But he did not last long—perhaps because he submitted too many drafts too late. LBJ always wanted an option and time to exercise it.

Some of the White House wordsmiths were old Johnson men, a few were inherited from Kennedy, some were actively recruited, and others found themselves on the speechwriting team almost by accident. Theodore Sorenson, a highly respected professional who had served Kennedy well, stayed on through the transition period. Reedy, Busby, and McPherson were attuned through long association to the Johnson mind and methods. Moyers was the principal architect of a number of important speeches and injected himself into the editing of drafts prepared by others in order to include his own ideas. Jack Valenti, the Houston advertising man who attached himself to LBJ the day Kennedy was killed, admired a touch of sentimentality and constantly urged other staff members to "Get some tears in it." Harry Middleton, a free-lance writer, had been engaged by Burke Marshall to write the report for the President's Commission on Draft Reform, then was asked to prepare LBJ's message to Congress on the subject, and gradually found himself eased in as a speechwriter on the White House staff. Benchley was hired because the President hoped his former association with *Newsweek* could be used to his own advantage, and when that naive plan failed to work, the young man was allowed to drift into helping out with speeches. Robert Hardesty, a Missourian, went to the White House on loan from the Post Office Department and stayed. Tom Johnson and Charles Maguire were White House Fellows before they became speechwriters. Califano's keen legal brain was focused on messages to Congress about various domestic programs. Will Sparks in a previous existence was in charge of public relations for a trade association.

LBJ's opportunity to foster competition among people working for him had never been greater than with this heterogenous crew, and he took full advantage of it. His habit of getting staff members to second-guess one another flourished among all these healthy egos.

"Frequently," said Christian, "you didn't know how many people were working on a certain subject, particularly a speech. He might get a draft of a speech from someone, hand out copies to four or five other people on the staff, and you wouldn't know who had all the copies. He'd say to me, 'Put this in Johnson City language,' or something, and I wouldn't have any idea who else was working on it and whether the guy that was might be doing the same thing."

As with Christian, so with others. LBJ enjoyed keeping people off-balance. The tactic sometimes gave rise to dissension, to be sure, but it also kept anybody from becoming complacent.

The competitive spirit even extended to finding or making up jokes for inclusion in speeches. When Peter Benchley, Harvard '61, went to work in the White House, he was instructed to get up a little humor for this purpose. What could be more logical? After all, he was the grandson of that very amusing fellow, Robert Benchley.

The trouble was, said the younger Benchley, he had no idea what the President would like to talk about so far as funny stuff went. As a result, he added ruefully, "You'd throw in bad jokes and it just didn't work out."

For some reason, Benchley said, Johnson had concluded that Ben Wattenburg, also a staff member, was a fine joke writer. So Wattenburg was assigned to come up with funny stories for speeches.

"He did what you had to do," Benchley explained, "which is go around and get jokes from people and assemble them. This caused some resentment because everybody was working on the jokes and the President would call Ben and say, 'Ben, I want jokes.' "

All this spotlight on one person—and a *man* at that!—did not set well with feminist Liz Carpenter, officially press secretary to Mrs. Johnson but unable to refrain from putting her finger into the LBJ speechwriting pie. She contributed a good many jokes herself and was determined to get credit for them. She organized regular weekly meetings in her office of five or six members of the speechwriting staff to sit down and hash out funny anecdotes or flip one-liners. This operation was somewhat successful, according to Benchley, although he reported that when Mrs. Carpenter's jokes were turned down "she'd go through the ceiling and tell everybody they were stupid."

A Texan herself, she favored extensive use of the Texas idiom in LBJ's speeches. Not always to his pleasure. Christian said Johnson "never forgave Liz for stuff like 'six-shooter coffee' and things like that early in his Administration."

When Clark Clifford was sworn in as Secretary of Defense, the President used a script prepared by Benchley which contained some light references to Clifford's home on Nantucket off Cape Cod. Mrs. Carpenter was furious.

"That's not Lyndon Johnson, that's Nantucket!" she screamed at Benchley. "Nobody goes to Nantucket except people with flat-chested wives. That's not Lyndon Johnson. That's not home country stuff."

She had one of her own sentences cut out of a speech she wrote for the President to deliver at a ceremony honoring Senator Hayden in Arizona. Bob Kerr was a member of the group flying out for the occasion and Johnson handed him a copy of the speech to read. Kerr let out a startled grunt when he came upon a sentence declaiming, "Carl Hayden's relationship to Arizona is like that of Adam to Eve." He showed the sentence to Reedy, who told me of the incident, and they agreed it must go.

Why? the proud author wanted to know.

"Think about it, Liz," Reedy urged. "Now just what did Adam finally do to Eve?"

She continued to protest, but Reedy said the sentence was eliminated.

The manufacture of jokes, while time-consuming, was only a minor part of the speechwriting process. As LBJ said in 1956 when questioned about his putative candidacy for the Democratic nomination for President, he was serious about everything he did. Persons who wrote material to be issued in his name were well advised to approach their work with appropriate solemnity. There was no other way to translate ideas into what McPherson described in his book as presidentialese—"that exalted language in which, custom had it, great public issues should be discussed."

The art of writing presidentialese had to be acquired. It was a style that came naturally to no one except after long practice. The basic purpose was to make whatever was written come out sounding profound, concerned, and dedicated to the solution of the particular problem being discussed.

A prime example of presidentialese was contained in a paragraph of President Johnson's 1965 State of the Union message: "The Great Society asks not only how much, but how good; not only how to create wealth, but how to use it; not only how fast we are going, but where we are headed." Alliteration was highly regarded, as in a sentence from a speech about the 1967 war in the Middle East: "This is a time not for malice, but for magnaminity; not for propaganda, but for patience; not for vituperation, but for vision."

Unfortunately, there was ample precedent for this kind of thing. Some speechwriter in 1952, when Eisenhower was running for President, had the old soldier utter these two remarkable sentences: "No fantastic fiat of history decreed that little South Korea . . . would fatally tempt Communist aggressors as their easiest victim. No demonic destiny decreed that America had to bleed this way in order to keep South Korea free and to keep freedom itself self-respecting."

Another President included these lofty words in his first inaugural address: "We can build a great cathedral of the spirit, each of us raising it one stone at a time, as he reaches out to his neighbor, helping, caring, doing. . . . We have endured a long night of the American spirit. But as our eyes catch the dimness of the first rays of dawn, let us not curse the remaining dark. Let us gather the light." That was Richard M. Nixon!

Although McPherson wrote the definition of presidentialese and was guilty of perpetuating his share of it, he disclaimed any admiration for this prose form. He especially disliked its use by LBJ, he said, because "I thought it put a wall between him and his audience and made him—already the artful politician—seem the more contrived."

Johnson, for reasons that constantly changed and were sometimes contradictory, was rarely satisfied with his speeches. He demanded that they be lightened up and then complained that efforts at humor made him appear foolish. "I'm not a funny President," he sharply reprimanded Benchley. Or a speech was without news value: "Where will the *Times* get a lead out of this?" Or it was too provincial. He constantly adjured his staff to keep in mind that the United States was not made up of just Washington, New York, Boston, Los Angeles, and San Francisco. There were many places and many people between the East Coast and the West Coast, he reminded the speechwriters, and they should remember those places and those people.

One of the staffers, Bob Hardesty, recalled that when he was asked to write speeches for LBJ, a job he coveted, Moyers "just scared hell out of me." Moyers told him, "You could be the best speechwriter in the world and it wouldn't suit Johnson's style." The difficulty lay in knowing what his style would be from one day to the next.

He bawled out his writers regularly, praised them once in a while, and on occasion made humble appeals to them for assistance. Whatever it took to keep them on their toes.

Hardesty and Sparks worked together until three A.M. one night on their second speech of the day. "It was terrible," Hardesty said, "and we knew it." So they were not cheered when they received word soon after returning to the White House following their late labors that the President wished to see them in his office immediately. They found Johnson behind his desk looking sad and patient.

"You know," he said in an unnaturally low voice, "I've got ambassadors going all over the world to get peace and I've got a potential strike on my hands and inflation's getting out of hand, and I've really got more to worry about than a speech. I can't write my own. I need some help. Now do you think you can take this draft back and do something with it?"

"Yes, sir!" the speechwriters replied in unison.

So that method worked when LBJ chose to use it. Hardesty said, "It was just the shot of adrenalin we needed."

At another time Johnson expressed outright enthusiasm for a speech Sparks wrote about the arts and humanities—just the right tone, he said. "By God," he told the pleased writer, "I've done more for the arts in this country than all those Georgetown jellybeans put together." Jellybean was a pejorative word in the hill country, even worse than drugstore cowboy.

LBJ liked enormously the "human" touches that he felt Valenti added to speeches he edited. The former advertising man believed strongly that Johnson must appeal to people "who will cry when an old lady falls down in the street." These two men had a similar fondness for corn and for what they called punchy sentences.

Johnson once told a reporter, "Jack is really an intellectual —he's a Harvard man himself, you know—and people would admit it if he didn't come from the wrong side of the Mason and Dixon Line." Valenti had indeed attended the Harvard Business School and was sufficiently well read to sprinkle classical allusions through his ghostly efforts. Calling him a Harvard man was no more than presidential license.

It was Valenti who aroused widespread risibility by saying in a speech before the Advertising Federation of America in mid-1965, "I sleep each night a little better, a little more confidently, because Lyndon Johnson is my President." Sam Houston wrote that such hero worship would have made him a bit uncomfortable, but added wryly, "I don't think the President minded very much."

The President himself caused some laughter when, escaping from his ghosts, he ad-libbed in a speech to soldiers in South

Korea that his grandfather had died at the Alamo in the lost battle which forever after caused Texans to swell with pride. This simply was untrue and his heroics were immediately challenged by the press. Johnson's defense was to deny that he made any such statement, even though it was recorded on tape. He had only been trying to establish rapport with the soldiers. When *Time* magazine jeeringly reported the incident, he wisecracked to Califano, "If Hugh Sidey [*Time*'s man in the White House] ever had a crowd like that, he'd claim he was a grandson of George Washington."

LBJ never hesitated to go outside the ranks of his own band of trained seals in his eternal quest for better speeches. Preferably the perfect speech.

He once asked Chester Bowles to write one for him. Bowles related the incident in a 1969 interview for the LBJ Library. The interview, covering sixty-seven typed pages, consisted mostly of Bowles talking about himself and what he had accomplished as Ambassador to India and how the country would be in much better shape if Johnson, Rusk, and McNamara had done as he advised them to do. But he finally did get around to telling about a conversation he had with the President.

"I'm not sure that you understand the aid program in India thoroughly," he said he told Johnson, "but I know your grandfather would."

"What do you mean by that?" asked an instantly interested LBJ.

"Your grandfather was a populist, an agrarian non-Marxist radical," Bowles explained. "He believed in lower freight rates and lower interest rates. He believed in schools and more doctors and rural roads. He believed in a better break for the little guy. Now that's what our foreign assistance program is all about. Those countries don't want communism or any other totalitarian ideology. They just want a better break. They want to see their resources used for their own benefit."

If Johnson, who so many times had steered foreign aid bills

through the Senate, thought this explanation gratuitous, he kept himself from saying so. Instead, he asked Bowles to write a speech for him elaborating on the points he had made. He said it would be an appropriate speech at a forthcoming dinner for editors that he had agreed to address. Bowles said he would do it.

"But I got through with it too late and missed my chance," he reported in the interview, adding with reflective modesty, "It would have been a good speech though."

(One wonders how closely together the two men were sitting in the Oval Office. When Bowles was in the Department of State in the Kennedy Administration and the Vice-President was traveling far and wide, LBJ confided to me, "Bowles is making enemies for us all over the world with his halitosis.")

Another effort at getting assistance from an outside writer also came to naught. The White House asked John Steinbeck to compose a few paragraphs about the meaning of America to be read at LBJ's inaugural in 1965. Steinbeck, then in Europe, obligingly complied with the request. But, according to Eric Goldman, the President refused to allow the contribution to be read at the inauguration ceremony because it was too good.

"It would upstage my speech," Goldman quoted LBJ as saying.

He was probably right. The President had some highly competent speechwriters, but even the best of them was hardly in Steinbeck's league.

12

LAUGHING ALONG
WITH LBJ

One of President Johnson's favorite stories for a long time, an improbable anecdote he told often to friends, ridiculed two men, Walter Lippmann and NBC's Fred Friendly, he felt had done him wrong. Telling this story was one way of getting back at them.

LBJ began his tale solemnly, explaining that Friendly was giving a lecture before a college audience in New York City when somehow the word "love" came into his talk. At this point a girl leaped to her feet and yelled, "You don't know what love is, Mr. Friendly! To you, love is just a big lay." The scene became confused and Friendly cut his speech short, the President said, adding that in the era of confrontation between generations this seemed a reasonable thing to do.

On that same day the television man had a lunch date with Lippmann at one of those fancy New York restaurants, Johnson continued, spinning out the story. While the two men were eating their shrimp cocktails, Friendly told his companion about the way his lecture had been interrupted.

Lippmann listened with interest and some evidence of bewilderment. Then he put down that little fork people use for eating shrimp cocktails and asked, "What's a lay?"

At this point in his story Johnson paused to allow his listeners to appreciate the naivete of a columnist who every day was telling the President how to run the country. Then he continued.

When Friendly reached home that evening, he repeated the account of his morning to his sixteen-year-old daughter and told her about Lippmann's question. And she looked at her father with big curious eyes and asked, "Who's Walter Lippmann?"

By the time he finished, LBJ was always choking with laughter. "Who's Walter Lippmann?" he would say through hawhaws. "Who's Walter Lippmann?"

This was the kind of private joke with which LBJ habitually entertained small groups—and, above all, entertained himself. His best apocryphal stories in this vein, usually sharp and often cruel, had to do with real persons.

Johnson was possessed not so much of a *sense* of humor as of humor itself. This quality of his, unrecognized by those persons who saw only the self-serving politician with the monumental ego, manifested itself both consciously and unconsciously. He could be funniest when he was not trying to be funny at all and did not even know he was being. At such times it was just as well not to laugh.

His conscious humor leaned heavily toward the genital and scatalogical. So does that of many other men, but they perform in country club locker rooms, so nobody minds. LBJ's specialty was off-color stories with a political flavor and he would tell them almost anywhere if that was the way he felt at the time.

The public jokes painfully assembled in the White House speech factory often fell flat when they were received by live audiences. As Liz Carpenter would have said, too many of them weren't Lyndon Johnson. But if he was in a relaxed frame of mind, talking to his down-to-earth kind of crowd, he might depart from his prepared text to come up with amusing and apropos

country-type stories. Through the years he built up a large store
of them, which he told over and over. Usually there would not be
more than one or two to a speech. He never came before an audience to reel off a string of japeries like a stand-up comedian.

A great deal of his success with such stories depended upon
his delivery. His Texas drawl would grow thicker, his manner
would become more elaborately offhand, as he swaggered and
slouched behind the podium. His big, ungainly frame was ideal
for imparting body English to the telling of his kind of story. His
gift for mimickry brought his characters—bucolic preachers, country politicians, small boys, grown men bewildered by the events
that had overtaken them—to life for his listeners and made them
laugh.

At a campaign rally for Representative Harley Staggers of
West Virginia, where Johnson rambled on far beyond his allotted
time without losing his audience, he told of a man who stayed out
late one night and came home more than a little drunk. He fell
into bed only to wake up two or three hours later with a raging
thirst. ("Some of you may not understand this story," Johnson
said in an aside, and the West Virginians tittered.) The poor suffering fellow moaned for his wife to bring him a pitcher of ice
water. She did and he drained half of its contents in a few gulps.
Raising his head, he stared blearily at his wife. "Martha, that's
great, really great," he said. "It's so good I want you to go wake
up the kids so they can have some."

Sometimes he would tell of a Texan—from the hill country,
naturally—who left home in 1861 to join the Confederate army,
assuring his neighbors he would be back home soon. The war
would be easy and quickly over, he said with great confidence,
"because we can lick those damyankees with broomsticks." More
than three years later the rebel came back home, looking thin and
bedraggled. The neighbors asked him what had happened. "The
trouble was," he explained, "the damyankees wouldn't fight with
broomsticks."

A story I heard Johnson tell many times concerned an

adolescent boy who had been converted from his evil ways at a revival meeting and was being baptized into the faith in a rural stream. After he had been immersed and his head lifted out of the water, a church deacon called from the bank of the creek, "Do you believe?" "I believe," the boy responded, and was promptly put under a second time. Again, as he emerged, the deacon called, "Do you believe?" "I believe!" the victim gasped. Down he went once more. When he was hauled up this time, the deacon cried, "What do you believe?" "I believe," the boy whimpered, "that this S.O.B. is trying to drown me."

LBJ had a number of other preacher stories he liked, most of them straight out of his country background. In one he told about a man in Johnson City who always slept through the preacher's sermon. Every Sunday this man would come to church and plant himself on the first row, after which he would promptly go to sleep and snore audibly during the entire sermon.

Finally the preacher got a little irritated, Johnson related, and one Sunday when the fellow was snoring away in the front row he looked out over the congregation and said in a low voice, "Will all you people who want to go to heaven please stand up?" Everybody rose except the sleeping man. After they sat down the preacher bellowed, "All you men who want to go to hell please stand up." The man started awake and jumped to his feet. He looked around the room in back of him and then stared at the preacher, somewhat frustrated, and said, "Preacher, I don't know what it is we're voting on, but looks like you and me are the only people for it."

The stories LBJ told in public rarely had the sole purpose of causing his listeners to laugh—although he welcomed and thrived on their laughter and laughed with them. As he once explained, he liked for his stories to make a point "because that way I don't bore even myself."

A little boy came into the house and told his mother there was a great, big old mean lion in the back yard. She reprimanded him, "That's just our dog and you know it. Now I want you to get down on your knees and pray to the Lord to forgive you for telling such a fib." After spending a little time on his knees, the boy came back to his mother and said, "The Lord said it looked like a lion to him too."

Johnson paused until the laughter subsided and then added forcefully, "Our country suffers today from poverty, from inadequate education facilities, from too much narrow nationalism. I hope you can see these lions and I hope the Lord thinks they are lions too."

In an appearance before the Pennsylvania delegation to the 1960 Democratic convention, Johnson remembered a congressman who in Washington had gained a fully earned reputation as a ladies' man. Back home for a visit, the congressman was instructed by local political bosses that things were not going well and he would have to get married to stop the gossip about his carryings-on. "Okay, boys," the pliant public servant agreed. "You know me—I'm an organization man all the way. Have you got the girl picked out?" (I saw David Lawrence, the Democratic boss of Pennsylvania, almost fall out of his chair laughing when Johnson told this story. But Kennedy got the delegation's votes.)

LBJ had political jokes for all occasions.

Back in the 1930s, when Franklin D. Roosevelt was uncordially known in the business community as "That Man" and *The New York Times* sold for five cents on weekdays, a Wall Street banker stopped at a newsstand every morning, picked up a copy of the *Times,* placed a nickel on the counter, glanced at the front page, put the paper back on the rack, and walked away. One morning the newsstand proprietor, unable to contain his curiosity any longer, asked the banker why he did this. "I'm looking for an obituary," he replied. "Why, mister," said the newsstand operator, "the obits are carried back in the second section, maybe on page thirty-eight or around there." "The one I'm looking for," the financier said coldly, "will be on the front page."

Then there was the Texan who needed a heart transplant and went to Houston to consult a surgeon who had successfully performed such operations. "You're in luck," the doctor said. "I can give you a good choice. This healthy twenty-three-year-old ski champion was killed in an avalanche and his heart is as good as ever if we hurry. Or we've got a twenty-year-old ballet dancer who died in an automobile accident and her heart's available. And then there's this seventy-eight-year-old Republican banker who just passed away here. You can have the heart you want." The man thought a moment and said, "I'll take the banker." The operation was successful. When the patient was ready to leave the hospital, the surgeon said, "I'm greatly interested to know why you chose the heart of the old Republican banker instead of taking one of those young hearts." And the man replied, "I just wanted to make sure I was getting a heart that had never been used."

To show that politicians did not always necessarily mean the partisan blows they exchanged, Johnson told about a Texas judge who received a telephone call late one night during the Great Depression from the member of the state legislature from his district.

"Judge," said the caller, "we've just abolished your court. We had to consolidate some courts for economy reasons and yours came up because it was the last one created."

"The legislature did that to me?" said the judge. "You surely didn't abolish it without a committee hearing."

"Oh, we had a hearing all right and heard witnesses."

"Who the devil would appear before a committee and testify that my court ought to be abolished."

"Well, the head of the bar association was there."

"Just let me tell you about him!" the judge exclaimed. "He's a shyster lawyer and so was his daddy ahead of him. Who else?"

"The mayor of your town came down and testified, Judge."

"I can tell you about him too. He stole his way into office.

He padded the ballot boxes. He counted the votes for him twice. Did anybody else testify?"

"The banker."

"Him! He charges usury rates every day just like his daddy and granddaddy did before him."

The friend laughed. "Judge, I don't think we'd better talk any more. Your blood pressure's getting up. Somebody did offer an amendment to abolish your court, but nobody testified against you at all. We fought the amendment and killed it and the bill has gone to the governor and he's already signed it. I was just kidding you."

"I understand. But why," and as LBJ quoted the judge his voice broke with grief, "why did you make me say those ugly things about three of the dearest friends I ever had?"

Johnson enjoyed taking pokes at the federal bureaucracy. One of his stories pictured a large bulldog so sex-oriented that his activities drew complaints from other dog owners in the small town neighborhood. The owner of the bulldog reluctantly had the necessary operation performed. But soon afterward the neighbors came to him and said the dog was again roaming the neighborhood, constantly followed by a cluster of smaller dogs. "He was just acting in a consulting capacity," Johnson explained, "and he was about as useful as some of the consultants we have drawing down Uncle Sam's money in Washington."

He also appealed to the instinctive anti-Washington feeling of many Americans with a yarn about a young boy in the hill country whose family "was having quite a problem with eating." The youngster sat down one night and wrote a letter addressed to the Almighty saying, "Dear Lord, I wish you would send Mother a hundred dollars to help us get along." The letter wound up on the Postmaster General's desk in Washington. That kindhearted gentleman was so touched by the appeal that he took a twenty-dollar bill from his wallet and mailed the money to the boy. A few days later another letter came to his desk and it said, "Dear Lord,

I want to say much obliged for the twenty bucks you sent us. The next time, though, please don't send it through Washington because they took a deduct of eighty percent."

In another vein was the case of a schoolteacher who was applying for a job in Blanco County. He came before the school board for an interview and a board member said, "There's some difference of opinion in our community about geography. We want to know where you stand. Do you think the world is round or is it flat?" The teacher really needed the job and wished to make no mistake. So he thought for a moment and gave what LBJ called a Dick Nixon reply: "I can teach it either way."

One of those imaginary friends drawn out of his hat by Johnson was losing his hearing and when he sought medical aid the doctor told him he would have to give up drinking. "Come back to see me in ninety days," the doctor ordered. The man showed up in the doctor's office at the appointed time. Tests showed no improvement in his hearing. "Did you stop drinking?" the doctor asked. "No, Doc, I didn't." "Why not?" the doctor demanded angrily. "I can't do anything for you if you won't follow instructions." "I know," the patient said humbly, "but, Doc, I decided I like what I drink a hell of a lot better than what I hear."

Another Johnson story, which he used to point up the importance of meeting new situations with a sense of lively curiosity, had to do with an army inductee who was being given the customary IQ test. The tester put a long question to the new soldier: "If you were standing alongside a railroad track and you saw a train coming from the east going eighty miles per hour and you looked the other way and saw another train coming from the west at sixty miles an hour and they were heading straight for each other with only a mile in between them, what would you do?" The inductee replied at once, "I'd holler for my brother to come quick." The tester asked, "Why in the world would you call your brother?" "Because," said the fellow whose IQ was being tested, "he hasn't ever seen a train wreck."

Newspaper reporters who followed LBJ around the country sometimes talked among themselves with wonder about the vast gulf between such harmless anecdotes and the stories with which the President, in moments of relaxation, entertained the pool of newsmen who rode with him on Air Force One. To this small audience he offered vivid accounts of the sexual habits of scores of prominent politicians. He delighted in giving graphic descriptions of the eccentricities of State Department personnel, reaching back to the time when FDR was President and Sumner Wells was, as Johnson said, "such a pain in the ass to Cordell Hull."

If he departed from personalities it was to reel off one obscene outhouse story after another, replete with the four-letter words that only then were beginning to appear sometimes in the pages of respectable publications. He told, for example, of the long-entrenched county sheriff who in one year had what threatened to be serious opposition. A group of the sheriff's advisers came together to discuss possible strategy. One of them suggested that they spread a rumor about the opponent having sexual intercourse with pigs. "Aw, hell," the sheriff objected, "nobody would believe that." "Maybe not," said the adviser, "but maybe we can make the son of a bitch go around denying it."

This was the same man who told Bill Brammer, after the former employee's novel about an LBJ-type politician was published, "Billy Lee, I tried to read your book but couldn't get very far because you used so many dirty words in it."

Again, the public Johnson and the private Johnson.

The impatient, sarcastic employer came to the fore when hardworking Jack Valenti thought it would be safe for once to take a night off and flew to New York with his wife for an evening at the theater. He had misjudged the situation; it was not safe. The President tried to reach him at home during the course of the evening only to learn of the pleasure outing. Early the next morning Valenti answered his phone to be greeted with, "Well, how's the playboy?"

LBJ's distaste for the elite took over in a comment reported by Califano. Late one night during the mob scenes in Washington that followed the assassination of Martin Luther King, Califano informed the worried President that he had heard a group was being organized in the riot-torn section of the city to march on Georgetown and burn it down. "Georgetown!" said LBJ, a sudden twinkle in his eye. "I've waited thirty years for this day."

His realistic cynicism was in evidence as one of a group of high-ranking business executives with whom he was meeting in the White House began a statement, "Now I'm just a country boy, but—" "Hold it!" Johnson broke in. "Down where I come from, if a man starts off by saying that kind of thing it always makes me put my hand on the pocket where I keep my billfold."

There was no humor, conscious or otherwise, in the account Johnson gave Phil and Katharine Graham of the birth of civil rights in Johnson City. The Washington *Post* Grahams were spending a weekend at the ranch at a time when LBJ was still in the Senate. The senator, who, Mrs. Graham said, "thought I was a little more liberal than my husband," kept twitting her about the inability of northern liberals to understand the practicalities of racial problems in Texas and elsewhere in the South.

Finally Johnson, turning serious, exploded, "You know, you think you fight for civil rights in the North. I want to tell you how civil rights came to Johnson City."

Then, Mrs. Graham went on to say in recalling the occasion in her interview for the LBJ oral history collection, the senator told about a gang of workers who years before had built a road through the town. He explained that there were two or three Negroes in the group. At that time Negroes were not permitted to stay in town after dusk, a restriction imposed in many other Texas towns. At the end of the first day on the job, the road contractor went to the Johnson City barber shop to get a shave. As he sat in the barber's chair the town bully, a hulking mean-mouthed fellow, came in and ordered, "You git them niggers out of town!"

As Johnson told it, the contractor got up out of the chair, removed the barber's towel from around his neck and put it aside, then left the shop with the town bully in front of him. Outside, the two men wrestled up and down Main Street, pummeling each other, until the contractor felled his opponent and clambered on top of him. He started knocking the bully's head against the pavement, LBJ related, and with each knock he bellowed, "Can I keep my niggers? Can I keep my niggers?"

In a Johnson story, the hero had to win and the bully finally gave in.

"And that," LBJ said to Mrs. Graham, "is how civil rights came to Johnson City."

That time he was not funning in the least.

13

LADY BIRD

In the weeks after LBJ became President, newspapers and magazines published column after column of stuff and guff, some of it more than a little gooey, about the new First Lady.

She was described by Marie Smith, a Washington *Post* reporter who had covered Mrs. Johnson as a Senate wife, a political campaigner, and a companion on her husband's foreign travels, as "a dark-haired, brown-eyed Texas beauty with a charm for winning friends, a shrewd brain for business, a persuasiveness in politics, and all the femininity her name implies." On top of all these desirable qualities, Miss Smith went on to say that Mrs. Johnson brought to the White House "the sunny friendliness of the Southwest; a picturesque speech as colorful as a Texas sunset; and a spirit of determination to measure up to the job and share the honors and privileges that are hers with as many people as possible." Somewhat purple prose, but not inaccurate.

A hardbitten friend of mine reacted sourly to this kind of thing, remarking to me, "Of course I don't believe most of what I read about her. She sounds too good to be true."

"I realize that," I replied. "And in fact in many ways she *is* too good to be true. But just the same that's the way she is."

This was something I knew about at firsthand. On the same day that Senator Johnson was stricken with a heart attack in 1955, my wife, several months pregnant, suffered a near-miscarriage. We were scared. All through that long Independence Day weekend I alternated between trying to keep her secluded and quiet and seeking by telephone the latest news about LBJ.

She was improved on the day after the Fourth, so I went to the office on Capitol Hill in the afternoon to help as well as I could to cope with the confused situation there. I mentioned to one of the secretaries that my wife had come close to losing the baby over the weekend. She must have said something about this confidence to Mrs. Johnson or to someone who passed it on to her.

However it happened, early that evening the telephone on the bedside table rang and my wife answered it to hear a woman who had not left her husband's side since he was brought to the hospital say in a soft voice, "Betty, this is Bird Johnson. I was so distressed to hear about your trouble and so relieved to know that you are better. I know how you must feel, having gone through the same ordeal myself."

The call was not merely a kindly gesture toward the wife of her husband's employee. It represented the reaching out of a sensitive, warmhearted woman to another woman, a virtual stranger, in a troublesome time for both of them. The instinct was born and bred in Mrs. Johnson.

Knowing this quality of hers, I was not in the least surprised when Lady Bird Johnson, before her husband had been in the White House a month, showed up one day at the D.C. General Hospital to go through the children's ward with Christmas presents and more than perfunctory cheerful words for each child. People who knew her well understood that there was nothing phony or make-believe in her performance. It was wholly in character.

235

On another level, so was a one-day inspection trip she made in the following month to the chronically depressed Appalachian Mountains country of Pennsylvania. Speaking like the politician she had trained herself to be, she told the press she considered herself a soldier in the war on poverty declared by her husband in his first State of the Union message to Congress. She made one formal and several informal speeches, visited factories and job retraining centers, and was received with warmth and enthusiasm by the crowds that met her everywhere she went during the day. Her talks were interlarded liberally with references to "Lyndon."

"This trip has been a real eye-opener to me," she said before one audience, "and I'll have a lot to tell the President when I get home tonight."

For years she had been having a lot to tell Lyndon Johnson. And he listened.

Nothing in her background or upbringing could have prepared Claudia Alta Taylor for the kind of life she would lead after marrying an importunate young LBJ on November 17, 1934, when she was a month short of her twenty-second birthday. If ever a woman transformed herself—deliberately, knowingly, painstakingly—it was she. A modest, introspective girl gradually became a figure of steel cloaked in velvet. Both metal and fabric were genuine.

Mrs. Johnson explained to me one evening in her Washington home, after LBJ was elected Vice-President but before he took office, how some of the changes had come about. Over a period of two or three hours, during an interview for a magazine article I planned, I learned much more about Lady Bird Johnson that I had known during the years I was on her husband's Senate staff.

The atmosphere was informal. Only the two of us were in the living room. We sipped scotch highballs—weak—as we talked. She was in a remembering mood. She spoke freely and without self-consciousness about the little East Texas town of

Karnack where she was born and brought up. Her father was the community's leading citizen, a landholder, planter, and merchant. The sign outside his general merchandise store read "T. J. Taylor, Dealer in Everything."

"We lived in the only brick house in town," Lady Bird Johnson remembered.

Her mother died when she was six. Aunt Effie, a gentle, sheltered lady, her mother's sister, moved down from the family home in Alabama to take care of the child. Two older brothers were away at boarding schools. The father was absorbed in his business. The girl in the brick house, her principal companions an aging genteel southern lady and one or two black household servants, grew up shy and bookish, a dreamer who pretended her dolls were kings and queens and made up stories about them.

"I had two heavy crosses to bear in my early teens," she told me. "One was the nickname Lady Bird. I hated it. The other was my hooked nose, which at one time I seriously considered having bobbed. But I never did, of course, and gradually I was able to come to terms with both my nose and my nickname."

She said she went through high school without having much contact with the outside world except on occasional trips to Alabama to visit kinfolks. "Aunt Effie did a great deal to develop my mind and spirit," she explained, "but she didn't really prepare me for anything else." The girl's school grades were excellent. Her appearance, she confided with a trace of wistfulness, left much to be desired.

"I knew nothing and cared nothing about clothes," she told me that evening in her home. "I thought it was frivolous to be concerned about such material things. I suspect I looked pretty dowdy."

Life began to change for her during her four years at the University of Texas, where she majored in journalism. She was still reserved, but she made friends, was elected secretary of the student chapter of Theta Sigma Chi, served on the executive council of the university's association for intramural sports. Her scholastic rating continued high. She planned a career in journalism or in business.

Those plans were sidetracked after LBJ's brief tempestuous courtship and their marriage. She went to Washington as the bride of a congressional secretary and returned with him to Texas when he was named state director of the National Youth Administration. She borrowed ten thousand dollars from her father to finance LBJ's first campaign for the House of Representatives in 1937. Back in Washington, she entered into the activities of a club for congressional wives. During the brief period of her husband's military service she ran his office. "This experience gave me confidence," she said afterward, "that I could make my own living if I had to."

She had become a politician's wife and a good one, but she was not herself a politician. Not yet.

"For years I simply went along and smiled and said howdy to people at barbecues and rallies when Lyndon came up for reelection," she said. "I didn't really get into things until that 1948 campaign."

She got into things in a big way then, as I well remembered. She flew all over Texas to plead her husband's cause before women's groups. At campaign headquarters in Austin, she greeted droppers-in and addressed envelopes. She telephoned students she had known at the University of Texas and those her husband had known at Southwest Texas State Teachers College, not only urging them to vote for LBJ but also cajoling as many of them as she could into doing volunteer work in the campaign. She went on the radio to explain why her husband should be sent to the United States Senate.

Mrs. Johnson admitted that none of this activity came easily at first. It went against her nature to talk to strangers and hand out campaign buttons on street corners. Making speeches was hardest of all.

"I had to brace myself to speak well in public about my husband and ask people to vote for him," she said. "What if they refused to listen? Or even laughed at me? In the beginning I always had such fears when I was going to make a speech. As time went on I came to realize that the people I talked to were like me and I didn't need to be scared of them."

She was deeply involved in the national campaign of 1960. She traveled 35,000 miles in seventy-nine days, including a tour through the South on a "Lady Bird Special" train, to speak well in public about her husband's candidacy for Vice-President. Near the end of the campaign she was at LBJ's side, a tight smile fixed on her face, as they forced their way through a crowd of near-violent hecklers bearing insulting placards in front of the Adolphus Hotel in Dallas where the candidate was scheduled to speak.

The shy girl from Karnack, Texas, had come a long way, baby. She was a full-fledged political partner of a man who lived politics every hour of every day.

She changed outwardly as well as inwardly. Gone were the drab dresses and flat shoes of her youth. She was married to a man who liked to see a woman arrayed in bright colors and who was known at times simply to buy a dress that struck his fancy and bring it home to her. So she transformed herself into a bird of colorful plumage. LBJ respected her bookishness because he considered it a proper feminine quality, but he also wished her to go with him to parties and political dinners. She became more of a social being than was her natural inclination and proved good at it. LBJ demanded that he be spared all details of managing a household, so the entire burden of doing that fell on her.

"Lyndon wants me to handle everything he thinks I am capable of handling," she explained. "He demands so much of me that I find I can do more than I would ever have believed I could. He's a great one for saying exactly what he wants done. Then he wants me to do it."

Mrs. Johnson had the utmost faith that what Lyndon wanted Lyndon got. One thing he wanted very strongly was a son and, as she once told me, she never doubted for a moment that their first-born would be a boy. And of course he would be named for his father. The Johnsons had no other name remotely in mind, so when the infant turned out to be a girl—born in the tenth year of their marriage after Mrs. Johnson had experienced four miscar-riages—she naturally was christened Lynda Bird. Their second daughter and final child was born three years later. She was named Lucy Baines. Later by her own choice she substituted an "i" for the "y."

Through the years of acting as her husband's political part-ner, running the various Johnson households in Washington and Texas, bringing up two daughters, using an inheritance from her mother to buy radio and television stations and overseeing their growth, Mrs. Johnson developed a sharply methodical mind. Some male chauvinist pigs, if the term had been invented then, might have thought it did not go well with her innate femininity. They would have been wrong. No conflict existed between the mind and the manner. The personality was not split.

The wife may have lived in the shadow of her husband, but Lady Bird Johnson was a "person in her own right" long before latter-day feminists induced housewives all over the country to start belligerently mouthing the words as a self-description. Al-though she never felt it necessary to take a consciousness-raising course in how to be disagreeable, Mrs. Johnson at no time under-went an identity crisis. She always knew who she was. The knowl-edge kept her strong and calm in moments of stress.

"There are two Mrs. Johnsons," said Jesse Kellam, who as general manager of the radio and television stations in Austin worked closely with her for many years, "so different you'd never believe they were the same person."

Kellam was talking about the businesswoman as contrasted to the politician's wife and the social hostess. He was qualified from long observation to speak of the difference. Actually, though, it was more seeming than real. That methodical mind of hers was strongly compartmentalized, enabling her to shift from one role to another without any clashing of gears and to allocate her hours with maximum efficiency. And it was a notable characteristic of Mrs. Johnson's that both her time and her money were used in a thrifty fashion.

She brought tremendous powers of concentration to whatever she undertook. Since she never allowed herself to become flustered, she was a quick learner. She learned and did whatever she considered necessary or desirable. After deciding that her speeches were not coming out in a manner satisfactory to her, she enrolled in a course in public speaking. When LBJ became Vice-President she attended Spanish classes three mornings a week so she could learn to communicate with visitors from Spanish-language nations. One evening at a party given at the Jenkins home in Washington for Vice-President and Mrs. Johnson, I observed with fascination that she spent an hour in learning from a talented young male guest how to dance the newfangled Twist.

Like everybody else around LBJ, and this would be particularly true of a wife, she was often caught up in the aura of perpetual excitement that surrounded him. But she was not swept away. Deeply devoted as she was to her husband, she never lost her sense of self. Or her sense of the fitness of things.

When Mrs. Johnson was sitting on a public platform, next to her husband while he stood up and made a speech, she invariably kept her face tilted upward and toward him with every appearance of listening as intently as if every thought he expressed was new and intensely precious to her. This posture made a great impression on the audience down below, which it undoubtedly was intended to do. But she did not hesitate if he went on too long to slip him a note with two words on it, "That's enough." On one occasion I saw her tug gently at his coattail. Soon afterward he stopped talking and sat down.

At times she spoke to the press with spontaneous candor. Asked by a reporter her opinion of LBJ's formal announcement in 1960 that he would go after the presidential nomination, she answered that she thought what he had said was "fine, strong, and thrilling," and immediately added, "There are a few things I'd like to discuss with him though." At the Los Angeles convention, with Johnson staging his hard belated drive for delegates, she told a press representative that she felt "no roaring confidence" he would win.

Mrs. Johnson could use her pretty southern ways offensively if the need arose. At a birthday party for Rayburn, when LBJ was in the Senate, I was chatting with her when we were joined by a newspaper friend of mine. He clearly had taken a drink or two above his quota and soon was addressing the senator's wife as "Lady Bird" and clapping her on the shoulder as her face froze into immobility. Finally lured away by uneasy me, the reporter called back over his shoulder, "See you again, Lady Bird." Her smile returned. "I hope not," she said.

When this woman went into the White House as First Lady of the land it was inevitable that she would bring different dimensions to the demanding unpaid job. Her immediate predecessor, Jacqueline Kennedy, for all her charm and beauty, was always and consciously removed from the commonalities of politics. Mamie Eisenhower continued as the President's wife to be the perfect spouse for an army officer. Bess Truman conscientiously stayed out of the limelight. The closest parallel to Lady Bird Johnson was Eleanor Roosevelt. Mrs. Roosevelt, however, developed her own constituency, which was not always the same as her husband's. Mrs. Johnson, although a highly individualistic person, was dedicated in whatever she did to the interests of the congressional secretary she had married some thirty years earlier and who now was President of the United States.

Ample evidence of this dedication is found in the journal she started keeping two or three days after LBJ became President which was subsequently published in book form.* Speaking of the nation's mourning for Kennedy, she thought first of "Lyndon, for whom it is the hardest of all to carry on." The published book was dedicated "To Lyndon, with love."

A close friend of the family remarked to me that the diary read like a long love letter to her husband. To some extent this was true and he may have been partly responsible. I learned from "sources," as the investigative journalists have it, that LBJ read the typescript and decreed a number of elisions. Still, there can be no question that Mrs. Johnson meant what she said about the man to whom she was married. Sophisticates had snickered unkindly when Jacqueline Kennedy meowed, "Lady Bird would crawl up Pennsylvania on her hands and knees over broken glass for Lyndon," but any exaggeration in the statement was slight.

When LBJ was talking in the summer of 1964 about not running for a term of his own, his wife wrote him a letter marked "Personal" which read in part: "You are as brave a man as Harry Truman—or FDR—or Lincoln. You can go on to find some peace, some achievement amidst all the pain. You have been strong, patient, determined beyond any words of mine to express. I honor you for it. So does the country. To step out now would be wrong for our country, and I can see nothing but a lonely wasteland in your future."

During an evening of relaxation and recreation with friends in Texas, Mrs. Johnson listened admiringly to her husband's stories about politics and ranching and pronounced them "earthy and colorful and true and fresh, though often rough." Her admiration did not keep her from noting with another part of her mind that he again was getting too fat. She wondered whether she should lash out at him angrily and sarcastically or simply "remind him for the nine hundred and ninety-ninth time" that he should exercise sufficient self-restraint to keep his weight down to the figure ordered by the doctor.

* *A White House Diary,* Holt, Rinehart and Winston, 1970.

243

LBJ's excess weight was a constant concern to her. She did not tell, but Sam Houston wrote in his book, about the President's complaint one Christmas that he had not received the customary box of homemade candy from a friend. "Maybe she's been too busy this year," his wife said evasively, "or perhaps she's ill." Teen-age Luci spilled the beans by exclaiming, "She didn't forget, Daddy. She sent you a box, but I think Mama hid it to keep you from putting on weight." According to Sam Houston, his brother irritably accused Mrs. Johnson of deceit and demanded that she produce the candy at once. Which, of course, she did.

She kept a wifely eye on his drinking, which was rarely excessive, as well as his eating. During one cocktail hour she thought LBJ was going after his scotch and seltzer with a bit too much enthusiasm and gently said so. "My doctor says scotch keeps my arteries open," he defended himself. "They don't have to be that wide open," she said with a smile.

This was unusual. The matrimonial chiding was much more likely to come from husband to wife. One day Mrs. Johnson was a few minutes late in appearing in the Rose Garden for an announcement the President was to make to the press and for which he had ordered his wife's appearance. LBJ publicly reprimanded her for not being on time and said it shouldn't happen again. She recorded in her diary that it was "a measured admonishment, dear man, from someone who had been up until five o'clock wrestling with problems of the magnitude he has."

At a more formal news conference, where the President had instructed her to sit on the platform at the front of the room, she felt pride in "his command of facts, his orderliness of presentation, the strength of what he said." At the same time, she expressed the wish that "there could have been a little more change of pace or humor."

In the published portions of her diary she never ventured beyond such mild criticism.

The journal itself and the manner of its creation reflected

Mrs. Johnson's methodical mind. She talked it into a tape recorder, trying to set aside time every evening to tell of the day's events and her reaction to them. If it became necessary on occasion to skip a day, she picked up the narrative later with information from her appointments list and her own shorthand notes set down in a pocket notebook. By the time she moved out of the White House she had recorded approximately one and three-quarter million words. It had all been thriftily done with an eye to future publication. With the assistance of Liz Carpenter, not to mention that of her husband, she edited this mass of material down to a volume of some eight hundred pages. The book was well received in the marketplace—much more so than LBJ's own story of his years as President. To his considerable and not surprising annoyance. Second best is no good, Booth.

Mrs. Johnson is clearly revealed in her diary as one of the world's champion self-improvers. She was rarely satisfied with herself. Instead of whining about what she regarded as her shortcomings, however, she was constantly resolving to do better next time.

When she saw herself on television in a brief taped interview, she was not pleased. Rather, she noted dispassionately that she looked as old and tired and frenetic as she felt. "If I'm not smart enough to get a moral out of this," she admonished herself, "I am not smart at all. No more unprepared things, no more things where I am not well briefed in what I am going to do."

Again, following a state visit from the president of Italy, she recorded her determination to have an aide stand beside her in future receiving lines. As it was, she said that by the time a guest's name was filtered down to her as she stood in third place in the line it was no longer distinguishable. She declared she would not be denied the moment of personal contact with each guest that she really wanted.

Joseph Hirshhorn came down from New York to discuss the terms on which he would donate a lifetime's accumulation of art treasures to the nation. Mrs. Johnson was eager to do everything possible to advance this project but feared she had made little headway. She mourned that she was the world's worst salesman. A First Lady, she said with a note of despair, should be "a show-man and a salesman, a clothes horse and a publicity sounding board" and have a genuine interest in people. She comforted herself with the thought that she did possess this last quality and valued it. (She need not have worried. The Hirshhorn Gallery in all its splendor exists in Washington today.)

Toward the end of her stay in Washington, after a final meeting of the Committee for the Preservation of the White House, Mrs. Johnson questioned whether the group had been sufficiently aggressive in its promotion efforts. She thought it would have been possible, if she had only managed better, to create a feeling among owners of paintings she wanted for the White House that it would be the smart thing and the patriotic thing to donate them. She concluded she had made too little use of the leverage of her position. "I came very late and timorously to the uses of power," she noted regretfully.

When public opinion polls showed LBJ at the low point of his popularity, his wife felt instinctively that her only reaction should be "to work harder, be staunch, and keep smiling." She admitted, however, that this was a difficult course to follow.

In the fall of 1967 she spent two days at Williams and Yale, where her appearance as a speaker was picketed by anti-war demonstrators. At Yale, where she spoke on the necessity of protecting the environment, she had the feeling that Kingman Brewster, president of the college, wished she were not there. Although she said his manner was eminently correct, she nevertheless sensed that "my presence here was really an imposition on him." She thought the campuses were artificially set apart from the world, isolated places where everybody had a tendency to think alike and act alike. But, being Lady Bird Johnson, she found in the experience a useful lesson: "I must not live only in the White

House, insulated against life. I want to know what's going on— even if to know is to suffer."

Self-improvement, every day in every way to get better and better.

She gave LBJ a birthday present of a wooden chest certified as a genuine antique brought to Texas by a German family in the 1840s. The gift, she reported, was not a resounding success. The recipient said to guests at his birthday party, "If I live long enough I guess Lady Bird will get enough of these chests." She felt chagrined and unworthy, saying in her journal, "There must be something I could give him that would surprise, excite, elate him." But she added that she could not think of any way to proceed except "to learn how to do my hair, keep my lipstick perfect, and be devoid of problems."

This was one of the few nonsensical statements in Mrs. Johnson's diary, for of course she could and did think of many things to do. She was as much of an activist in her field as her husband was in his.

One part of her area of responsibility was entertainment with a purpose. In the first month of 1964, she and the President gave a dinner for the chairman and ranking members of all the Senate committees, the leadership on both sides, and their wives. After dinner she took the ladies upstairs for a tour of the White House family quarters, which most of them had never seen. She showed them the plaque in her bedroom designating it as the room where Lincoln slept. The guests also saw a smaller plaque added by Mrs. Kennedy before she moved out, which read, "In this room lived John Fitzgerald Kennedy with his wife Jacqueline during the two years, ten months and two days he was President of the United States." Mrs. Johnson recorded no comments by her or her guests about this addition.

The Johnsons invited Attorney General and Mrs. Robert Kennedy and Senator Ted Kennedy and his wife to a state dinner for Ireland's President De Valera. They did not show up. "They are off, I think," Mrs. Johnson excused their absence, "on a money-raising campaign for the Kennedy Library." Perhaps. There was not much socializing between the Johnson family and the kinfolk of the late President.

Regularly scheduled luncheons were held at the White House for what Mrs. Johnson called, somewhat regrettably, "Women Do-ers." The attendants devoted their attention to such subjects as the problems of urbanization, safeguarding the environment, getting rid of unsightly junkyards, and beautifying the parks of Washington by extensive flower plantings. Considerable action came out of these luncheons. It was not in Mrs. Johnson's nature to be simply a glorified women's garden club president. For one thing, she and her Women Do-ers prodded the President into hammering ambitious highway beautification legislation through Congress. LBJ referred to it as "Lady Bird's bill" and did some of his famed arm-twisting to secure its approval.

Mrs. Johnson's self-assigned task of leading the way toward a more beautiful America occupied much of her attention. When the executive committee of the United States Conference of Mayors met in Washington, she invited its members to the White House. She had planned the occasion as a "tea and thank you" session and was gratified when it turned into a substantive meeting with the mayors giving enthusiastic reports of what was being done to make their cities look better. The Governors' Conference met in the Capital City and she arranged a tree planting by the state executives' wives on a stretch of land along the Potomac in Virginia. The temperature was twenty-nine degrees and the earth was muddy, but the trees were planted.

Beautification efforts were not the sole concern of the Women Do-ers. Their first luncheon of the year in 1968, when the national atmosphere had turned nasty on all sides, dealt with the problem of crime in the streets. After short speeches offering pertinent suggestions by several women and a few words from the President himself, Mrs. Johnson opened the meeting to ob-

servations from those who had been listening. One of the hands
that went up belonged to Eartha Kitt, the singer and performer.
Miss Kitt had been smoking ferociously and tossing her long hair
contemptuously all through the speeches.

Now she rose, her voice throbbing with passion, to denounce
the Vietnam war as the principal cause for crime. She pointed her
finger at her hostess as she unloosed her diatribe: "You are a
mother too, although you have had daughters and not sons. I am
a mother and I know the feeling of having a baby come out of my
guts. I have a baby and then you send him off to war. No wonder
the kids rebel and take pot. And, Mrs. Johnson, in case you
don't understand the lingo that's marijuana!"

Mrs. Johnson saw that the press representatives present were
racing their pencils over their notebooks. She knew she would
have to reply. But she remained silent while two other women
made rejoinders to Miss Kitt and were applauded. Then she
turned to look directly at her difficult guest and, her voice trem-
bling ever so little, spoke her own piece.

"Because there is a war on," she said, "and I pray that there
will be a just and honest peace, that still doesn't give us a free
ticket not to try to work for better things—against crime in the
streets, and for better education and better health for our people.
I cannot identify as much as I should. I have not lived the background that you have, nor can I speak as passionately or as well,
but we must keep our eyes and our hearts and our energies fixed
on constructive areas and try to do something that will make this
a happier, better educated land."

It was hardly a polished oration, but the applause from the
luncheon attendants indicated that the round had gone to her. So
did the ensuing press reports.

Mrs. Johnson's journal included snapshots of the woman as
well as portraits of the First Lady. On December 23, 1963, as
the month of mourning ended, she noted with pleasure that "I
have put my small wardrobe of black dresses, worn every day

since that day in November, in the back of the chest and put on my Christmas red." Sprinkled throughout after that entry are descriptions of dresses she wore on various occasions. They were in bright colors. After going through fittings for a spring wardrobe, she confessed to feeling "slightly ridiculous" that clothes should take up so much of her time. The modest, thrifty girl from Karnack believed it was probably wrong to spend so much time and money on clothes. And yet, she admitted, this thought was accompanied by "a sort of vain, feminine, increasingly delighted feeling that I do look rather well in them, a bit younger and slimmer than I used to."

She gave details about intimate talks she enjoyed with her daughters. They were grown up now, but their mother still remembered with a pang how when they were little girls they often protested, "Why are you always going out, Mama?" Once, she recalled, Lynda had said forlornly, "Mama, Washington is sure meant for the congressmen and their wives, but it is not meant for their children." Now, in the White House, they were busy with beaus and their own social doings. The mother welcomed their confidences and talked with them as equals.

At times Mrs. Johnson expressed a continuing sense of wonder at finding herself where she was. After being in the receiving line at an Eleanor Roosevelt Memorial Foundation luncheon: "In walked a guest list that comprised a large part of the power structure of New York—from the financial side, the philanthropic, those interested in human welfare, and, I imagine, those just interested in society." After a day of ceremonies in connection with the National Gallery of Art Awards: "All in all, it was a precious day to me, afforded entirely by my role here in the White House, and not earned by my knowledge or myself." After a visit with the Laurance Rockefellers in Tarrytown, New York: "This will be a day to remember in the life of Lady Bird Taylor of Karnack and Mrs. Lyndon Johnson of Johnson City— a day with the Rockefellers and the Astors and the Goulds."

Her time was not spent exclusively with big names and VIP's. She and her husband were living temporarily in the White House, but Texas was home and they often entertained old Texas friends—visitors to and residents of Washington. The Bill Whites were frequent guests both at the White House and at the presidential retreat, Camp David. Dale Miller, a low-key and highly successful lobbyist for various Texas enterprises, and his wife Scooter were longtime friends. Among the Johnsons' favorite guests were the Homer Thornberrys. Thornberry, a Federal judge, had succeeded Johnson in his seat in the House of Representatives. Jack Pickle, who in turn succeeded Thornberry, had worked hand in hand with LBJ for years before he came to Washington. The Johnsons saw as much as they could of several other Texas congressmen and their wives. Liz Carpenter was a White House employee, but long before becoming one she and her husband had been close to Representative and Mrs. Lyndon Johnson and they remained close. There were many others, persons with whom the presidential couple could let down their official faces and feel at home.

All during her time in the White House, Mrs. Johnson was making plans for the LBJ Library. This project had its inception as far back as 1957 when Johnson's mother suggested the establishment of a community center in Johnson City to house memorabilia of both the Johnson and Baines families. LBJ liked the idea. Juanita Roberts was placed in charge of collating and classifying papers that should go into it. Dorothy Territo, a professional librarian, was borrowed from the Library of Congress and subsequently was added to the staff.

After Johnson became President, the dream expanded. An agreement was reached with the University of Texas that it would build the library and an LBJ School of Public Affairs on its Austin campus. Mrs. Johnson journeyed with members of the university's board of regents and architects to the existing presidential libraries to garner ideas for their project.

A visit to the Truman Library in Independence, Missouri, caused her, as she said, to see presidential papers from a new perspective. She deplored the idea of LBJ's library containing only thousands of gray anonymous boxes of documents, "hidden from the world on shelves behind locked doors, awaiting the very few scholars who came." She thought a more dramatic display could be made of the documents through the use of brightly colored boxes, secure behind glass but visible to the visting public. Also, she said the library-museum should contain dramatic presentations highlighting her husband's outstanding achievements. Although the scholars who came might be few, she foresaw that other people would come in considerable numbers.

The strong-willed southern lady had her way. The Lyndon Baines Johnson Library, opened in May 1971, unquestionably possesses color. Located on fourteen acres of the university campus, just across the way from a stadium which can seat eighty thousand football-crazed southwesterners, the library accurately reflects the LBJ personality. It speaks to the visitor with more than a hint of the hyperbole with which he frequently expressed himself.

Some unkind observers have said the massive eight-story concrete structure resembles an Egyptian pharaoh's tomb.

Inside, show-and-tell museum exhibits are featured on the first two floors. Bemused visitors can view a stunningly variegated collection of photographs, art objects, and mementoes surrounding the LBJ presidency. There is a wall mural of Johnson etched in metal, larger than life (what else?), and in five different poses. Short motion pictures present summaries of his Great Society programs. There is an auditorium with a seating capacity of one thousand. Mrs. Johnson herself appears in a movie about the ranch and the family life there.

On the second floor, a fittingly named Great Hall has a ceiling four stories high. The archives housing the claimed thirty-one million documents reposing in the library are visible behind glass on the four floors. The papers are stored in thirty-six thousand boxes, forty-two hundred of which are visible to persons gaping up from the floor of the Great Hall. Each of the bright red buckram-colored boxes on the front row is embossed with a gold presidential seal, which LBJ was fond of having placed on everything from cigarette lighters to cowboy boots. The gray boxes Mrs. Johnson disliked are there but cannot be seen.

In addition to Johnsonian papers, the library offers reminders in abundance that LBJ was a highly visible and constantly voluble man. When he was in the White House, a cameraman was always on hand to record him conducting a cabinet meeting, addressing Congress, talking to a foreign head of state, kissing the Heart Baby of the Year, pulling his dog by the ears, anything and everything he did. Most of the celebrated photographs are in the library, along with more than half a million unpublished photographic negatives of Johnson in action.

Unlike his successor, Johnson never bugged the entire White House. But he was concerned about having his own statements and speeches preserved for posterity. The library contains more than four thousand hours of video tape by and about him. They include virtually every public utterance he made while he was President. The oral history collection holds recordings of interviews with hundreds of persons who at one time or another had undergone the experience of contact with LBJ.

Mrs. Johnson welcomed the inflow of tourists pouring into the building at the rate of two thousand per day. But she also took particular pride in researchers who came to study. On one of my visits to the library, she came into the room where I was engrossed in papers and exclaimed, "I'm so glad to see somebody *using* this place."

Johnson lived to see the library completed and in operation. He was a frequent visitor to it and on occasion addressed seminars held there. His widow continued to maintain an office there after his death, administering the affairs of the LBJ Foundation and an organization called Friends of the LBJ Library.

During the time that this ambitious project was in the planning stage, Mrs. Johnson, as the President's troubles mounted, returned repeatedly to the question of when he should make it clear to the country that he would not go for another term. In 1964, she had said the President wanted her to help him get out, but she thought she could only say, "Stay for now." Not far into his full term, however, she set March 1968 in her mind as the time when he should make a firm statement that he would not be a candidate for reelection. For the first time she had decided that her husband could be happy in retirement, busying himself with matters at the ranch and perhaps doing some teaching at the University of Texas. As for herself, she yearned to go home for good. She expressed doubt that either of them could "endure" another four-year term, adding that she would face the prospect of another campaign "like an open-ended stay in a concentration camp."

After the President made the announcement she had longed for, she issued her own brief statement to the press. "We have done a lot," she said. "There's a lot left to do in the remaining months. Maybe this is the only way to get it done."

Mrs. Johnson was and is one of the most remarkable and admirable women I have known in my life. Some people, I realize, were never enchanted by her. They made fun of her accent and her southern colloquialisms ("y'all come, hear?") and what they regarded as her studiously Pollyannaish approach to life. She was accused by a few of being a coldly ambitious person, a wife more interested in her husband's career than in her husband. She did not appear to good advantage on television or newspaper photos. Somehow, the camera lens turned the warmth of her brown eyes into an opaque hardness and accentuated what the girl in Karnack had disliked about her nose. Her speeches showed the effects of lessons in the "elocution and action" school of public speaking. The wide, toothy smile at times seemed forced and artificial, the animated gestures exaggerated.

Most of these criticisms were unjustified, in my admittedly prejudiced opinion, and some were of no real importance. I saw Mrs. Johnson as a woman who genuinely cared about people, a woman of independent spirit and keen intelligence with an unusually wide range of interests.

The wife of the President wrote in her journal about the joys of a family Christmas. She noted with amusement that there was quite a flap in the newspapers when her daughter Lucy changed the spelling of her name to Luci. She recorded that on a visit to New Zealand and Australia, where almost everybody was Lady This or Lady That, she felt like an imposter when she signed the guest books "Lady Bird Johnson." After her first two months in the White House, she said, "If I'm going to win the battle to keep us all close together, I'll need to apply equal time to the girls, along with Lyndon's business, and my public duties, and my own pursuits." She neglected none of them.

She never wavered in her devotion to her husband, although it can scarcely be doubted that, as people used to say of a woman married to a man who could be difficult, she had a lot to put up with. He demanded nothing less from her than perfection according to his standards. He expected complete tolerance of his own lapses from perfection.

From the time I knew Johnson there were always rumors about him and other women, usually secretaries on his staff. After he became President gossips in Washington loved to speculate about his supposed relationship with this or that newswoman, television personality, or dancing partner. I knew nothing about the truth of the rumors and gossip, although any onlooker could see that he enjoyed the company of women.

After his death, Mrs. Johnson was questioned about this side of his personality by Barbara Walters on the "Today" show. She replied forthrightly, "Lyndon was a people lover and that did not exclude half the people in the world—women. Oh, I think perhaps there was a time or two . . ."

She broke off the sentence at that point, but then added, "If all those ladies had some good points that I didn't have, I hope I had the good sense to learn a little bit from it."

The durable relationship between LBJ and his wife was

tested by far greater stresses than most marriages are called on to withstand. Lady Bird Johnson did not falter and Johnson knew, as he once said, that she was "always there."

Her last entry in her published White House journal quoted a line of poetry: "I seek, to celebrate my glad release,/The Tents of Silence and the Camp of Peace."

"And yet," she said, "it's not quite the right exit line for me because I have loved almost every day of these five years."

Honest to the end.

14

LBJ'S LONG RIDE

At a time when Johnson was in the Senate, Bobby Russell, a favored nephew of the senator from Georgia, telephoned me one day in Washington from the ranch. He and Senator Russell were guests of the majority leader.

"What's going on down there, Bobby?" I asked.

The young man, whose outgoing spirit more than matched his uncle's reserve, told me excitedly of deer hunts, venison sausage breakfasts, fast automobile trips over the LBJ acres, people coming in to stay up late talking about ranching and politics.

"I can tell you one thing," Bobby chortled, "It's a great ride if you can keep from falling off."

So it was. Riding with Johnson was never dull. Many fell off along the way, although some of them later clambered back aboard. Many stayed the course. LBJ was never deserted and alone, no matter how often he said he felt that way.

Sagacious political commentators held that finally he himself fell or was pushed from the presidency. Johnson vigorously

257

disagreed with this concept. He maintained that he stepped down of his own free will for the good of the country.

A couple of days after his announcement that he was counting himself out for another term, I encountered Warren Woodward, the former LBJ employee who had become a vice-president of American Airlines. Woodward told me he was one of a small group of intimate friends called in by Johnson the evening before so he could give them, as he said, "a fuller and personal explanation" of his decision.

I listened intently and immediately on reaching my office that morning I wrote down Woodward's report of what the President had said. It is, in my opinion, authentic Johnson in content and tone.

"I'm just fed up to here," LBJ told his friends, dramatically placing one hand on his neck, "with the way things have been going."

He went into detail:

"I think I've done more for the Negro people than any President since Lincoln. And what happens? Martin Luther King goes to Memphis and precipitates a riot and all the so-called liberals say it's my fault.

"No Administration has done more for education. But college students boo the mention of my name and accuse me of killing babies.

"I guess I was born in the wrong place and brought up at the wrong time. I was always taught to believe that patriotism—love of country—was a good thing. But, you know, patriotism isn't the 'in' thing now. I wake up in the morning and read in the papers that fifty or sixty American boys have been killed in Vietnam. And then I turn on the TV and Fulbright or Bobby Kennedy or Morse is making a talk saying it's all my fault and we ought to just turn Asia over to the Communists.

"It does look like the country is badly divided and I've become a symbol of the division. I hope that by getting out of the race I can make moves during the next nine months or so without being accused of political motivations. I'm going to be working for the country the best way I can," he said, "and I hope you-all will help me.

"But," he added, looking around at these loyal friends, among whom were several White House staff members, "if you've got to get out and take care of yourselves, I'll understand and you won't hear any words of blame from me."

Woodward said several of the men, including him, had tears in their eyes as the President concluded.

The statement about neither seeking nor accepting was added to the speech at almost the last moment before the President went on the air. The body of the address, over which McPherson and Clark Clifford had labored through nine drafts, was devoted to announcing a bombing halt in North Vietnam and plans for peace negotiations. After the final draft was handed over to Johnson, he told Busby of the addition he wished to make and, as he had so many times before, this talented aide wrote the language.

Evidence that the decision was not sudden is found, however, elsewhere than in Mrs. Johnson's diary. Bill White told me that eighteen months earlier, during a visit to Camp David, he had been informed by the President "in strictest confidence" that he would not be a candidate for reelection. White, a newspaperman of such deep-rooted integrity that he probably was not even tempted to do otherwise, sat on the sensational news during the ensuing year and a half.

Despite his wife's urging, Johnson may have wavered at times. Two weeks before he took himself out of the running, he told Senator Thruston Morton, an old Republican friend from Kentucky who had announced he would not be a candidate for reelection, "You know, I haven't made up my mind what to do."

Only three days before making the fateful statement, Johnson talked by telephone with Edwin W. Pauley, a California oil man prominent in Democratic party affairs for many years. The two men had known each other since LBJ was a congressional secretary. In this telephone conversation, Pauley gave his old friend the unvarnished and dismaying results of a public opinion survey in California. It showed Robert Kennedy running well ahead of Johnson. Senator Eugene McCarthy was a strong third. The poll gave Johnson no more than a third of the vote, Pauley recalled in an interview for the oral history collection.

"Well, Ed, you've told me enough," the Californian reported LBJ as saying. "If the people don't want me I don't want to run."

Yet he stubbornly contended after leaving office that he could have won if he had chosen to run again in 1968. In the first of his televised interviews with Cronkite for the Columbia Broadcasting System in late 1969, he declared he stepped out because his wife, "one of the wisest and certainly the most trusted counselors I've had," did not want him to be a candidate again. He disdained the notion that the determination of Kennedy and McCarthy to fight him for the nomination had anything to do with the matter.

"If you're asking me in an indirect way whether I had any doubt about my election as President," he told Cronkite, "the answer is an absolute, positive no."

His central argument was that he could have been nominated by the Democratic convention and would have beaten Nixon in the November election. In fact, he said, he felt more confident of victory in 1968 than he had in 1964.

LBJ labored mightily in the television interview to present his case convincingly to the country. The big, rubbery face grinned and scowled as he bent it toward Cronkite. His hands swept the air in gestures which proclaimed that here was a man who had nothing to conceal and spoke the truth. His voice took on that earnest, wheedling tone of reasonableness I had heard him employ so many times. How could any listener not believe him if he believed himself? How could anyone fail to understand the facts he made so clear? Self-confidence was mingled with self-pity as he undertook to prove once and for all that he was not "run out of the presidency."

That was the point he sought so hard to make. A man from the hill country might magnanimously take an action against his own interests if it appeared to serve the greater good of others. But a man from the hill country would never avoid a fight because he was afraid. Never. No, sir; we don't grow any cowards down my way. My daddy can whip your daddy. I can lick any kid on the block. Don't ever believe for a moment that Lyndon Johnson of Johnson City was run out of the presidency.

Many people did believe exactly that and Johnson's argument did not change their minds. Patrick Moynihan, a man of sufficient political flexibility to serve in two Democratic and two Republican administrations, argued later in a memo to Nixon that Johnson had been toppled by a mob. For a time this was commonplace thinking.

The theory ignored the fact that the President was not thrown out of office but served the full term for which he had been elected. He chose, whether for the reasons he advanced or for other reasons, not to offer himself for another term. That the decision came hard was evidenced by the tear which trickled down one furrowed cheek as he announced it to the national television audience. But it was his own decision.

Garry Wills, an unusually perceptive newspaper columnist, wrote from the perspective of some six years later: "Johnson's motives were clearly mixed. He hoped, by not seeking reelection, to gain added leverage for ending the war. The Tet offensive, signaling North Vietnamese ability and intention to fight on, probably had greater effect on Johnson than did the McCarthy and Kennedy challenge to his renomination."

To those who knew how Johnson had come to agonize over the war this seemed a valid judgment.

In any case, there he was, on April 1, 1968, a self-proclaimed lame duck President.

LBJ told a small group of women reporters, in an off-the-record session, "I'm going to be in charge right up till the last minute." This statement, although his feeling was understandable, departed from reality. During the remaining months of the year the President's power suffered a steady erosion. It could not have been otherwise.

His principal efforts were devoted to trying to wind down the war. He still had many individual friends on Capitol Hill and was able to obtain passage by Congress of a tax surcharge measure and a fair housing bill. But the body as a whole was not interested in any new proposals from the White House. Before long some other President would be presenting his own programs. For the present the lawmakers had swallowed as much of the Great Society as they could digest.

LBJ understood how these things went. But he retained, for the time being, control over the Federal departments. He directed their heads to prepare detailed records of the accomplishments of his Administration for future inclusion in the library in Texas.

Some of the Cabinet members were restive. Several double-crossed him by last-minute official actions that enraged him.

The burdens of office did not appreciably ease with the diminution of power. So far as I could tell, Johnson did not slow down at all after he knew a date certain when he would no longer be President. The focus of his activities had changed, but in many basic ways he was the same man for whom I had gone to work in 1953. A bit more relaxed in manner, to be sure, but even that development had come about only recently.

Certainly it had come about since the time early in 1967, only a year before, when I talked with him about a trip I was preparing to make to Korea. Not at his behest, I hasten to add, but in connection with a public relations job I was doing for the government of that country. LBJ had instructed Marvin Watson, who stood very close to him, to tell me to give Walt W. Rostow, his special assistant for national security affairs, a full report when I returned. He would want to know about my projected interview

with Korean President Park Chung Hee and what the South Ko-
reans required to keep them fighting on the United States side in
Vietnam. As always, he was insistent on knowing everything—
everything—that could be learned. The result, which was of
course the one he desired, was that I spent about as much time in
the Republic of Korea gathering information for him as I did attending to my own business.

By contrast, he was easy and unhurried when I went to see
him with the suggestion that I would like to write a magazine
piece about his unsuccessful 1941 campaign for the Senate. Yes,
he said, it was a good idea and he would be glad to cooperate. He
gave me the names of persons who had figured in that campaign
and said he would instruct them to talk freely to me. Come back
to see me, he invited, after I had gathered the basic information
and he probably could add to it. He grinned at my proposed title,
"The Time LBJ Got Beat."

Johnson appeared at his friendly best at a reception he and
his wife set up for Watson after his appointment of that valuable
friend as Postmaster General was confirmed by the Senate. The
aide Mrs. Johnson had determined early in the game must be on
hand to help her with guests' names in the receiving line was
present, but he was not really needed. The presidential couple
knew all of us and greeted each individually as we came along.
The speeches were short and unstudied. Afterward the host and
hostess mingled with the guests on the White House lawn, chatting and laughing as though trouble had never entered their
world.

A much larger affair, but one marked even less by formality,
was a dinner and lawn party the President and Mrs. Johnson gave
one summer evening for more than two hundred old friends,
nearly all of them originally from Texas or still living there. Some
were important in the governmental scheme of things; most were
not. In either case, there was no longer anything they could do to
advance the fortunes of LBJ. He arranged the party, Willie Day

Taylor told me, "just for fun." It was not in honor of anyone or anything.

The President had as much fun as anybody. In a long, rambling after-dinner speech, made without notes, he managed to mention by name and with reference to some personal incident of the past, scores of his guests. His reminiscent remarks brought guffaws and shouts of approval from the uninhibited assemblage.

"And there's Booth Mooney," he said at one point, leering down at the table where he had spotted me, "who did his best to keep me from coming to the Senate at all."

So it went with one guest after another. It was a virtuoso performance, wholly in one phase of the LBJ tradition. He might have been holding forth at a backyard picnic on the ranch in Blanco County, relaxed, boisterous, "joshing" his guests and even himself. Here was a Lyndon Johnson the television audience never saw.

It was an LBJ the guests themselves had seen often in the past, although not in these surroundings. During the course of the evening I found myself in one of the White House men's rooms with several gentlemen. They were clearly having the time of their lives. As one of them attended to his business he stopped laughing long enough to ask solemnly of his friends, "Who ever thought when we started out with Lyndon that we'd be peeing in the White House?"

That was as close to an expression of awe as I heard all evening. These were the home country folks doted on by Liz Carpenter—who was present at the party. They had known old Lyndon for a long time.

Some of the Washington columnists were writing again about a "new" Lyndon Johnson. This time they saw a subdued but unchastened man who still refused to admit the error of his ways, a man embittered and made paranoid by the failure of his Vietnam policy, a man no longer strong enough to smite his critics hip and thigh. Such columnists drew out of their creative imaginations a portrait that was false or at best distorted in almost every feature. Johnson was quieter—at times—than he once had been, yes, and the years and events had caused him to place some restraints—at times—on the more excessive aspects of his personality. But the fact that the leopard's spots may have faded a bit in color did not deny their continued existence. He was no more a new Johnson than he had been in his first news conference as President.

When I first went to work for Johnson he was constantly exhorting his staff, "Just because we're getting fat and forty let's not give up looking for new ideas." He continued to use the admonition after he became President, changing it only to say "fat and fifty." Now he had turned sixty—but not soggy—and he was still relentlessly on the search for innovative ideas. He never stopped coming up with ambitious ones of his own.

He outlined some of them to his companions on Air Force One as he and Mrs. Johnson were flown back to Texas after Nixon's inauguration on January 20, 1969. The group included Rostow, who was to join the academic world in Texas; Hardesty and Middleton, former speechwriters for the President; Tom Johnson, who had been an assistant press secretary, and Mary Rather, still the other Johnson's personal secretary. According to her, LBJ discussed several definite projects with which he and they would immediately begin to occupy themselves in Texas. As was to be expected, each had a top priority.

His modest program included building and staffing the library and the LBJ School of Public Affairs at the university, getting Mrs. Johnson's diary ready for publication, writing his own book, and preparing himself for the series of long interviews with Cronkite which would be broadcast over a period of several months.

On the day before Johnson left Washington, the *Post* published an editorial estimate of his Administration. The newspaper, which had strongly opposed the nation's deepening involvement in Vietnam, gave the President credit for eventually turning the conflict around and heading for a gradual American disengagement. But the editorialist was more interested this time in the positive achievements of the Johnson years. The *Post* summed them up:

"The list of legislative accomplishments runs on and on from the 1964 Civil Rights Act to rent supplements, voting rights, model cities, medicare, control of water pollution, immigration reform, job training, educational aid. And while some of this was the finishing of unfinished business, well begun before his time, some of it broke new ground. A landmark aid to education act, for elementary and secondary schools, cracked a constitutional and political impasse over church-school relationships, and it was brought into being not by past momentum or by parliamentary manipulation but through the innovation and sheer determination of the President."

Every close observer of the national political scene knew about the legislative record. More surprising was the understanding shown in the editorial of the basic source of Johnson's strength and his own failure at times to recognize it.

"It is often said of Mr. Johnson," the editorialist wrote, "that his trouble came from incapacity to inspire, and thus to lead. He would say, on the contrary, that he was victimized by Easterners and intellectuals and liberals and the Kennedy people who scorned him for his regionalism and his roughness, his table manners and the twang of his voice. There is truth in both, and also irony, because the sad thing is that his origins are the best thing about him, and the thing he has going for him whenever he is himself, and he didn't know it. Or maybe he just wasn't confident enough about it."

His origins *were* "the best thing about him." LBJ felt that himself, yet he deliberately went out of his way to invite comparisons between him and the elite he scorned and envied. It was a game which he could not possibly win but one he continually initiated. In this unnecessary and futile game he was forever pitting the plain country folks against the big city sophisticates, the graduate of a teachers' college in Texas against Rhodes scholars and men who talked with the accent of Harvard, cattleman hats against top hats.

Back home to stay, however, he became wholly himself without defensiveness.

Johnson watchers had predicted confidently that there would be noise from the banks of the Pedernales. They expected that within a short time, as soon as he was decompressed, the old pol would start yelling and poking at the Democratic party and issuing homilies on what should be done for the good of the country. It was inconceivable, they agreed wisely, that LBJ, after more than thirty years in elective office, could hold himself back from storming around as though he were still in the center of things.

The prognosticators erred. For a long time what came mostly from Blanco County was a great quiet.

He adopted a deliberate policy of shying clear of activities that might put him back in the public view. He instructed his staff to turn down invitations to speak or contribute articles to periodicals. He had a strong desire to stay away from controversy involving the new setup in Washington.

"Whatever I say," he told Busby, who remained a close confidant, "they'll twist it around to say that I'm criticizing the President. I'm not mad at anybody. I don't want to fight with anybody. The only way to stay out of scrapes is to stay where I belong—on the ranch."

He was busy with the projects he had discussed on the flight from Washington. The interviews with Cronkite brought front-page newspaper headlines and some incredulous editorials when they appeared on television, but Johnson made no other national news. He saw few reporters and had little to say to those he did see. He took up the affairs of the ranch as if he had never been away. He and Mrs. Johnson visited with neighbors and had friends out from Austin for barbecues. After his library was opened, following a monster dedication ceremony, he visited it frequently and sometimes delighted tourists by being discovered at his desk in the replica of the Oval Office on the top floor of the building. When several thousand South Texans staged an "Appreciation Day" for their congressman and Johnson's friend, Representative Kika de la Garza, LBJ showed up to praise the honoree and to be welcomed with great enthusiasm by people who, as de la Garza said, "knew him as their friend."

In such ways as these the ex-President submerged himself in the life of the region that meant more to him than any other place in the world.

Visiting him at the ranch, I found him giving instructions to hired hands dressed in the uniform of the cow country instead of barking orders to white-collared minions scurrying around with papers nervously clutched in their fists. The ranch hands were the more independent breed. When the boss arrived in his big white car, they listened to what he told them, their faces woodenly expressionless, and either nodded without a word or said "Okay" and went about their work.

On one occasion the men were engaged in herding together cattle for spraying preparatory to a trip to market. LBJ told me they had kept four hundred head of cattle unnecessarily penned up in the summer heat for an extra half hour because somebody had goofed and the spray was not ready. But he never raised his voice in speaking to the men, never used a swearword, bawled out nobody.

"I'm just trying to be suggestive," he explained as he drove off to another part of the pasture. "I don't want to give orders unless I have to. But dammit," he added, "they're sure as hell bollixing up this spraying job."

When we returned to the ranch house at noon, I found it was taken for granted that I would join him and Mrs. Johnson and two or three office employees for the lunch that was already temptingly spread. I explained that such a pleasant interlude would cause me to be late for an appointment, important to me, I had in Austin. No further explanation was necessary. Johnson understood business.

Before I left, though, he said, "Come on in the office for a moment."

I went with him into the room and he reached into a desk drawer and started hauling out small packages. As he handed me each one he told its contents. Cigarette lighter. Cuff links. Medallion paperweight. Playing cards—"Your wife plays bridge, doesn't she?" Earrings—"Maybe she'll like these." A small metal bust. The bust was of himself and the medallion had his likeness on one side and a brief quote from one of his speeches on the other. All the items bore the presidential seal.

"Had these made up to give people when I was in Washington," he explained, "and some were left over. I thought you might like to have them."

That was the last time I saw him.

LBJ made his final public appearance before a sizable audience during a symposium held at the library on December 12, 1972, to mark the opening to researchers of the presidential papers on civil rights. Black and white leaders in the struggle of the 1950s to make some start at ending racial discrimination were present. Participants in the seminar included such men as Chief Justice Warren, Senator Humphrey, Roy Wilkins, Clarence Mitchell, Burke Marshall.

Also present was Gerry Siegel, the former general counsel for the Senate Democratic Policy Committee, who had been Majority Leader Johnson's strong right hand in getting the groundbreaking civil rights legislation of 1955 through Congress. Before the meeting began, Siegel told me, he came upon a small group in which his old boss was talking thirteen to the dozen. LBJ was so engrossed that he did not see his former employee. Besides, he was not one to interrupt himself to greet anyone.

Siegel listened to Johnson for a time, a familiar enough experience for him, without being able to catch his eye. Finally he stepped forward to extend his hand and say mischievously, "Mr. President, I'm Gerry Siegel."

He intended his greeting as a joke, perhaps having forgotten that to LBJ a joke was a funny and probably salacious story.

Johnson snapped his eyes toward Siegel. "Hell, Gerry, I know who you are," he said, just as if they were still in the Senate chamber, and took up his monologue where he had left off.

When the session began and Johnson was presented to the crowd, he said his doctors had advised him against making a speech. Nevertheless, he remarked, "I'm going to speak anyway because I have something to say."

What he had to say on the subject of civil rights was colloquial and roughly eloquent. He told apropos stories that made the audience laugh. There was no laughter but a respectful silence when at one point he faltered between sentences, then without apology or ostentation removed from a small bottle a nitroglycerin tablet and downed it before proceeding. It was a sobering reminder, Siegel said in telling me of the day at the library, that here was a man who had withstood several heart attacks and could constantly be on the verge of another.

The time for laughter was over. Johnson ended his talk in a deeply serious vein.

"We have proved that great progress is possible," he said, looking around the auditorium. "We know that much still remains to be done. And if our efforts continue, and if our will is strong, and if our hearts are right, and if courage remains our constant companion, then, my fellow Americans, I am confident we shall overcome."

Applause, naturally. But no sooner had he finished than two black men made their way to the podium to deliver unscheduled speeches of their own. They protested that the seminar included only speakers who held to the Establishment line on civil rights. They called upon those present to pass resolutions demanding more aggressive action. They declared that a followup meeting should be scheduled with more militant speakers on the program.

The two did not go unheard. But neither did they go unchallenged. Clarence Mitchell, director of the NAACP, arose in the audience to say forthrightly, "If President Johnson had the courage to come out in Texas and speak against white demagoguery, wherever I am I'm going to come out and speak against black demagoguery." He proceeded to do so in measured terms.

Johnson had gone to sit in the audience after his own speech. He listened closely to the protesters and to Mitchell's reply, then stood up to walk slowly and with obvious effort back to the rostrum. He denounced nobody, but expressed understanding of the dissident opinions that had been set forth. Reason still offered the only solution, he said tiredly but with conviction. All persons concerned about civil rights must reason together.

Time was when he would have stood beaming with arms stretched above his head as spontaneous prolonged applause sounded through the hall. Now, however, he sank wearily back into his seat.

The fire in his belly, burning low though it was, had not yet died out. Even if, as he said, he was swallowing nitroglycerin tablets "like a goldfish gulping crackers."

On the last day of 1972, a Sunday, he was full of plans in an early morning telephone call to Busby in Washington. He asked his old friend to come up with names of some "new and exciting thinkers" for a planned guest lectureship series at the Library. Also, he said, he would be wanting ideas for the commencement address he had agreed to deliver at the University of Virginia. He declared his intention of getting "really active" during the new year.

"After the inauguration," he told Busby, "we'll have four years behind us and I think I can speak up a little more. I've got some programs up there they're kicking around and I'd like to go more places and see more people again."

With a final "Thanks for everything," a sentence I had heard him utter hundreds of times and which I had written in letters for his signature thousands of times, he hung up the telephone.

The former President died on January 22, 1973, of a heart attack suffered as he was alone for a nap in his bedroom at the LBJ ranch.

His last words were a command. It was spoken urgently over his bedroom telephone to a Secret Service man assigned to him: "Send Mike immediately!"

When Mike and another agent arrived on the run, they found Johnson unconscious on the floor. He died on a plane hurrying him to a San Antonio hospital.

15

L'ENVOI

Ah, well, I did not set out to compose a valentine, either sentimental or comic, featuring LBJ. He created his own portrait, and
sometimes it seemed a caricature, all through his life. What I have
undertaken to do is simply to present some portions of the com-
posite whole that came under my ken—mostly firsthand, sometimes secondhand. In doing so, I became convinced that there is
no way to arrive at a complete understanding of this complex,
driving, driven man. I do feel, however, that I have come closer
to an understanding than I was able to do during the years I
worked for and with him. At least a partial explanation of this is
that little time was available then for making a sustained effort to
analyze what made Lyndon run. All associated with him were too
busy with the tasks immediately at hand. "I want everybody here
to come up with one brand new idea every day," he once told a
meeting of his top Senate staff.

His quest for new ideas was unceasing. Yet it was Lyndon
Johnson's destiny to serve as President during a time of ferment

when ideas, no matter how new, based on old concepts—of progressivism, of neo-populism, of FDR's New Deal brought up to date, of unrelenting opposition to communism as a monolithic force—no longer captured the hearts and minds, a phrase he was fond of using, of large numbers of Americans. Such concepts were not up to meeting the stresses of the latter half of the sixties. But Johnson could not abandon them.

After John Morley, the distinguished British politician and historian, returned from a visit to the United States during the Theodore Roosevelt Administration, he was asked by a woman at a dinner in London what he thought of TR. Morley began a pontifical reply: "You may take every adjective on every page of the *Oxford Dictionary,* good, bad, indifferent, and you will find some to apply it . . ."

"That's too complicated," the questioner interrupted impatiently. "Can't you tell us in half a dozen words?"

"In half a dozen words," Morley responded, "half St. Paul, half St. Vitus."

If Lord Morley had not been interrupted, his reply might have served to give a fair description of LBJ.

"He spoke as an American primitive," Haynes Johnson wrote of him in the Washington *Post,* "and left a legacy as an American original. He was both great and gross, full of promise and imperfections. He did more than the country realized or appreciated, and accomplished less than his own dreams."

Harry McPherson, who knew him so well, did his own summing up in *A Political Education:* "He was a manipulator of men when the young were calling for everyone to do his own thing; a believer in institutions such as government, universities, business and trade unions, when these were under constant attack on the campuses; a paternalist in a time of widespread submission to youth values and desires."

If a liberal thought ever came into Johnson's mind, Wayne Morse had said, he would have a brain hemorrhage.

In one of his self-appraisals, Johnson one day in 1961 met Carl Rowan, the journalist he later was to name director of the United States Information Agency, and said, thrusting his finger against the other man's chest, "Mr. Roe-ann, you don't know me. But one of these days you're gonna discover that I'm a goddam sight more liberal than some of these so-called liberals you've been cottoning up to."

At a moment during the 1960 Democratic convention when things were not going well, Johnson said to me, "I take things harder than most people, can't help it." To be sure. But that was the reverse side of the figurative coin on which was expressed his literal motto: "If you're going to be a bear—be a grizzly."

Every adjective on every page of the *Oxford Dictionary*. Good. Bad. Rarely indifferent, though.

One facet of his personality not really difficult to understand, although it puzzled many observers, was the admixture of scorn and respect with which he regarded the intellectual community. LBJ the onetime schoolteacher admired book learning. LBJ the pragmatic politician from the hill country recognized an overeducated fool when he saw one. He was unable satisfactorily to segregate his ambivalent positions and the failure aroused more anger than sorrow within him. Sure, he knew and often said that many persons who called themselves intellectuals or unprotestingly permitted the term to be applied to them lacked sense enough to pour piss out of a boot. But he could not forget that his mother had drilled into him the everlasting value of education. He never really resolved the inner conflict.

On their side, most of the self-styled intellectuals seemed to find keen pleasure in downgrading Johnson and, in the end, reviling him in scathing terms. They said he was a slob who appealed to the slobbishness of the beer-guzzling, television-watching, pay-check-greedy, and *unintellectual* middle class. Who but a slob would proclaim that he thrilled to the sight of the American flag in a foreign land? Or display his operation scar to reporters and photographers? Or say "Amurrica" in his speeches, for Christ's sake? The intellectuals made their case against **LBJ** with sneers that fed their own sense of superiority.

In this as in other areas that affected him personally, Johnson showed a striking incapacity to protect and defend himself. He was a genius at pressing issues but singularly inept at putting his own best foot forward. Worst of all, he would stand high on any list of men who habitually spoke the truth as though it were a lie. The dynamic vitality emanating from everything he said or did served only to emphasize this flaw.

Being himself an uncommonly purposeful man, he assumed that every action of all persons had to have a logical purpose. This caused him to be innately suspicious of the motives of other men. Small talk was not only a bore but also, he felt, was a screen thrown up to keep him from discovering those hidden motives. But he would root them out. By God, he would!

LBJ was not a single actor alternately playing the roles of hero and villain. He was an entire cast of characters: bulldozing ambitious politician, sentimental family man, Mr. Vanity, frustrated schoolmaster, locker room raconteur, hardheaded businessman, Uriah Heep, journalism instructor, paternalistic employer, moody self-analyst, friend in time of need. The list could be extended. No wonder he confused close associates as well as hordes of wondering outsiders.

He burned with an unquenchable passion to be number one in everything he did. He had an insatiable craving for accomplishment. He wanted desperately to do it all and he wanted to do it all at once. Getting second place for his debate team caused him to throw up. All the Senate Democrats ought to vote with their leader. All his committee reports must be unanimous. When he was a candidate for office his earnest determination was to get as nearly one hundred percent of the votes as possible. The American people owed it to their country to unite behind their President. He never fully comprehended why he could not be loved by all and fretted when the popularity polls showed this was far from the case.

The folks in the Lyndon Baines Johnson Library like to tell about a group of third grade students who were being shown through the imposing building. Halfway through the tour, one of the youngsters turned to another and asked in an awed voice, "What is a President, anyway?" His schoolmate replied without hesitation, "Why, he's the principal of the whole world."

LBJ would not have quibbled at that definition. It was what he wished to be.

INDEX

279